Lecture Notes
in Business Information Processing   76

Series Editors

Wil van der Aalst
  Eindhoven Technical University, ...

John Mylopoulos
  University of Trento, Italy

Michael Rosemann
  Queensland University of Technology, Brisbane, Qld, Australia

Michael J. Shaw
  University of Illinois, Urbana-Champaign, IL, USA

Clemens Szyperski
  Microsoft Research, Redmond, WA, USA

Marten van Sinderen
Pontus Johnson (Eds.)

Enterprise
Interoperability

Third International
IFIP Working Conference, IWEI 2011
Stockholm, Sweden, March 23-24, 2011
Proceedings

 Springer

Volume Editors

Marten van Sinderen
University of Twente
Centre for Telematics and Information Technology (CTIT)
7500 AE Enschede, The Netherlands
E-mail: m.j.vansinderen@utwente.nl

Pontus Johnson
KTH - Royal Institute of Technology
Industrial Information and Control Systems
10044 Stockholm, Sweden
E-mail: pontus@ics.kth.se

ISSN 1865-1348   e-ISSN 1865-1356
ISBN 978-3-642-19679-9   e-ISBN 978-3-642-19680-5
DOI 10.1007/978-3-642-19680-5
Springer Heidelberg Dordrecht London New York

Library of Congress Control Number: 2011922266

ACM Computing Classification (1998): J.1, H.3.5, H.4, D.2.12

Typesetting: Camera-ready by author, data conversion by Scientific Publishing Services, Chennai, India

Printed on acid-free paper

Springer is part of Springer Science+Business Media (www.springer.com)

Preface

One of the characteristics of our economy today is that enterprises increasingly (need to) compete and collaborate in a global market, using the Internet and other technical means to overcome the traditional barrier of geographical distribution. Another characteristic is continuous and rapid change and innovation, which may be internal or external to individual enterprises, but nevertheless affecting the way these enterprises can perform in relation to other enterprises and their market environment. The success of an enterprise therefore more and more depends on its ability to seamlessly interoperate with other agile enterprises, and to be able to adapt to actual or imminent changes, instead of making some product or providing some service in the most efficient way.

The role of the current Internet for enterprise interoperability is essential but at the same time still limited in light of its potential. The future Internet should be much more than a universal access and communication infrastructure. It should be able to empower enterprises to innovate by creating new business value in competition and together with other enterprises, based on relevant knowledge about each other and the market. It should do so in a sustainable and socially responsible fashion, making efficient use of physical resources with a minimal environmental footprint. Therefore, the Internet as we know it should evolve into a universal business support system in which enterprises enjoy interoperability services that can be invoked on the fly according to their business needs. Such interoperability services may require physical sensing capabilities as well as extensively exploiting knowledge assets.

This background provided the inspiration for the International IFIP Working Conference on Enterprise Interoperability, IWEI 2011, held March 22–23, 2011, in Stockholm, Sweden. IWEI 2011 was the third in a series of international events on enterprise interoperability. Previous events took place in Munich, Germany (2008), and Valencia, Spain (2009). The IWEI series of events aim at identifying and discussing challenges and solutions with respect to enterprise interoperability, with the purpose of achieving flexible cross-organizational collaboration through integrated support at business and technical levels. Contributions to the development of the following results are highlighted: a scientific foundation for specifying, analyzing and validating interoperability solutions; an architectural framework for addressing interoperability challenges from different viewpoints and at different levels of abstraction; a maturity model to evaluate and rank interoperability solutions with respect to distinguished quality criteria; and a working set of practical solutions and tools that can be applied to interoperability problems to date.

The special theme chosen for IWEI 2011 was "Interoperability and Future Internet for Next-Generation Enterprises." This means that special attention was given to the interoperability needs of next-generation enterprises and how these needs are shaped and supported by the emerging Future Internet.

IWEI 2011 was organized by the IFIP Working Group 5.8 on Enterprise Interoperability in cooperation with INTEROP-VLab. The objective of IFIP WG5.8 is to advance and disseminate research and development results in the area of enterprise interoperability. The IWEI series of events provide an excellent platform to discuss the ideas that have emerged from IFIP WG5.8 meetings, or, reversely, to transfer issues that were raised at the conference to the IFIP community for further contemplation and investigation.

This volume contains the proceedings of IWEI 2011. Out of 47 submitted full papers, 15 papers were selected for oral presentation and publication (31.91% acceptance rate). In addition, five short papers were selected for oral presentation and publication in a companion book. The selection was based on a thorough reviewing process, in which each paper was scrutinized by at least three experts in the field. The papers are representative of the current research activities in the area of enterprise interoperability. The papers cover a wide spectrum of enterprise interoperability issues, ranging from foundational theories, frameworks, architectures, methods and guidelines to applications and case studies.

The proceedings also include the abstracts of the invited talks at IWEI 2011, given by two renowned keynote speakers: Andreas Friesen (Research Program Manager of Service Science, SAP) and Gérald Santucci (Head of the Unit on Networked Enterprise & Radio Frequency Identification, INFSO DG, EC).

We would like to take this opportunity to express our gratitude to all those who contributed to IWEI 2011. We thank the keynote speakers for their excellent and forward-looking talks; we thank the authors for presenting the accepted papers, which resulted in valuable information exchange and stimulating discussions; we thank the reviewers for providing useful feedback on the submitted papers, which undoubtedly helped the authors to improve their work; and we thank the attendants for their interest in this working conference. We are indebted to IFIP TC5 and WG5.8 for recognizing the importance of enterprise interoperability as a research area with high economic impact. Finally, we are grateful to KTH, the Royal Institute of Technology, for hosting IWEI 2011.

March 2011   Marten van Sinderen
                                                                    Pontus Johnson

Organization

IWEI 2011 was organized by IFIP Working Group 5.8 on Enterprise Interoperability, in cooperation with INTEROP VLab.

Executive Committee

General Chair	Pontus Johnson	KTH, Sweden
Program Chair	Marten van Sinderen	University of Twente, The Netherlands
IFIP Liaison	Guy Domeingts	INTEROP-VLab/University Bordeaux 1, France
Local Organization	Joakim Lliesköld	KTH, Sweden

International Program Committee

Stephan Aier	University of St. Gallen, Switzerland
Khalid Benali	LORIA – Nancy Université, France
Peter Bernus	Griffith University, Australia
Ricardo Chalmeta	University of Jaume I, Spain
David Chen	Université Bordeaux 1, France
Antonio DeNicola	LEKS-IASI-CNR, Italy
Guy Doumeingts	INTEROP-VLab/GFI, France
Yves Ducq	Université Bordeaux 1, France
Ip-Shing Fan	Cranfield University, UK
Ricardo Goncalves	New University of Lisbon, UNINOVA, Portugal
Claudia Guglielmina	TXT e-solutions, Italy
Sergio Gusmeroli	TXT e-solutions, Italy
Axel Hahn	University of Oldenburg, Germany
Jenny Harding	Loughborough University, UK
Roland Jochem	University of Kassel, Germany
Paul Johannesson	KTH, Sweden
Leonid Kalinichenko	Russian Academy of Sciences, Russian Federation
Bernhard Katzy	University of Munich, Germany
Kurt Kosanke	CIMOSA Association, Germany
Lea Kutvonen	University of Helsinki, Finland
Jean-Pierre Lorre	PEtALS Link, France
Michiko Matsuda	Kanagawa Institute of Technology, Japan
Kai Mertins	Fraunhofer IPK, Germany
Jörg Müller	Technische Universität Clausthal, Germany

Philipp Offermann   Deutsche Telecom T-Labs, Germany
Andreas Opdahl   University of Bergen, Norway
Angel Ortiz   Polytechnic University of Valencia, Spain
Hervé Panetto   UHP Nancy I, France
Hervé Pingaud   École des Mines d'Albi-Carmaux, France
Raul Poler   Polytechnic University of Valencia, Spain
Raquel Sanchis   Polytechnic University of Valencia, Spain
Ulrike Steffens   OFFIS, Germany
Raymond Slot   Hogeschool Utrecht, The Netherlands
Bruno Vallespir   Université Bordeaux 1, France
Alain Wegmann   Ecole Polytechnique Federal de Lausanne,
                            Switzerland
Xiaofei Xu   Harbin Institute of Technology, China

Additional Reviewers

Camlon Asuncion   Thomas Knothe
Alexis Aubry   Holger Kohl
Luiz Olavo Bonino da Silva Santos   Mario Lezoche
Markus Buschle   Pia Närman
Moustafa Chenine   Matthias Postina
Michele Dassisti   Waldo Rocha Flores
Luís Ferreira Pires   Brahmananda Sapkota
Christian Fischer   Teodor Sommestad
Ulrik Franke   Vikram Sorathia
Bettina Gleichauf   Sergey Stupnikov
Sven Glinizki   Johan Ullberg
Hannes Holm   Sven Wusher
Frank Jaekel   Esma Yahia

Sponsoring Organizations

IFIP TC5 WG5.8
INTEROP-VLab
KTH, Royal Institute of Technology
CTIT, Centre for Telematics and Information Technology

Table of Contents

Keynotes

Full Papers

Session 1

Session 2

Session 3

Session 4

Session 5

On Challenges in Enterprise Systems Management and Engineering for the Networked Enterprise of the Future

Andreas Friesen

SAP Research Center CEC Karlsruhe, SAP AG, Vincenz-Priessnitz-Strasse 1
76131 Karlsruhe, Germany
andreas.friesen@sap.com

Abstract. Since 20 years, many traditional firms transform their orientation from products to services, among them also many potential SAP partners, competitors and customers. Powered by globalization, competition, and the Internet, that process happens globally and at accelerating speed. It breaks existing product supply chains and transforms them into a volatile network of collaborating businesses – the business value network. The network forms around service value propositions of the participants that lead to joint value creation. While SAP and other players have developed quite a sophisticated understanding of on premise software solutions and accompanying services, the field of on-demand software services is relatively new to the industry, and the underlying principles of value creation in many successful new service businesses are often a miracle. Business value networks will become increasingly important in the world's economy in the future. Their appropriate IT support must efficiently realize business collaborations and interactions between globally spread organizations. In the past, Enterprise Interoperability has been often seen as a synonym for Enterprise Application Integration at intra- or inter-organizational level. In the future, the ability to adapt to changing market and business requirements together with the ability to reflect the business adaptations on the level of the connected ICT systems will constitute key challenges for the support of business network formations. Enterprise Interoperability will have to address business value networks not only from ICT viewpoint but also as socio-technical systems from the business and operational perspective. Over the past years, SAP Research was involved into intense research that has taken place to explore the Internet of Services. New ways of developing, hosting, aggregating, mediating and finally consuming services have been described and tested. The developed Service Delivery Framework will be presented as a foundation for a Future Internet platform for business value networks demonstrating the key roles and relationships involved in the formation and value creation of business value networks from the business, operational and technical perspective.

Keywords: enterprise systems management; enterprise systems engineering; networked enterprise.

Brief Biography

Andreas Friesen holds a doctorate degree in computer science. After his PhD studies on security and trust in service-oriented architectures he joined Siemens Corporate

M. van Sinderen and P. Johnson (Eds.): IWEI 2011, LNBIP 76, pp. 1–2, 2011.
© IFIP International Federation for Information Processing 2011

Technology where he worked on multimedia security topics. In 2004 he started to work for SAP Research as senior researcher. Over the past years he was leading a number of EU-funded research projects in the areas of Enterprise Interoperability and Application Integration in Service-oriented Frameworks, Semantic Web Services, Application of Formal Methods in software engineering and business process modeling. Since 2010 he leads a new research program at SAP Research called Service Science.

As member of the SAP Research team he has contributed to a variety of technology transfers to SAP product development teams including use of semantic technologies in business applications, software engineering for the next generation business applications, enterprise interoperability in service-oriented business frameworks, and collaborative business process modeling.

Andreas Friesen is author of over 30 scientific publications published in international conferences, workshops and journals and is member of programme committees of various international conferences and workshops and different working groups related to service science, software and service engineering, and business process modeling.

Research Roadmap for Future Internet Enterprise Systems

Gérald Santucci

Networked Enterprise & Radio Frequency Identification (RFID), INFSO DG, EC
B -1049 Brussels, Belgium
infso-desk@ec.europa.eu

Abstract. In this presentation, we will introduce and explain a research road-map for Future Internet enterprise systems. This research roadmap has been developed by the community of scientists, developers and other stakeholders in the context of the "Future Internet Enterprise Systems" cluster, managed by the "Internet of Things and Networked Enterprise" unit of the Information Society and Media General-Directorate of the European Commission.

Keywords: research roadmap; Future Internet; enterprise systems.

Brief Biography

Gérald Santucci has been working in the Information Society and Media Directorate-General of the European Commission since February 1986. In March 2007, he was appointed Head of the Unit Networked Enterprise & Radio Frequency Identification (RFID). The unit's portfolio includes some 40 R&D projects, grouped around two clusters, which address the development of ICT-based systems supporting the Future Internet Networked Enterprise and the shift from contactless technologies towards the "Internet of Things".

The adoption by the European Commission, in March 2007, of a Communication on RFID has constituted a first milestone towards the achievement of a European policy framework regarding RFID. Work underway includes: the continuous monitoring of a Commission Recommendation on the implementation of privacy and data protection principles in RFID-enabled applications, with special emphasis placed on privacy impact assessment and RFID signs/logos; a Commission Communication on the Internet of Things, which covers fourteen different lines of action, in particular governance, privacy and data protection, and the 'right to the silence of the chips'; and a Mandate to European Standardization Organizations on privacy and security aspects of RFID. Gérald is the acting chairman of the Expert Group on the Internet of Things, composed of some 50, stakeholders from Law, Economics and Technology, which is tasked with advising the European Commission on Internet of Things evolution and associated public policy challenges. In addition, Gérald is highly committed to develop and strengthen cooperation with Europe's international partners, such as Japan, China, Korea, U.S., Brazil and India, in order to promote the exchange of information and best practices and the definition of global or harmonized standards and regulations in the emerging field of Internet of Things.

Over the years, Gérald has gained extensive experience in the activities of the Directorate-General through his involvement in research management, including heading the Unit "Applications relating to Administrations" (i.e., eGovernment) 1999-2002, the Unit "Trust and Security" 2003, and "ICT for Enterprise Networking" 2004-2006. During the period from 1986 to 1989, Gérald managed the preparatory work that led to the AIM (Advanced Informatics in Medicine) exploratory action, which still exists today in the form of the ICT for Health unit of DG Information Society and Media. In 1991-1993, he was involved in the Uruguay Round Trade Negotiations with respect to Semiconductors (tariffs, rules of origin, direct investment) and drafted a Commission Communication on the European Telecommunications Equipment Industry.

In November 2008 Gérald Santucci received the Honourable Mention in the Asset Tracking Forum segment of the ID People Awards ceremony at the seventh ID WORLD International Congress in Milan. This recognition underlined Gérald's untiring efforts to drive forward and foster a coherent European approach to RFID that ensures common standards, harmonized legislation as well as compatible guidelines.

Gérald holds a Master's degree from the Institute for Political Studies in Paris, and a Ph.D. in Microeconomics from the University of Paris 12 Val-de-Marne.

A Manufacturing Core Concepts Ontology for Product Lifecycle Interoperability

Zahid Usman, Robert Ian Marr Young, Nitishal Chungoora, Claire Palmer, Keith Case, and Jenny Harding

Wolfson School of Mechanical & Manufacturing Engineering, Loughborough University, Loughborough, UK, Post Code LE11 3TU
{Z.Usman,R.I.Young,N.Chungoora,K.Case,
C.Palmer3,J.A.Harding}@lboro.ac.uk

Abstract. This paper proposes a manufacturing core concepts ontology (MCCO) aimed at providing support for product life cycle interoperability. The potential focus of the work is interoperability across the production and design domains of product lifecycle. A core set of manufacturing concepts and their key relationships are identified in MCCO. Semantics are captured formally through heavyweight logic using rigorous rules and axioms. Three different levels of specialization have been identified according to the degree of specialization required. Each level provides an immediate route to interoperability for the concepts specialized from that level. MCCO enable knowledge sharing across design and production domains through core concepts. A successful initial experimental implementation has been done to demonstrate the working of MCCO.

Keywords: semantics, core concepts, interoperability, manufacturing ontology, knowledge sharing, product lifecycle, design and production.

1 Introduction

Technology and knowledge have been recognized as the key factors for production [1]. Information and Communication Technologies (ICT) have become an integral part of most organizations. Manufacturing organizations have moved from traditional manual drawings and design to Computer Aided Technologies (CAx). Software based approaches like Enterprise Resource Planning (ERP), Manufacturing and Materials Resource Planning (MRP), Product Lifecycle Management (PLM) etc are being employed rapidly. ICT are key to the manufacturing competence, competitiveness and jobs in Europe [2]. With machines replacing men, a mechanism of interoperability is required for machines to communicate across different domains.

Interoperability is "the ability to share technical and business data, information and knowledge seamlessly across two or more software tools or application systems in an error free manner with minimal manual interventions" [3]. To highlight the importance of interoperability a study in 1999 at NIST showed that U.S.$ 1 billion are spent per year by the U.S. automotive sector alone for solving interoperability problems [4].

M. van Sinderen and P. Johnson (Eds.): IWEI 2011, LNBIP 76, pp. 5–18, 2011.
© IFIP International Federation for Information Processing 2011

The multiples of this amount when other sectors like, services, health care, logistics, telecom, etc are considered from around the globe, the figures would definitely highlight this as a major problem. It has also highlighted the need to minimize the cost incurred in solving interoperability problems.

To make a system interoperable it is of extreme importance to formally capture & incorporate the semantics of concepts. A survey highlighted that almost 70% of total costs of interoperability projects is spent on solving issues of semantic mismatches[5]. Semantics can be captured formally by using ontologies based on rigorously formalized logical theories [6] i.e. heavyweight ontologies. Several definitions of ontology which is a borrowed term from philosophy are found in literature. The most quoted one being "An ontology is an explicit specification of a conceptualization" [7]. The one preferred for this work though is "a Lexicon of the specialized terminology along with some specifications of the meanings of the terms involved" [8]. This definition covers both the lightweight and heavyweight ontologies. The definition and use of concepts are captured by formalizing ontologies with rigorous logic based rules and this is what makes the ontologies formal or heavy weight.

To fulfill the requirements of manufacturing knowledge sharing core ontologies are generally developed from foundation ontologies [9]. In the domains of design and production an extended heavyweight ontological foundation needs to be explored and developed further [10]. A novel method for developing a novel common semantic base in the form of a multilevel heavyweight MCCO to assist sharing knowledge across design and production domains of product lifecycle is proposed in this paper.

2   The Need for a Heavyweight Manufacturing Ontology

2.1   Lightweight Ontologies

Knowledge capturing and sharing has been done partially through database approaches like ERP, MRP, PLM, etc software tools. Limited success has been achieved in providing the information through databases [11] because they have an underlying structure based on lightweight ontologies. Lightweight Ontologies in manufacturing have loosely formalized semantics making concepts open to multiple interpretations. These are also not understood well enough by computers for interoperability. There exists a lack of generally agreed terminology and underlying concepts not being defined explicitly in the manufacturing enterprise architectures area [12].

The current major route to interoperability is to use international standards. But, when it comes to knowledge sharing across different domains they have their own issues. ISO standards relevant to the manufacturing (mainly from ISO TC 184/ SC4) are very focused on their narrow domains of interest, e.g.:

- ISO 10303-STEP-Standard for The Exchange of Product date model AP239-Product Lifecycle Support (PRODUCT LIFECYCLES), AP224-Feature based manufacturing and mainly machining, AP1-Overview and fundamental principles, etc.,
- ISO 13584-Part Library (PLIB),

- ISO 15531-industrial MANufacturing management DATa (MANDATE),
- ISO13399-Cutting Tool Standard,
- Etc.

In a very specific and narrow domain of discourse the relevant standards are very useful. Definitions of terms in a narrow domain can be loose since their meanings are already understood by the concerned community. Across a broader domain like product lifecycle where more than one standard are required, interoperability through standards becomes an issue. To share knowledge across standard a common understanding among them is required. Most of the relevant ISO standards have non formalized text based semantics. Consistency lacks not only across standards but even within the same standards as well, e.g. the definition of 'component' in ISO standards:

- 'Component' definition in ISO-10303-1: "A product that is not subject to decomposition from the perspective of a specific application",
- 'Component' definition in ISO-10303-AP224: "The component specifies either a Single_piece_part or another Manufactured_assembly used to define an assembly",
- 'Component' definition in ISO 19439:2006 [general]: "Entity that is part of, or capable of becoming part of, a larger whole".

The semantics being text based and different within and across standards raise an issue for knowledge sharing through standards. The design and production domains of product lifecycle would require different set of concepts but they need to have a commonly understood formal semantic base for interoperability and knowledge sharing.

2.2 Heavyweight Ontologies Approach

Heavyweight ontologies can potentially overcome this problem of standards and lightweight ontologies. Heavyweight ontologies can formally define concepts, control their use, capture knowledge and provide a route to share across design and production. They offer better reasoning capability compared to the databases with fixed form and formats. Heavyweight ontologies have the potential to provide a rigorous common semantic base. Therefore, research potential is there to work on precisely and rigorously defined manufacturing ontology as a common semantic base. No common semantic base in the form of a heavyweight core manufacturing ontology is available for interoperability across design and production.

Foundation ontologies like DOLCE, SUMO, OCHRE, OpenCyc, BFO provide the first stage of a common understanding. They provide formally axiomatised domain independent set of concept e.g. *AbstractEntity, ConcreteEntity, Endurant, Perdurant,* spatial and temporal concepts, etc. But these are developed to cover everything therefore they are broadly based and generic [13]. Thus, the common semantic base provided by foundation ontologies will be too generic for interoperability across product lifecycle domains. Thus, concepts from foundation ontologies can serve as a basic backbone for the creation of the more specialized/viewpoint-dependent MCCO.

Heavyweight manufacturing ontologies available as of now are incomplete and do not cover the whole of product lifecycle and need to be completed and developed more [14]. Ontologies for the product lifecycle and manufacturing need to be developed further and tested [13, 15]. Also, the lack of core manufacturing ontologies to provide a common understanding for various strands of manufacturing [12, 16] needs to be overcome. Therefore, heavyweight product ontology capturing the semantics will help focus others on knowledge management issues [14].

3 Manufacturing Core Concepts Ontology

MCCO is formed by identifying a core set of concepts formalized in heavyweight logic. Three different levels with increasing degrees of specialization have identified for formalizing concepts.

3.1 Core Concepts and Relationships within MCCO

Capturing production knowledge requires different types of concepts. A detailed discussion on this is not possible in this paper. The UML diagram in fig 1 summarizes all the categories of concepts, key concepts in each category, and some of the key relationships identified between the concepts.

Features and *Part Family* category contains the most important one. *Features* and *Part Family* concepts and their specialized concepts at three different levels are key to capturing and sharing knowledge in product lifecycle [17, 18]. In this paper the feature concepts are used to show the implementation of the multi level ontology, to show implementation of core concepts, to prove their specialization and their ability to provide a route to sharing knowledge across design and production domains.

3.2 Levels of Specialization of Concepts

The domain specific concepts developed directly from the foundation ontology lack the required level of interoperability. The design and production concepts can be directly specialized from very generic foundation ontology concepts. Foundational concepts enable knowledge sharing only through a level having nothing to do directly with either design or production. Some intermediate concepts are required in addition which are more concerned with the product lifecycle and its sub domains. Design and production layers of concepts can have a common underlying layer which can provide the route to interoperability and knowledge sharing at a more specialized level. Since the layers above the foundation ontology contain concepts relatively more specialized they provide a common base for interoperability at a more specialized level.

Each intermediate level of concepts has a higher degree of specialization with concepts closer to the specific domain. Each level acts as a semantic base for the concepts specialized from that. This gradual specialization of concepts is thus required for providing a route to share knowledge at more specialized levels. Various levels are required to specialize concepts from the foundation to the specific domains. As shown in fig. 2 the number of levels identified in this research work are three [19] based on the degree of specialization required.

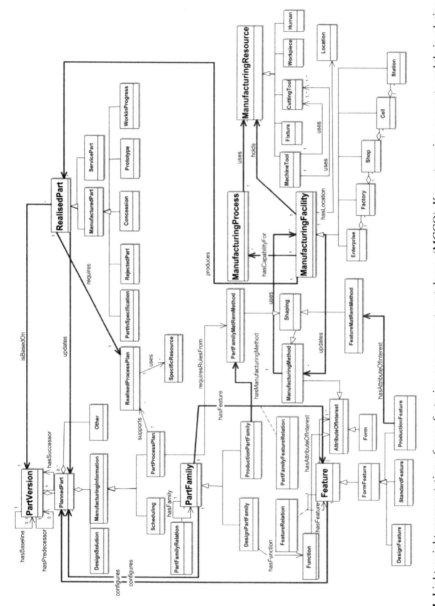

Fig. 1. Light weight representation of manufacturing core concepts ontology (MCCO): Key categories, concepts and their relationship

Fig 2 summarizes the manufacturing core concepts ontology and its application. It shows two main layers. The bottom layer represents MCCO. While the top layer represents the implementation and evaluation. MCCO at the bottom layer with its three levels of specializations. Top Layer represents the interoperable specialized ontologies and knowledge bases (KB) developed from MCCO. This layer may contain some further specialized concepts according to requirement. The Interoperability across design and production has been tested by querying the relevant knowledge between the two domains. The exploration of core concepts and their relations in MCCO is vital for the successful implementation.

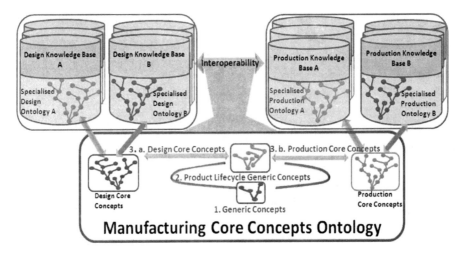

Fig. 2. MCCO, its specialization levels and its implementation scheme

3.2.1   Generic Core Concept Level

This level is to provide a link of product lifecycle concepts to other domains like business domain etc if required. These concepts are more specific as compared to foundational concepts like entity, event, quality, quantity etc. Concepts like *activity, activity occurrence, feature, dimension, tolerance, part, part family* etc, are present in this level. These concepts are applicable to any domain.

3.2.2   Product Lifecycle Generic Core Concept Level

A set of concepts generic to the product lifecycle domains are also required to act as a common level for the specific product lifecycle domains like design and production. Product lifecycle generic concepts are specialized from generic concepts and are applicable to any of the specific product lifecycle domains like design and production but not outside product lifecycle. Concepts like *ProductFeature, ProductPartFamily, GeometricDimensions, GeometricTolerance*, are some of the product lifecycle generic concept level.

3.2.3   Product Lifecycle Domain Specific Core Concept Level

This contains concepts specific individually to each product lifecycle domains like design and production. Concepts like *ProductionFeature* and *ProductionPartFamily'* are production specialization of product lifecycle generic concepts. Similarly *Design-Feature'* and *'DesignPartFamily'* are design specializations of product lifecycle generic concepts. The design and production concepts can either be used directly for capturing knowledge or can be further specialized to develop customized ontologies.

4 An Example of Concepts Specialization

Specialization of concepts is not a simple process. Most specializations of concepts require other concepts, relations, function and rigorous rules & axioms. The three specialization levels have been elaborated by taking the *Feature* concept and showing its journey through the levels. The formalization of definitions, knowledge capture and sharing are also demonstrated. It is appropriate to use *Feature* as this is one of the key concepts for interoperability and has simpler relations and axioms. Moreover, the ontology is developed more with respect to *Feature*.

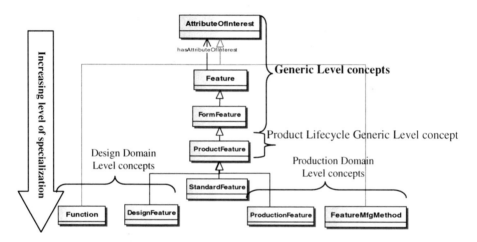

Fig. 3. Feature specializations, lightweight representation

Feature concepts start from the generic *"Feature"* concept. Feature as defined in oxford dictionary is "a distinctive attribute or aspect of something". So *'Feature'* is defined as "anything having an attribute of interest". *Feature* is at the generic level of the ontology. *Feature* thus can be the dark hair of a person, or the ability of a person to run fast etc. The *Feature* in the product lifecycle domain will have some form or shape. This leads to the specialization of *Feature* as a *FormFeature* which should have a *Form* as its *AttributeOfInterest*. A *FormFeature* may be associated to a *Product*. The *FormFeature* thus gets specialized in to a *product feature* where it has an associated *product*. The domain specific concepts *DesignFeature* and *ProductionFeature* can be direct specializations of *from form* or *product feature*. So, *Design Feature* is a *product/form feature* having *function* as a compulsory attribute of interest and *ProductionFeature* is a *ProductFeature / FormFeature* having *ManufacturingMethod* as an *AttributeOfInterest*. The concept of *StandardFeature* is generic to both design and production which is a *ProductFeature / FormFeature* having both *Manufactur-ingMethod* and a *Function* as attributes of interest. Fig. 3 shows the lightweight UML representation of *feature* specializations.

5   Formalization of Concepts

To formally define concepts, control their use, capture knowledge and populate facts, heavyweight logic is embedded in MCCO. Common logic (ISO/IEC 24707:200) based Knowledge Frame Language (KFL) provided by Highfleet is used for heavy-weight formalization. Axioms and rules are there at all levels of MCCO. The more generic the concepts the lesser the number of constraints on them and the higher is the level of interoperability. The formalization of *Feature* concept and its specializations in KFL are elaborated.

First of all the concepts and relations are declared in the ontology e.g. the concepts '*feature*' and '*AttributeOfInterest*' and relation *hasAttributeOfinterest* which relates a *feature* to its *attribute* are declared in ontology for defining *feature*.

Similarly specializations of *feature* i.e. *FormFeature, ProductFeature, Design-Feature, ProductionFeature* and their respective attributes of interest *Form, Product, Function, ManufacturingMethod*, along with their key relationships are declared in MCCO.

The declaration of concepts, relations and functions is followed by the most impor-tant part of formalization i.e. Axiomatization, which makes the ontology heavy-weight. Rules and axioms have been divided in two parts i.e. 'Semantic Rules' and 'Knowledge Rules'. Semantic Axioms formally capture and control the meanings of terms. They are subdivided into 'Defining Axioms' and Controlling Axioms'. Defin-ing Axioms formally capture the definition of concepts e.g. to capture the definition of *Feature* following axioms is embedded in ontology.

```
(=>  (Feature ?f)(exists(?AOI)

    (and (AttributeOfInterest ?AOI)

        (hasAttributeOfInterest ?f ?AOI))))

:IC hard "Feature has an Attribute of Interest"
```

The above axiom means in simple English "if there is a *feature* ?f then there has to exits an *attribute of interest* ?AOI related to *feature* by the relation *hasAttributeOf-Interest*". This captures formally the definition of *feature* and puts it as a hard integ-rity constraint (IC) in MCCO. This would prevent loading any *feature* without its *attribute of interest*. Similarly definitions of all specializations of *feature* i.e. *Form-Feature* at generic level, *ProductFeature* at product lifecycle level and *StandardFea-ture, ProductionFeature & DesignFeature* at domain specific levels can be captured. Other type of semantic axioms and rules i.e. 'Controlling Axioms' are similar and they make the facts assertion fool proof in accordance with formal definitions e.g. a *ProductionFeature* cannot be asserted with *function* as its *attributes of interest* as it belongs to *DesignFeature* and similarly a *DesignFeature* cannot have a *Manufactur-ingMethod* as its *AttributeOfInterest*.

Knowledge rules are divided into two parts as well. The first type is 'knowledge capturing rules' which formally capture the actual domain specific knowledge e.g. the rule below captures the knowledge relating *NeckWidth parameter* of a *feature* and the *CuttingTool* available to machine that and places it as a soft IC. This IC fires and warns the designer whether the value of *NeckWidth* is out of range with respect to available *CuttingTool*. The facts are still populated because soft ICs are there to warn only.

```
(=>(and(Groove ?g) (NeckWidth ?n)

       (hasParameter ?g ?n) (hasValue ?n (mm ?r1)))

   (inInterval ?r1 (interval in 8 12 in)))
:IC soft "NeckWidth value is out of range (8mm to 12mm)
for machining with standard tooling"
```

The second of the knowledge rules types i.e. 'Inference rules' make the inference of facts from the already loaded facts e.g. A *StandardFeature* has both *function* and *ManufacturingMethod* as its *attribute of interest*. Therefore, it has both *DesignFeature* and *ProductionFeature* in it, and they should be inferred whenever a *Standard-Feature* is asserted in knowledge base. The rule below does exactly that when a *StandardFeature* is asserted in knowledge base.

```
(<=(and    (DesignFeature    (DesignFeaturefor ?sf))

    (hasAttributeOfInterest (DesignFeaturefor ?sf)?f)

    (hasAttributeOfInterest (DesignFeaturefor ?sf)?fm))

 (and (StandardFeature ?sf) (Function ?f) (Form?fm)

      (hasAttributeOfInterest ?sf ?f)

      (hasAttributeOfInterest ?sf ?fm)))
```

In simple English the above rule implies: if there is a *StandardFeature* ?sf, having *Function* ?f and *Form* ?fm as its attributes of interest then infer a *design feature* 'DesignFeaturefor' having same *Function* and *Form* as those of *StandardFeature*.

6   Experimental Validation of the MCCO

The experimental implementation of MCCO is focused on the critical concepts and their relationships, on the basis that if these can be rigorously defined the rest of MCCo will be straight forward to implement. MCCO is loaded in the Integrated Ontology Development Environment (IODE). The following aspects of ontology have been tested: 1. Capturing of semantics, 2. Controlling concepts, 3. Capturing Domain Knowledge 4. Inferring Knowledge 5. Route to knowledge sharing through MCCO.

6.1   Testing Definition and Specialization of Feature Concepts

This experiments test the assertion *ProductionFeature*. This verifies two things: 1. Definition of *ProductionFeature* has been captured, 2. *ProductionFeature FormFeature*

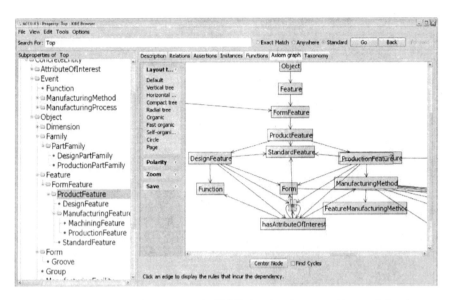

Fig. 4. A portion of MCCO ontology in IODE showing feature and its specializations

is indeed a specialization of *ProductFeature* which is a specialization of *FormFeature* which is a specialization of *Feature*.

According to the definition, a *ProductionFeature* has a *ManufacturingMethod* as its *AttributeOfInterest*. First the *ProductionFeature* is asserted without *Manufacturing-Method* to test the definition. As shown in fig. 5 the assertion has been cancelled.

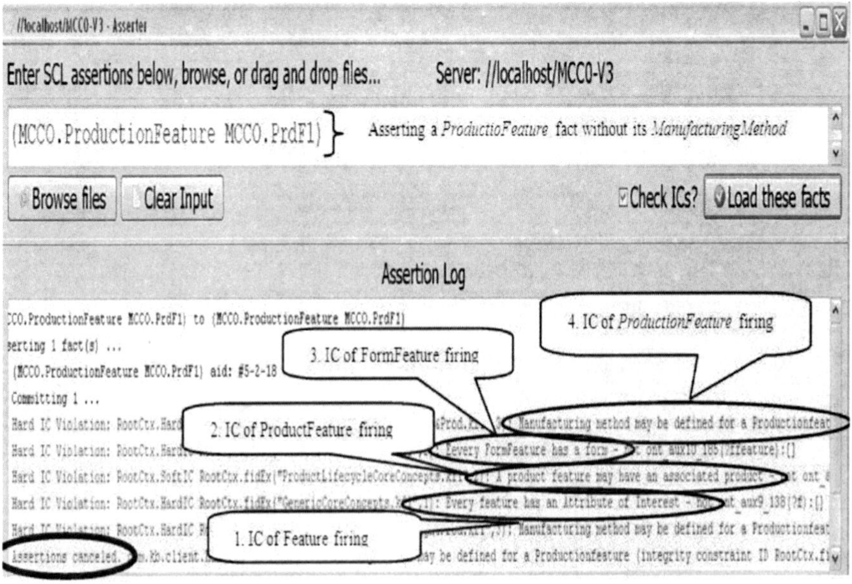

Fig. 5. Asserting a production feature without manufacturing method

The IC cancels the assertion and notifies the user that a *ManufacturingMethod* may be defined for it. But this is not the only IC which has fired. ICs from generic concepts *Feature* and *FormFeature* as well of product lifecycle generic concept *ProductFeature* have also fired. This is due to the specialization.

A *ProductionFeature* inherits ICs from all three levels of specialization.

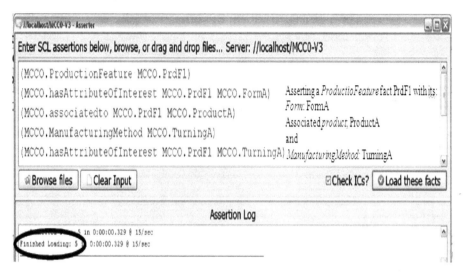

Fig. 6. *ProductionFeature* asserted with all its *AttributesOfInterest* and associated *Product*

ProductionFeature is specialized from the product lifecycle generic concepts *ProductFeature* which is specialized from the generic concept *FormFeature* which in turn is specialized from the generic concept *Feature*. After that a production feature is asserted with *ManufacturingMethod* 'TurningA' as its *AttributeOfInterest*, 'ProductA' as its associated *Product,* and 'FormA' as its other *AttributeOfInterest*. The assertion is accepted as shown in fig 6. This is because all the ICs coming from all three levels have been taken care of and the assertion satisfies all of them. This shows that the definition of *ProductionFeature* has been successfully captured. Firing of ICs from all levels confirms the integrity driven specialization of concepts at different level.

6.2   Testing Inference of Knowledge and Route to Knowledge Sharing

A sample of DesignFeature, ProductionFeature and StandardFeature facts have been asserted in the KB having a common form. A query is run find out the *DesignFeature* and *ProductionFeature* as well as *StandardFeature* having common form. As shown in fig 7 Form 'CirGroove' is the common form for all feature facts. Once a *ProductionFeature* with common a *Form* as that of a *DesignFeature* is identified, the knowledge about the *ProductionFeature* can be queried and fed back to the *DesignFeature* with the same form. Common form comes from *FromFeature* thus the concepts *Form* and *FormFeature* provided the route to interoperability between design and production features. The *DesignFeature* 'DesignFeaturefor StdGroove' and *ProductionFeature*

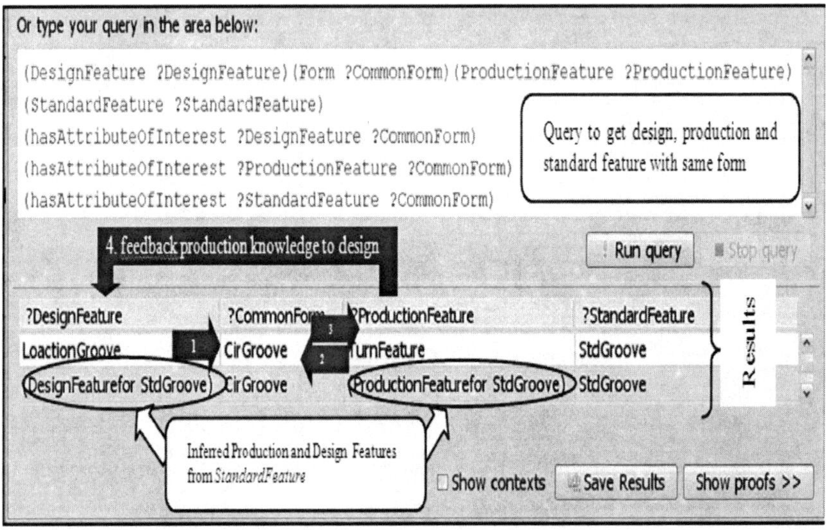

Fig. 7. Route to knowledge sharing and inferred facts

'ProductionFeaurefor StdGroove' are inferred from the *StandardFeature* StdGroove. So this also showed that knowledge can be inferred automatically using MCCO rules and axioms.

7 Conclusion

The focus of the work is to provide an ontological foundation for sharing manufacturing knowledge across production design and production. However, the underlying technological base can provide an understanding of production quality, cost and time-scales. This has a potential to provide further linkages to a business perspective. This approach does not ensure full interoperability but it does ensure the understanding of the extent to which interoperability is possible. A core set of concepts has been formally defined in MCCO and these concepts have been used to capture as well as share production knowledge. Three different levels of specialization i.e. generic, product lifecycle generic and domain specific level have been identified for MCCO. Feature concepts have been successfully specialized at the three levels and other concepts in MCCO are being specialized. The behaviors of concepts have been controlled. Knowledge has been captured and inferred successfully using core concepts and the expressive power of common logic. The ability of core concepts to provide a route to communicate, identify and share the knowledge across design and production domains has been demonstrated through the *Feature* concepts.

Future research direction is aimed to explore a more detailed level of Interoperability between design and production features at parametric level. Manufacturing method for features and part families from knowledge sharing context is being explored using a meta-level underpinning. Actual industrial implementation remains to be explored. The formalization of concepts in MCCO which are borrowed from various ISO-standards and encoded in common logic based formal definitions. MCCO can be extended to explore interoperability across other product lifecycle domains like services, operation and disposal.

Acknowledgments. This research work is funded by the Innovative Manufacturing and Construction Research Centre (IMCRC) under the Interoperable Manufacturing Knowledge Systems (IMKS) project (IMCRC project 253). The authors would also like to thank the research team in IMKS project for their support and cooperation.

References

1. Frankovič, B., Budinská, I.: The Role of Ontology in Building of Knowledge Systems for Industrial Applications. In: 4th Slovakian-Hungarian Joint Symposium on Applied Machine Intelligence, Herlany, Slovakia (2006)
2. ICT for Manufacturing, Report of Meeting with Group of Representatives of Five Expert Panels, Brussels (2005)
3. Ray, S., Jones, A.: Manufacturing interoperability. Journal of Intelligent Manufacturing 17(6), 681–688 (2006)
4. Brunnermeier, S.B., Martin, S.A.: Interoperability Cost Analysis of the U.S. Automotive Supply Chain. National Institute of Standards and Technology, U.S.A (1999)
5. Bussler, C., et al.: Context Mediation in the Semantic Web: Handling OWL Ontology and Data Disparity Through Context Interchange. In: Bussler, C.J., Tannen, V., Fundulaki, I. (eds.) SWDB 2004. LNCS, vol. 3372, pp. 140–154. Springer, Heidelberg (2005)
6. Uschold, M., Gruninger, M.: Ontologies and Semantics for Seamless Connectivity (2004)
7. Gruber, T.R.: Toward Principles for the Design of Ontologies used for Knowledge Sharing, pp. 907–928. Academic Press, Inc., London (1995)
8. Schlenoff, C., et al.: ISO-18629 The Process Specification Language (PSL): Overview and Version 1.0 Specification, NISTIR 6459. National Institute of Standards and Technology, Gaithersburg, MD (2000)
9. Young, R.I.M., et al.: Manufacturing knowledge sharing in PLM: a progression towards the use of heavy weight ontologies. International Journal of Production Research 45(7), 1505–1519 (2007)
10. Chungoora, N., Young, R.I.M.: The configuration of design and manufacture knowledge models from a heavyweight ontological foundation. International Journal of Production Research (2010)
11. Abramovici, M., Sieg, O.C.: Status and development trends of product lifecycle management systems. In: IPPD Conference, Wroclaw (2002)
12. Chen, D., Doumeingts, G., Vernadat, F.: Architectures for enterprise integration and interoperability:Past, present and future. Computers in Industry 59, 647–659 (2008)
13. Borgo, S., Leitão, P.: Foundations for a core ontology of manufacturing, Bragança, Portugal (2007)
14. Lee, J.-H., Suh, H.-W.: Ontology-based Multi-layered Knowledge Framework for Product Lifecycle Management. Concurrent Engineering 16(4), 301–311 (2008)
15. Zhou, J., Dieng-Kuntz, R.: Manufacturing Ontology Analysis and Design: Towards Excellent Manufacturing. IEEEXplore, 39–45(2004)
16. Leimagnan, S., et al.: MASON: A proposal for an ontology for manufacturing domain. In: Proceedings of the IEEE Workshop on Distributed Intelligent Systems: Collective Intelligence and Its Applications (DIS 2006), IEEEXplore (2006)

17. Gunendran, A.: An Information and Knowledge Framework to Support Multiple Viewpoints in the Design for Manufacture of Injection Moulded Products, PhD Research Thesis, Loughborough University (2004)
18. Gunendran, G., Young, B.: Methods for the Capture of Manufacture Best Practice in Product Lifecycle Management. In: International Conference on Product Lifecycle Management 2008. Inderscince Publishers (2008)
19. Usman, Z., et al.: A Manufacturing Foundation Ontology for Product Life Cycle Interoperability. In: Interoperability for Enterprise Software and Applications. Springer, Coventry (2010)

A Construction Approach of Model Transformation Rules Based on Rough Set Theory

Jin Li[1,2], Dechen Zhan[1], Lanshun Nie[1], and Xiaofei Xu[1]

[1] School of Computer Science and Technology, Harbin Institute of Technology, 92 West Dazhi Street, Harbin 150001, China
[2] School of Computer Science and Technology, Harbin Engineering University, 145 Nan Tong Street, Harbin 150001, China
miaookok@163.com, {dechen,nls,xiaofei}@hit.edu.cn

Abstract. Model transformation rules are the central part of model transformation. Many model transformation approaches provide some mechanisms to construct transformation rules in industrial and academic research. However, transformation rules are typically created manually in these approaches. As far as we know, there are no complete solutions that construct transformation rules automatically. In this paper, we propose a rough set based approach to construct transformation rules semi-automatically. Construction approach of rough set is improved in order to support the transformations between different meta-models, then the corresponding algorithm to construct transformation rules is presented. We also provide the measurement indicators of transformation rules to support selecting proper rules from many rules which meet transformation requirement. Three kinds of experiments for problems with distinct complexity and size are given for the validation of the proposed method.

Keywords: Model transformation, Model transformation rules, Rough set theory.

1 Introduction

Model-driven architecture (MDA) is an approach for the development of software systems. Model transformation is a core part of MDA and plays an indispensable role in many different application domains, for instance, to generate code from models, to derive higher-level models from legacy models, to support model driven interoperability, or to compose service models for enterprise interoperability.

However, model transformation involves many repetitive difficulties. Model transformation consists of transformation rules which describe how a set of elements of the source model are transformed into a set of elements of the target model through transformation relationships [2]. With increasing in number and size of models, the relationships implicated among models reflect gradually more and more uncertainty, incompleteness and inconsistency, etc. Therefore, the efficient design of transformation rules has become a major challenge to model transformation.

A lot of researchers in both academic and industry study on how to implement model transformation and construct transformation rules. For example, model

M. van Sinderen and P. Johnson (Eds.): IWEI 2011, LNBIP 76, pp. 19–35, 2011.

transformation has been well achieved especially in database domain [3].Usually there are two kinds of approaches for constructing transformation rules. One is that domain experts and model transformation designers capture mapping relationships between source and target metamodel elements, then define transformation rules based on these mapping relationships. It depends on domain experts and model transformation designers to not only understand the knowledge of modeling and model transformation, but also discover the semantic relationships among source and target models, especially implicit relationships. The other is that matching relationships can be discovered from a set of input metamodels through data mining methods [4], and then transformation rules are designed according to these matching relationships [5]. It gives enough attention to metamodel transformations, however complex and uncertain relationships among source and target models are difficult to derive and selection from rules set is also a challengeable task.

We introduce rough set [6-8] into the construction process of transformation rules. In doing so, we try to discover both explicit and implicit matching relationships and specify transformation rules. Then we also provide measurement indicator for selecting the proper transformation rules [9]. The rest of this paper is structured as follows. In Sect. 2, we propose the motivating example which will be used throughout the paper. Section 3 provides the core concepts and main algorithms and illustrates the construction process of the example. Section 4 designs three kinds of experiments in order to respectively analyze three quantities' influence on transformation rules. Sect. 5 presents related work. Finally, Sect. 6 concludes the paper and further work.

2 Motivating Example

As the transformation from UML class diagram to relation database model is very common in the field of software system development, in this section, we introduce an example, entitled UCD2RDM, to construct transformation rules which describe how UML class diagram is transformed into relational database model. Both source and target metamodels are illustrated in Fig. 1.

UML class diagram consists primarily of *Class*, *Relationship* and *Property*. Each *Class* has zero or more *Properties*. The type of each *Property* can be defined by built-in type or another *Class*. The relation among *Classes* is specified by *Relationship*. *Relationship* can be extended to describe the more concrete relations, for example *Association*, *Composition*, *Aggregation*, *Generalization* and *Dependency*, etc. Relational database model is composed of *Table*, *FKey* and *Column*. A *Table* contains one or more *Column*, and zero or more *FKey*. An *FKey* is also a *Column*.

We define a source model conforming to UML class diagram and a target model conforming to relational database model. Both models describe the relationships among teachers, students and courses of some educational institution.

The class *Teacher* can teach one or more courses (*Course*). The class *Student* can select one or more courses (*Course*). According to the teacher's title information, *Teacher* has a subclass (*Professor*). *Student* has also a subclass (*Master*). Only the class *Professor* can supervise the master (*Master*). The model of the educational institution is shown in Fig. 2.

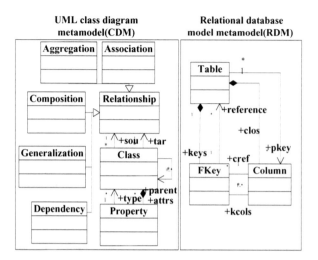

Fig. 1. Source and target metamodels of UCD2RDM

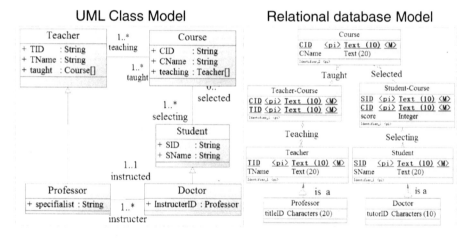

Fig. 2. Source and target models of UCD2RDM

In Fig. 2, there are three kinds of transformation rules which are used to transform elements of UML class diagram into elements of relational database model.

- The first rule describes how to transform *Class* into *Table* through the mapping between the properties of *Class* and the columns of *Table*;
- The second rule expresses the correspondence between *Relation* and *Table*. It consists of the matching relationships between the *Relation*'s name and the *Table*'s name, and the mapping relationship between the crucial properties of *Relation* and the foreign column of *Table*;
- The last rule presents the mapping relationships between the identity property of *Class* and the important column of *Table*.

3   Rough Set and Discovered Rule Based on Rough Set

3.1   Rough Set Theory

Rough set theory is a mathematical tool to deal with vagueness and uncertainty. It has capability to effectively analyze uncertain, incomplete and inconsistent data, discover dependent and implicit relations, and construct mapping rules [10]. The process of constructing rule in rough set is composed of three steps. The first step is to classify the data according to the equivalence relations. The second step is to format the data in order to generate the decision table. The last step is to calculate the data belong to the decision table and construct the mapping rules [11].

This paper extends rough set theory to construct transformation rules with three major improvements. Firstly, we present more precisely domain using source and target metamodels in order to discover the mapping among source and target metamodels. Secondly, we redefine the traditional property set to get a new property set that has two kinds of properties: composed by source metamodels and decision properties composed by target metamodels. Finally, we extend the decision table and other correlative concepts. The work will help discover and construct transformation rules.

3.2   Basic Concept

For the convenience of description, we introduce some related definitions of model transformation [18]. We also extend some basic notions of rough set theory (i.e. decision tables and decision function) that will be useful in this paper.

Definition 3.1 (Directed-role graph): A directed-role graph is defined as

$$RG = (L, \otimes, \oplus) . \tag{1}$$

Where
  -   $L = N \cup R \cup U \cup D$ is a non-empty finite set of alphabets,
  -   N is a non-empty symbol finite set of nodes,
  -   R is a non-empty symbol finite set of relations,
  -   U is a non-empty symbol finite set of roles,
  -   D is a non-empty symbol finite set of domain,
  -   $\otimes(R) = [\ldots, U \times N, \ldots]$ is a relational function , and describes that the node plays a role in the relation,
  -   $\oplus(N,R,U) = (\min(N,R,U), \max(N,R,U))$ is a cardinality function, and it presents times that a node plays a special role in the relation. $\min(N,R,U)$ denotes the minimal times and $\max(N,R,U)$ denotes the maximal times.

Definition 3.2 (Model): A model is defined as

$$M = (RG, \gamma, \xi) . \tag{2}$$

Where $RG = (L, \otimes, \oplus)$ is a directed-role graph; γ is also a directed-role graph, and it can be denoted as $RG_\gamma = (L_\gamma, \otimes_\gamma, \oplus_\gamma)$; each L has a mapping function $\xi: L \rightarrow L_\gamma$, and ξ

describes all of elements, such as node, relation, role and domain, come from the finite symbol set of RG_γ.

Definition 3.3 (Metamodel): Given two model $M_1=(RG_1, \gamma_1, \xi_1)$, $M_2=(RG_2, \gamma_2, \xi_2)$.
if $\gamma_1=M_2$, that is $RG_\gamma=(L_\gamma, \otimes_\gamma, \oplus_\gamma)=(RG_2, \gamma_2, \xi_2)$
then M_2 is called the metamodel of M_1, which denotes $M_1:M_2$.

Definition 3.4 (Model match): A model match is defined as

$$MMatch= \text{Match} (\{sm\}:MM_s,\{tm\}:MM_t) . \tag{3}$$

MMatch builds the relationships between the source$\{sm\}$ and target$\{tm\}$ metamodels.

Definition 3.5 (Model transformation): A model transformation is defined as

$$MT= \cup \text{Match} (\{sm\}:MM_s,\{tm\}:MM_t) . \tag{4}$$

MT is a process in which elements of source models are transformed into elements of target models according to *MMatch*.

Definition 3.6 (Model transformation rule): A model transformation rule is defined as

$$MTR=\{sm\}:MM_s \rightarrow \{tm\}:MM_t . \tag{5}$$

If the conditions of the source metamodel are satisfied, the conditions of the target metamodel would be deduced.
　　Because model transformation language ATL provides simply structure, we use it to describe transformation rules.

Definition 3.7 (Decision table of transformation rules): A decision table of transformation rules is defined as

$$RT = (M, V, \Gamma) . \tag{6}$$

Where

- $M=SM \cup TM$ is a non-empty set of finite model elements,
- $SM=\{sm_1,sm_2,...,sm_i\}$ is the finite element set of the source model,
- $TM=\{tm_1,tm_2,...,tm_j\}$ is the finite element set of the target model,
- $V=V\gamma_{SM} \cup V\gamma_{TM}$ is the set of values that associate for every element of metamodel, $\gamma_{SM}=\{smm_1,smm_2,...,smm_k\}$ is the finite element set of the source metamodel and $\gamma_{TM}=\{tmm_1,tmm_2,...,tmm_l\}$ is the finite element set of the target metamodel, in general, γ_{SM} is called the decision property set and γ_{TM} is called the decision property,
- $\Gamma: M \times \gamma_M \rightarrow V$ is a determine function, $\gamma_M=\gamma_{SM} \cup \gamma_{TM}$ is the finite element set of the source and target metamodel, and Γ determines the metamodel element of each model element.

For $\forall mm \in \gamma_{SM}$, $sm \in SM$, then has

$$V_{\gamma_{SM}} = \bigcup_{mm \in \gamma_{SM}} V_{mm}, \Gamma_s : SM \times \gamma_{SM} \to V_{\gamma_{SM}} .$$

(7)

For $\forall mm \in \gamma_{TM}$, $tm \in TM$, then has

$$V_{\gamma_{TM}} = \bigcup_{mm \in \gamma_{TM}} V_{mm}, \Gamma_T : TM \times \gamma_{TM} \to V_{\gamma_{TM}} .$$

(8)

In decision table decision properties can be unique or not. When some condition properties are satisfied, decisions, operations and actions in decision properties will be executed.

Definition 3.8 (Indiscernibility relation): Let $RT=(M, V, \Gamma)$ be a decision table, and $B \subseteq \gamma_{SM}$. Then an indiscernibility relation Δ_B is generated from B and SM with the form

$$\Delta_B = \{(w_1, w_2) \in SM \times SM : \Gamma(w_1, smm) = \Gamma(w_2, smm), \forall smm \in B\}$$

(9)

if $(w_1, w_2) \in \Delta_B$, then w_1 and w_2 are called as the indiscernibility relation of B.

Indiscernibility relation is the main concept of rough set theory. The source model is divided into the equivalence class according to indiscernibility relation, which is denoted as SM/Δ_B.

Definition 3.9 (Indiscernibility relation of the decision value): Let $RT=(M, V, \Gamma)$ be a decision table, and $B \subseteq \gamma_{SM}$. Then an indiscernibility relation of the decision value Δ_B is generated from B and RT with the form

$$\delta_B : SM \to \rho(V\gamma_{TM})$$
$$\delta_B(w) = \{ i : \exists w' \in SM \text{ s.t. } w\Delta_B w', t(w) = i, 1 \le i \le r(\gamma_{TM}) \} .$$

(10)

Where $\rho(V\gamma_{TM})$ denotes the power set of $V\gamma_{TM}$, and $t(w)$ denotes the value of model element w in the decision property set γ_{TM}.

Definition 3.10 (Indiscernible decision table): Let $RT=(M, V, \Gamma)$ be a decision table, and $B \subseteq \gamma_{SM}$. δ_B is an indiscernible decision function; $SM/\Delta\gamma_{TM}$ is the indiscernible partition over the source model SM,

$$\text{if } \theta(\delta_B) = \{ \forall(p, q) \in SM \times SM, \text{ then } \delta_B(p) = \delta_B(q) \} .$$

Where RT is called the indiscernible decision table; $SM/\theta(\gamma_{SM})=\{W_1, W_2, \ldots, W_n\}$, W_i $(i=1,2,\ldots,n)$ is the equivalence class of the condition property and $i=1$ to n; $TM/\theta(\gamma_{TM})=\{X_1, X_2, X_m\}$, $X_j(j=1,2,\ldots,m)$ is the decision class of transformation rules and $j=1$ to m.

Definition 3.11 (Property reduction): Let $RT=(M, V, \Gamma)$ be a decision table, and $B \subseteq \gamma_{SM}$, $smm_j \in B$

(1) if $\Delta_B = \Delta_B - \{smm_j\}$ is true, the metamodel smm_j is redundancy to the set B, else smm_j is necessary to B;

(2) if all properties of B are necessary, B is independent;

(3) set $B' \in B$, if B' is independent and $\Delta'_B = \Delta_B$, B' is one of simplified set of B.

Definition 3.12 (Decision matrix of transformation rules): Let $RT = (M, V, \Gamma)$ be a decision table, then a decision matrix $CM(RT)$ is defined as

$$CM(RT) = (m_{ij})_{n \times n} \ . \tag{11}$$

Where $SM/\theta(\gamma_{SM}) = \{W_1, W_2, \ldots, W_n\}$, $\tau(W_i)$ is the value of the equivalence class W_i in the set of condition properties; $m_{ij} = \{ \tau \subseteq \gamma_{SM} : \tau(W_i) \neq \tau(W_j) \ \Pi \ \delta_B(W_i) \neq \delta_B(W_j) \}$

Decision matrix of transformation rules is a symmetric matrix, namely $CM(RT)$ is an upper triangular matrix.

Definition 3.13 (Decision function of transformation rules): Let $CM(RT) = (m_{ij})_{n \times n}$ be a decision matrix, a decision function of the condition equivalence class is defined as

$$B_i = \bigwedge_{j} \bigvee_{smm \in m_{ij}} smm = (\bigvee_{k<i} \bigwedge_{smm \in m_{kj}} smm) \wedge (\bigvee_{l<i} \bigwedge_{smm \in m_{il}} smm) \ . \tag{12}$$

Where $i = 1$ to n, and let B_i be minimal disjunctive normal form (DNF) according to the idempotent rule $a \wedge a = a$, the absorption rule $a \wedge (a \vee b) = a$, and the distributive rule $a \wedge (b \vee c) = (a \wedge b) \vee (a \wedge c)$.

Decision matrix of transformation rules describes the relationships between equivalence classes($SM/\theta(\gamma_{SM})$) and decision classes($SM/\theta(\gamma_{TM})$). These relationships can be presented using the form $W_i \rightarrow X_j$. W_i, called as the precondition of transformation rules, is the minimal disjunctive normal form. X_j, called as the decision of transformation rules, is the elements of the target metamodel. We use three measurement indicators[10], i.e. support, accuracy and coverage, in rough set theory to evaluate transformation rules. Support, denoted as support $(W_j \wedge X_i)$, means the number of objects which satisfy both X_i and W_j in decision table. Accuracy, denoted as accuracy $(W_i \rightarrow X_j) = \text{support}(W_i \wedge X_j)/\text{support}(W_i)$, is the confidence of the decision of transformation rules. Coverage, denoted as coverage $(W_i \rightarrow X_j) = \text{support}(W_i \wedge X_j)/\text{support}(X_j)$, means the applicability of transformation rules.

3.3 Algorithm for Transformation Rules

In this section, we present a construction algorithm, entitled rsCRT, based on the generation algorithm of rough set theory using UCD2RDM in Sect. 2. There are four sub-algorithms in rsCRT. The main construction process of transformation rules is the following:

(1) Firstly, decision table is generated by Def. 6. Its construction algorithm is shown in Sub-algorithm 1;

(2) After generating the decision table, the compatibility of the decision table should be detected according to Def. 8. If the decision table is incompatible, it

should be redesigned through indistinguishable function δ_B defined by Def. 9. The specific detection and operation is written in Sub-algorithm 2;

(3) Before building the decision matrix, the decision table should be rewritten according to equivalence class and decision class. The decision matrix is built according to Sub-algorithm 3;

(4) Finally, the decision function B_i, established based on the decision matrix, is converted into minimal disjunctive normal form to construct transformation rules. The rules with the same source and target metamodels are merged and calculated their measure indicators. The creation algorithm of transformation rules is written in Sub-algorithm 4.

Sub-algorithm 1. Generating Decision Table

```
Input: MS=(RG_s,γ_s,ξ_s), MT=(RG_T,γ_T,ξ_T)
Output: model_tran_rule_dec_table
model_tran_rule_dec_table(schema)={n,r,u,c,t};
List queryRelList,queryUseList,queryCarList;
void queryRUCList(String tempNodeInstance){
    for(m=1 to |{⊗(r)}|)
        if(⊗(r)[m].n==tempNodeInstance){
            queryRelList.add(⊗(r)[m].r);
            for(n=1 to |⊕(n,u,r)|)
                if(⊕(n,u,r)[n].n==tempNodeInstance)&
                   ⊕(n,u,r)[n].u==⊗(r)[m].u&
                   ⊕(n,u,r)[n].r==⊗(r)[m].r))
                    queryCarList.add(⊗(r)[m].u);}  }
    for(i=1 to |RG_s(L)|){
        meta_model_Element=ξ_s(RGS(L_i));
        queryRUCList(meta_model_Element);

    Value=queryNodeSchemaValue(meta_model_Element);
        for(j =1 to queryRelList.length()){
            rValue=queryRelSchemaValue(queryRelList[j]);
            uValue=queryUseSchemaValue(queryUseList[j]);
            cValue=queryCarSchemaValue(queryCarList[j]);
            model_tran_rule_dec_table.add(row)=({nValue,
    rValue, uValue, cValue, ξ_T(RGT(tempNodeInstance })); }
    }
```

In Sub-algorithm 1, to reduce decision table of UCD2RDM, we use n to describe the node of source metamodel (i.e. *Class,Relationship,Propery*), and r to denote the relation of source metamodel (i.e. *Association,Inheritance,Composition*), and u to present the node's role participated in the relation, such as *attr*, *type* and *parent* etc, and c to indicate the number of the role, and t to reveal the elements of target metamodel(i.e. *Table,Fkey* and *Column*).

Table 1. Decision table of transformation rules

decision class	equivalence class	number of source metamodel	condition property				decision property
			n	r	u	c	t
	W1	2	0	0	6	3	0
	W2	2	0	1	0	1	0
	W3	2	0	0	6	3	0
	W4	1	0	1	6	3	0
X1	W5	1	0	0	6	3	0
	W6	1	0	0	6	3	0
	W7	1	0	1	6	3	0
	W8	6	1	0	6	3	0,2
	W9	4	1	1	6	1	0
X2	W10	3	2	2	2	1	1,2
X 3	W11	2	2	2	1	1	2

Sub-algorithm 2. Redesigning Compatible Decision Table

```
Input: model_tran_rule_dec_table
Output: model_tran_rule_dec_table
for(i=1 to |model_tran_rule_dec_table(row).length|)
  row_i= model_tran_rule_dec_table(row)[i];
  for(j=i+1 to
|model_tran_rule_dec_table(row).length|)
      row_j= model_tran_rule_dec_table(row)[j];
        if(row_i.n==row_j.n&row_i.r==row_j.r &
        row_i.u==row_j.u&row_i.c==row_j.c){
            if(row_i.t<>row_j.t){
                row_i.t=row_i.t+row_j.t ;
                row_j.t=row_i.t;} }
```

We apply Sub-algorithm 2 in UCD2RDM and get the incompatible information which is shown as follows:

$$\delta_B(TID)= \delta_B(TName)=\{1,2\}, \quad \text{that is } |\delta_B(TID)|=|\delta_B(TName)|\neq 1$$

$$\text{similarly,} \quad \delta_B(CID)= \delta_B(CTName)= \delta_B(SID)= \delta_B(SName)==\{1,2\}$$

So the decision table should be redesigned through Sub-algorithm 2. The result is shown in the right part of Table 1 (i.e. condition property and decision property).

Sub-algorithm 3. Building Decision Matrix

```
Input: the equivalence class W_i (i=1,2,…,n),
the decision class X_j(j=1,2,…,m),
model_tran_rule_dec_table
Output: the decision matrix CM
String[] TM/θ(γ_TM)={X_1,X_2,…,X_n},SM/θ(γ_SM)={W_1,W_2,…,W_m};
for(i=1 to |SM/θ(γ_TM)|){W_i= SM/θ(γ_TM)[i];
   for(j=1 to |TM/θ(γ_TM)|){X_j= TM/θ(γ_TM)[j];
       if(ξ_s(RG_s(W_i))∈X_j){
           X_j.add(RG_s(W_i));
```

$$\text{Support}(W_i, X_j) = |W_i \cap X_j|\,;\,//\text{support}$$
$$\text{SI}(W_i, X_j) = |W_i \cap X_j|\,/\,|W_i|\,;\,//\text{accuracy}$$
$$\text{CI}(W_i, X_j) = |W_i \cap X_j|\,/\,|X_i|\,;\,//\text{coverage}\qquad\}\quad\}$$

```
String[][] m_ij={smm∈γ_s:smm(X_j)≠smm(X_j)&Γ(X_i,ξ_s(RG_s(X_i))
           = Γ(X_j,ξ_s(RG_s(X_j)}
     CM(model_tran_rule_dec_table)=(m_ij)_nxn;
```

In Sub-algorithm 3, the decision class $SM/\Delta\gamma_{TM}$ is defined as following:

$X_1 = Teacher \cup Professor \cup Course \cup Student \cup Master \cup$
  $Teaching \cup Selecting \cup Supervising$

$X_2 = TID \cup CID \cup SID \cup TName \cup CName \cup SName$

$X_3 = title \cup tutor$

We apply this algorithm and obtain the decision matrix. The result is shown in Table 2. The equivalence class W_{10} is defined by Def.3.10 and def.3.11 based on the results of incompatibility.

Sub-algorithm 4. Constructing Transformation Rules Set

```
Input: the decision matrix CM
Output: {MTR}
List rulefirstList, rulelastList, ruleList;
for(i=1 to CM.col.length){
    row_i= model_tran_rule_dec_table(row)[i];
    String rulefirst, rulelast;//save a rule
    for(j=1 to i)
        if(i==j)
            for(k=i to CM.row.length)
                rulefirst= rulefirst∧m[i][k];
        else
            for(k=1 to i)
                rulefirst= rulefirst∧m[k][i];
        rulelast= rulelast∨row_i.t;
        rulefirstList.add(disformat(rulefirst));
        rulelastList.add(rulelast); }
    for(i=1 to rulefirstList.length)
        for(j=i+1 to rulefirstList.length){
            if(rulefirstList[i]==rulefirstList[j])
                if(rulelastList[i]<>rulelastList[j])
rulelastList[i]=rulelastList[i]∨rulelastList[j];
rule=rulefirstList[i]→rulelastList[i];
rule.SI=    rulefirstList[i].SI+    rulefirstList[j].SI;
rule.CI= rulefirstList[i].CI+ rulefirstList[j].CI;
    ruleList.add(rule);
    rulefirstList.del[j];
    rulelastList.del[j];  }
    ruleset_rulepara(schema)={rule,rule.SI,rule.CI};
    for(m=1 to ruleList.length){
MTRuleSet.add(row)[m]=({ruleList[m].rule,
ruleList[m].SI,ruleList[m].CI}));
    out(MTRuleSet);
```

Table 2. Decision matrix of transformation rules

decision class	Equivalence class	decision matrix of transformation rules											transformation rules		measurement indicator
		X1									X2	X3	precondition	decision	(SI,CI)
		W1	W2	W3	W4	W5	W6	W7	W8	W9	W10	W11			
	W1		ruc		r	c		r	n	nrc	nruc	nruc	(n,0)∧(r,0)	(t,0)	(1.0,0.10)
	W2			ruc	uc	ruc	ruc	uc	nru c	nu	nruc	nru	(u,0), (n,0)∧(c,1)	(t,0)	(1.0,0.10)
	W3				r	c		r	n	nrc	nruc	nruc	(n,0)∧(r,0)	(t,0)	(1.0,0.10)
	W4					rc	r		nr	nc	nruc	nruc	(r,1)∧(c,3), (n,0)∧(r,0)∧(u,6)	(t,0)	(1.0,0.05)
X1	W5						c	rc	nc	nrc	nru	nruc	(n,0)∧(r,0)	(t,0)	(1.0,0.05)
	W6							r	n	nrc	nruc	nruc	(n,0)∧(r,1)	(t,0)	(1.0,0.05)
	W7								nr	nc	nruc	nruc	(r,1)∧(c,3), (n,0)∧(r,1)∧(u,6)	(t,0)	(1.0,0.05)
	W8									rc	nruc	nruc	(n,1)∧(r,0), (n,1)∧(c,3), (n,1)∧(r,1),	(t,0)∨ (t,2)	(1.0,0.30) (1.0,0.55)
	W9										nruc	nru	(n,1)∧(c,1), (u,6)∧(c,1)	(t,0)	(1.0,0.20)
X2	W10											uc	(u,2)	(t,1)∨ (t,2)	(1.0,1.00) (1.0,0.27)
X3	W11												(u,1)	(t,2)	(1.0,0.18)

Table 3. Set of transformation rules and measurement indicator

order	transformation rules	support	accuracy	coverage
1	$(n,0) \wedge (r,0) \rightarrow (t,0)$	5	1.00	(1.0,0.25)
2	$(n,0) \wedge (c,1) \rightarrow (t,0)$	2	1.00	(1.0,0.10)
3	$(r,1) \wedge (c,3) \rightarrow (t,0)$	1	1.00	(1.0,0.05)
4	$(n,0) \wedge (r,1) \rightarrow (t,0)$	1	1.00	(1.0,0.05)
5	$(r,1) \wedge (c,3) \rightarrow (t,0)$	1	1.00	(1.0,0.05)
6	$(n,0) \wedge (r,1) \wedge (u,6) \rightarrow (t,0)$	1	1.00	(1.0,0.05)
7	$(n,1) \wedge (r,0) \rightarrow (t,0) \vee (t,2)$	6	1.00	(1.0,0.30) (1.0,0.55)
8	$(n,1) \wedge (c,3) \rightarrow (t,0) \vee (t,2)$	6	1.00	(1.0,0.30) (1.0,0.55)
9	$(n,1) \wedge (r,1) \rightarrow (t,0)$	4	0.50,0.50	(1.0,0.20)
10	$(n,1) \wedge (c,1) \rightarrow (t,0)$	4	0.50,0.50	(1.0,0.20)
11	$(u,6) \wedge (c,1) \rightarrow (t,0)$	4	0.50,0.50	(1.0,0.20)
12	$(u,2) \rightarrow (t,0) (t,0) \vee (t,2)$	3	0.50,0.50	(1.0,1.00) (1.0,0.27)
13	$(u,1) \rightarrow (t,2)$	2	1.00	(1.0,0.18)

We apply Sub-algorithm 3 and get the transformation rules, as shown in Table 3. The transformation rules can be selected according to their measurement indicators, for example, we can select the rule through coverage. The highest coverage of the rule between *Class* and *Table* is 0.25, and the coverage of the rule between *Relation* and *Table* is 0.30, and the coverage of the rule between *Property* and *Column* is 0.27. The three kinds of transformation rules described using ATL are shown in Fig. 3. Note that according to the inclusion relationship between *Class* and *Property*, like *Table* and *Column,* the rule between Property and Column is consisted in the rule *Class2Table* and *Relationship2Table.*

These sub-algorithms are central components of rsCRT, so they determine the time complexity of rsCRT. Sub-algorithm 1 is used to generate the decision table through searching elements of the source and target model according to the mapping relationships, so the decision table is created in $O(N^2)$, and N is equivalent of $\max\{|\{\otimes(r)\}|, |\oplus(n,u,r)|\}$; in Sub-algorithm 2, the decision table is detected through searching itself. The number of cycles is equal to the record number of items in the decision table, so the compatibility problem is solved in $O(N^2)$; the number of the decisional class($|TM/\theta(\gamma_{TM})|$) is less than the number of the equivalence class ($|SM/\theta(\gamma_{TM})|$), and the number of the equal class is less than the number of the decision table in Sub-algorithm 3, so the decision matrix is built in $O(N^2)$; in Sub-algorithm 4, the number of transformation rules is equal to the number of the equivalence class, so these transformation rules are constructed in $O(N^2)$. Although the same rules are merged in Sub-algorithm 4, the number of cycles is not more than $|SM/\theta(\gamma_{TM})|^2$. Therefore the time complexity of rsCRT is $O(N^2)$, and $N=\max\{|\{\otimes(r)\}|,$ $|\oplus(n,u,r)|\}$.

4 Experiment

To validate the proposed approach, we designed three kinds of experiments in order to respectively analyze three quantities' influence on transformation rules (i.e. Class2Table, Relationship2Table and Property2Column), i.e. the sample's number, the number of the source metamodels and the property reduction. In each experiment, seven intervals of the sample's number are investigated. They are [0, 50], (50,100], (100, 150], (150, 200],...,(300, 350]. For each interval, 350 instances which are randomly generated are executed and averages of the three measure indicators are calculated. Java is used for programming in all of simulation.

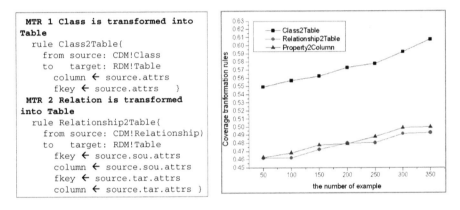

```
MTR 1 Class is transformed into
Table
    rule Class2Table{
        from source: CDM!Class
        to    target: RDM!Table
            column ← source.attrs
            fkey ← source.attrs    }
MTR 2 Relation is transformed
into Table
    rule Relationship2Table{
        from source: CDM!Relationship)
        to    target: RDM!Table
            fkey ← source.sou.attrs
            column ← source.sou.attrs
            fkey ← source.tar.attrs
            column ← source.tar.attrs }
```

Fig. 3. Transformation rules of the example   **Fig. 4.** Comparisons of the number of samples

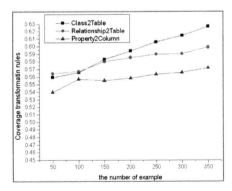

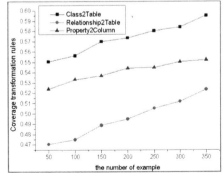

Fig. 5. Comparisons of the number of source metamodels

Fig. 6. Comparisons of the property reduction

Experiment 1 Number of samples
The average Coverage (Class2Table, Relationship2Table, and Property2Column) is shown in Fig. 4. The average Coverage of Class2Table varies from 0.5489 to 0.6072, and the average Coverage of Relationship2Table rises from 0.4619 to 0.4928 and the average Coverage of Property2Column increases from 0.5243 to 0.5522.

Experiment 2 Number of the source metamodels
In order to verify whether the detailed information of the source and target metamodels affects the construction and measurement of transformation rules, we expand the role elements of UCD2RDM, such as *sou*, *tar* and *child*. The result of the measurement indicators is shown in Fig. 5.

Experiment 3 Property reduction
The property reduction plays an important role in rough set theory. In this experiment, the condition properties, such as the property c, are reduced to observe the change of the average Coverage The result is shown in Fig. 6.

The first experiment demonstrates that the more the number of the mapping relationships is, the larger the average of the measurement indicators of the transformation rules is. For instance, the average Coverage of Class2Table varies from 0.2500 to 0.6072. In the second experiment, the more the number of the source metamodels is, the larger the average of the measurement indicators of the transformation rules is, in particular Relationship2Table and Property2Column. The third experiment denotes the average of the measure indicators become large when some properties whose values fluctuate are eliminated. For example, the average Coverage of Property2Column increases observably after eliminating property c in the source metamodels.

5 Related Work

Shane [12] presents a transformation language based on graph transformation and defines transformation rules through a group of production rule, while Karsai [13] proposes another transformation language to describe the mapping between the source model into target model using the theory of graph transformation and graph rewriting. Dhamanka [14] proposes an approach to create complex links in the beginning of a mapping. However, the complex mapping should be divided into smaller parts to produce transformation rules. David [15] gives emphasis to use set and relational algebra to describe transformation rules. The definition of relation is too strict to expand the set of transformation rules. So the coverage of the method is not widely. The solution in [16] provides a mechanism which name is Clio to produce transformations based on a set of relationships. Clio has a shortage that the definition of the relationships is not extended, so creating complex kinds of model transformation has become a challenge. Similarity Flooding has evolved in [17] to define transformation rules for difference metamodels. The major work gives an algorithm which is the basis of metamodel matching transformations. Design Pattern [18] is one of the first solutions to integrate modeling units to generate transformation rules. It can discover the relation between the source and target models. It is not adapted to match elements in metamodel-level, so it can not support the production of more complex mappings.

The work from [19] uses matching transformations and weaving models to semi-automate the development of model transformation. The weaving model can be used to discover and save the different kinds of relationships among metamodels. Our approach can not only construct transformation rules but also evaluate these transformation rules. In a paper of Zoltán[20], their approach is applied to derive transformation rules on the basis of the prototype of the source and target models using the inference logic method. Wimmer [21] use an object-based idea to derive ATL rules for model transformation. Because both approaches use mappings between terminal models to construct transformation rules, the rules will have the influence of the size of terminal models.

The INTEROP [22] approach is generally used to solve the transformations from and to the enterprise model level and usage of ontologies. In paper [23], starting from the ATHENA interoperability architecture, Bernhard Bauer presents a methodical approach to transform ARIS into UML and BPDM. However, the source and target models are conforming to UML2 and the approach doesn't support the other metamodels.

6 Conclusions and Future Work

In this paper we use rough set to semi-automate the production of transformation rules and present an approach to construct transformation rules. The approach supports the matching of different metamodels. Transformation rules constructed by our approach are accompanied by measurement indicators supporting selection of transformation rules.

We analyzed the construction theory of rough set from several aspects related to the complexity of transformation rules. Firstly, we have improved the construction approach of rough set to support the mapping between different metamodels. Secondly, we have presented the algorithm rsCRT to construct transformation rules. We provided the measurement indicators of transformation rules according to rough set. These indicators consist of support, accuracy and coverage.

To validate the construction approach, we designed three kinds of experiments in order to respectively analyze three quantities' influence on transformation rules, i.e. the sample's number, the number of the source metamodels and the property reduction. The result denote that the more the number of the mapping relationships and the source metamodels is, the larger the average of the measurement indicators of the transformation rules is, and the average of the measure indicators become large when some properties whose values fluctuate are eliminated. Future work is to optimist transformation rules constructed through our approach transformation. For this reason, we plan to analysis the transformation rules and compose some transformation rules to improve the efficiency of model transformation.

Acknowledgments. Research works in this paper are partial supported by the National Natural Science Foundation of China (60773064), the National High-Tech Research and Development Program of China (2009AA04Z153, 2008GG1000401028).

References

1. Mukerji J, Miller J.: MDA guide version1.0.1. OMG (2003),
   http://www.omg.org/cgi-bin/doc?omg/03-06-01.pdf
2. Kleppe, A., Warmer, J., Bast, W.: MDA Explained: The Model Driven Architecture: Practice and Promise. Addison-Wesley, Boston (2003)
3. Agrawal, R., Srikant, R.: Quest Synthetic Data Generator,
   http://www.almaden.ibm.com/cs/quest/syndata.html
4. Han, J., Kamber, M.: Data Mining: Concepts and Techniques. Morgan Kaufmann, San Francisco (2006)
5. Varró, D.: Model transformation by example. In: Wang, J., et al. (eds.) MoDELS 2006. LNCS, vol. 4199, pp. 410–424. Springer, Heidelberg (2006)
6. Pawlak, Z., Skowron, A.: Rough sets rudiments. Bulletin of IRSS 3(3), 67–70 (1999)
7. Liyun, C., Guoyin, W., Yu, W.: An Approach for Attribute Reduction and Rule Generation Based on Rough Set Theory. Journal of Software 10(11), 1206–1211 (1999)
8. Swiniarski, R.W., Skowron, A.: Rough set methods in feature selection and recognition. Pattern Recognition Letters 24, 833–849 (2003)
9. Øhrn, A.: Discernibility and rough sets in medicine: tools and applications, Trondheim, Norway (1999)
10. Pawlak, A., Slowinski, R.: Rough set approach to multi-attribute decision analysis. European Journal of Operational Research 72(3), 443–459 (1994)
11. Pawlak, Z., Skowron, A.: Rough sets and Boolean reasoning. Information Sciences 177(1), 41–73 (2007)
12. Shane, S.: Combining generative and graph transformation techniques for model transformation: An effective alliance? In: Proc. of the 2nd OOPSLA Workshop on Generative Techniques in the context of Model Driven Architecture. ACM Press, Anaheim (2003),
    http://cui.unige.ch/~sendall/files/
    sendall-mda-workshop-OOPSLA03.pdf
13. Karsai, G., Agrawal, A.: Graph transformations in oMG's model-driven architecture. In: Pfaltz, J.L., Nagl, M., Böhlen, B. (eds.) AGTIVE 2003. LNCS, vol. 3062, pp. 243–259. Springer, Heidelberg (2004)
14. Dhamanka, R., Lee, Y., Doan, A., Halevy, A., Domingos, P.: iMAP: discovering complex semantic matches between database schemas. In: Proceedings of ACM SIGMOD 2004, pp. 383–394. ACM, New York (2004)
15. David, K., Stuart, A.: A relational approach to defining transformations in a metamodel. In: Jézéquel, J.-M., Hussmann, H., Cook, S. (eds.) UML 2002. LNCS, vol. 2460, pp. 243–258. Springer, Heidelberg (2002)
16. Miller, R.J., Hernandez, M.A., Haas, L.M., Yan, L.-L., Ho, C.T.H., Fagin, R., Popa, L.: The Clio Project: Managing heterogeneity. SIGMOD Record 30(1), 78–83 (2001)
17. Melnik, S.: Generic Model Management: Concepts and Algorithms. Ph.D. Dissertation. LNCS, vol. 2967. Springer, Heidelberg (2004)
18. Tian, Z., Yan, Z., Xiaofeng, Y., et al.: MDA Based Design Patterns Modeling and Model Transformation. Journal of Software 19(9), 2203–2217 (2008)
19. Del Fabro, M.D., Valduriez, P.: Towards the efficient development of model transformations using model weaving and matching transformations. Software and System Modeling 8(3), 305–324 (2009)
20. Balogh, Z., Varró, D.: Model Transformation by Example Using Inductive Logic Programming. Software and System Modeling 8(3), 347–364 (2009)

21. Wimmer, M., Strommer, M., Kargl, H., Kramler, G.: Towards model transformation generation by-example. In: Proceedings of HICSS-40 Hawaii International Conference on System Sciences, p. 285. IEEE Computer Society, Los Alamitos (2007)
22. Panetto, H., Scannapieco, M., Zelm, M.: INTEROP noE: Interoperability research for networked enterprises applications and software. In: Chung, S., Corsaro, A. (eds.) OTM-WS 2004. LNCS, vol. 3292, pp. 866–882. Springer, Heidelberg (2004)
23. Bauer, B., Müller, J.P., Roser, S.: A Model-Driven Approach to Designing Cross-Enterprise Business Processes. In: Chung, S., Corsaro, A. (eds.) OTM-WS 2004. LNCS, vol. 3292, pp. 544–555. Springer, Heidelberg (2004)

Third Party User Interaction Control in SIP Networks

Ivaylo Atanasov and Evelina Pencheva

Technical University of Sofia, Faculty of Telecommunications
8 Kliment Ohridski blvd., 1000 Sofia, Bulgaria
{iia,enp}@tu-sofia.bg

Abstract. A lot of attractive applications in addition to manipulation of session related signaling involve specific processing at media level such as playing media, prompting and collecting media from the user, mixing media streams etc. One of the ways of provisioning applications in managed all IP-based multimedia networks, is based on Open Service Access (OSA) service platform. The paper investigates the capabilities for OSA third party control on user interactions in multimedia networks where the session management is based on Session Initiation Protocol (SIP). The focus is on the interoperability between OSA application control on session-related user interactions and media services in SIP networks. OSA user interaction interfaces are mapped onto SIP signaling. The behavior of the OSA gateway is modeled by synchronization of application view on user interaction call and SIP session involving media resources. A formal approach to functional verification of OSA gateway is proposed.

Keywords: Open Service Access, Media services, Interface to protocol mapping, Formal testing of functional behavior.

1 Introduction

Media services refer to different type of functions such as playing media, prompting and collecting media from the user, and mixing media. Many of existing multimedia applications use media services. In a managed all Internet Protocol-based network, session control relies on Session Initiation Protocol (SIP) [1]. SIP signaling is used to control media resource functions which provide media services to users.

Multimedia applications may be provided by three types of application servers [2].

SIP-based application servers host a wide range of value-added multimedia services. Along with the services like presence and availability, messaging and conferencing, SIP-based application server may be programmed to provide media services controlled by VoiceXML scripts [3], [4]. A mechanism for providing an interoperable interface between SIP-based application servers and media servers is defined in [5], [6].

The second alternative for service provisioning is Customized Applications for Mobile Network Enhanced Logic (CAMEL) Service Environment which offers

M. van Sinderen and P. Johnson (Eds.): IWEI 2011, LNBIP 76, pp. 36–49, 2011.

capabilities for supporting legacy services such as call control, user interaction, user status etc. The interworking between CAMEL services and SIP session control is defined in [7].

Open Service Architecture (OSA) allows third party access to communication functions in a network neutral way. Using OSA Application Programming Interfaces (APIs), application developers can create attractive applications without specific knowledge about underlying network technology and control protocols. Interoperability between OSA applications and specific network functions requires special type of application server called OSA gateway. The OSA gateway is responsible for translation of OSA interface method invocations into control protocol messages and vice versa.

The OSA User Interaction (UI) service provides API for call-related and call-unrelated user interactions [8]. The user interaction supports sending information or sending and collecting information. The mappings of OSA UI API onto CAMEL Application Part protocol and Short Message Service are defined in [9] and [10] respectively. No mapping of OSA UI API onto SIP signaling is defined. As SIP is considered to be a key control protocol in all IP-based multimedia networks, the mapping between OSA UI API and SIP would allow third party control on both session management and media services.

In this paper we investigate the interoperability between OSA application control on user interactions and SIP-based media services. We provide mapping of OSA UI API onto SIP signaling following [11]. As the OSA application view on user interactions has to be synchronized with the SIP session state in media resources, we suggest a formal approach to specification of functional behavior of OSA gateway.

The paper is organized as follows. In Section 2, we discuss aspects of OSA deployment in managed all IP-based multimedia networks and present in brief the OSA User Interaction service. In Section 3, we define an interoperability mapping between OSA UI API and SIP protocol. A formal description of OSA gateway behavior is provided in Section 4, where a SIP session state model representing the states of media resources is proposed and the behavioral equivalence between SIP session handling and OSA application user interaction handling is proved. Before concluding the paper we present an example of OSA application control on media services.

2   OSA Application Control in Managed All-IP Multimedia Networks

Internet Protocol Multimedia Subsystem (IMS) is service control architecture intended to provide all types of multimedia services based on IP connectivity [12]. In the IMS control architecture, Application Servers run applications some of which may reside in a third party network as shown in Fig. 1. The OSA gateway provides interoperability between third party control and network functions. The OSA gateway communicates with Serving CSCF (S-CSCF) which is responsible for user registration and session management which rely on SIP signaling. Media

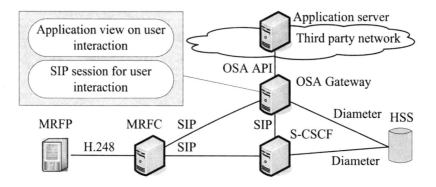

Fig. 1. Open access to media services in IMS

Resource Function Controller (MRFC) and Media Resource Function Processor (MRFP) together provide mechanisms for media services such as conferencing, announcements to users or bearer transcoding in the IMS architecture. The MRFC handles SIP communication to and from the S-CSCF and controls the media resources of MRFP using H.248 protocol. The MRFP provides media resources requested and instructed by the MRFC. The Home Subscriber Server (HSS) is a database which stores the user profiles. The access to user data in the HSS is based on Diameter signaling.

The OSA User Interaction service distinguishes between two levels of user interactions. Generic user interaction supports sending information or sending and collecting information from users. Call-related user interaction allows interactions with users engage in call.

In cases of OSA application control on user interactions in IMS, the OSA gateway is responsible for the translation of OSA methods into SIP messages and vice versa. The OSA gateway provides interoperability between the state machines representing the application view on user interaction and the SIP session with MRFC. In the next section, we define an interoperability mapping between OSA User Interaction interface methods and SIP messages.

3   Mapping of OSA User Interaction Interfaces onto SIP Protocol

The OSA User Interaction API provides the third party applications with access to the functions such as playing media, prompting and collecting media from the user via the OSA Interface Class methods. At the OSA gateway, the OSA Interface Class methods need to be mapped, or translated, onto the relevant SIP methods. The present paper is not exhaustive in covering all the mappings that can be expected. In particular, only general cases of normal operations are covered and exception scenarios are not considered. The elaborate mapping requires also parameters mapping which is beyond the scope of the paper.

The OSA *createUI* and *createUICall* methods are used to create a new User Interaction object for non-call related and call related purposes respectively. The invocation of these methods results in SIP session establishment with MRFC as shown in Fig. 2.

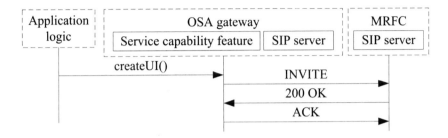

Fig. 2. Creation of OSA UI object and session initiation with MRFC

The OSA asynchronous *sendInfoReq* method sends information to the user. This information can be sent by SIP INFO request which controls media resources within the established session with MRFC as shown in Fig. 3. The INFO request may be used for initial or subsequent *sendInfoReq* method. The information to be sent to the user is transferred in the body of INFO request, for example as an XML script.

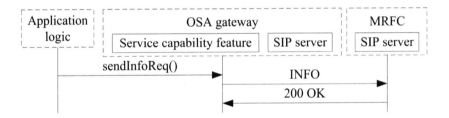

Fig. 3. Mapping of *sendInfoReq* method onto INFO message

The OSA asynchronous *sendInfoRes* method informs the application about the start or the completion of a *sendInfoReq* method. This response is called only if the application has requested a response and can be mapped onto SIP INFO request as shown in Fig. 4. The user interaction report is transferred in the INFO request body.

The SIP INFO request can be used to indicate that the request to send information was unsuccessful which is reported to the application by invoking of OSA *sendInfoErr* method. The user interaction error code is transferred in the body of the INFO message.

The OSA *sendInfoAndCollectReq* method that plays an announcement or sends other information to the user and collects some information from the user

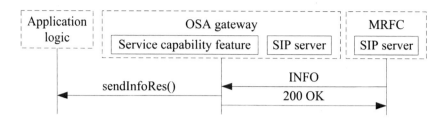

Fig. 4. Mapping of *sendInfoRes* method onto INFO message

can be mapped onto SIP INFO message as shown in Fig. 5. The information collected that has to be returned to the application using the *sendInfoAndCollectRes* method is sent by INFO message also.

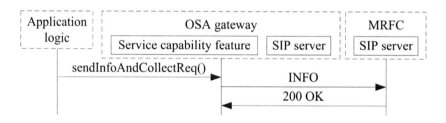

Fig. 5. Mapping of *sendInfoAndCollectReq* method onto INFO message

The INFO message is used to transfer the indication that the request to send information and collect a response was unsuccessful which is reported to the application by *sendInfoAndCollectErr* method as shown in Fig. 6.

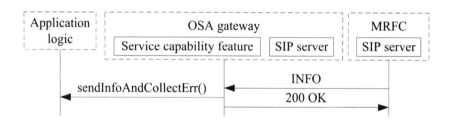

Fig. 6. Mapping of *sendInfoAndCollectErr* method onto INFO message

The OSA *release* method requests that the relationship between the application and the user interaction object be released. It causes the release of the used user interaction resources and interrupts any ongoing user interaction. The result is termination of the SIP session with the MRFC as shown in Fig. 7.

The OSA *createNotification*, *changeNotification*, *destroyNotification*, *enableNotifications*, and *disableNotifications* methods of the IpUIManager

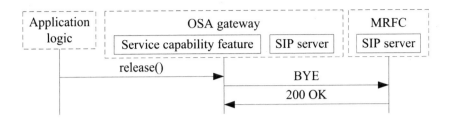

Fig. 7. The application initiated release of user interaction resources

are used to create, change, destroy, enable, and disable notifications for user initiated interactions.

Fig. 8 shows the call flow for *createNotification* method. The OSA gateway requests the S-CSCF to observe for certain SIP events to be notified to the application. Initial filtering information will be uploaded to the HSS and from here to the S-CSCF, e.g. when the user gets registered. User-related data in the HSS are updated by Diameter signalling.

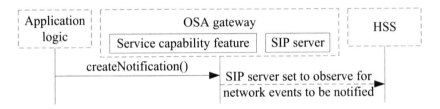

Fig. 8. The application subscribes for notifications related to user session

The OSA *reportEventNotification* method notifies the application of an occurred network event which matches the criteria installed by the *createNotification* method. Fig. 9 and Fig. 10 show the call flows for *reportEventNotification* triggered by SIP requests and SIP answers respectively.

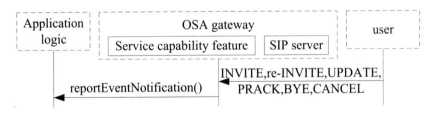

Fig. 9. Notification triggered by SIP requests

The OSA *userInteractionAborted* method indicates to the application that the User Interaction service instance has terminated or closed abnormally (e.g. a link failure to the MRFP). This event is reported by MRFC using SIP BYE message.

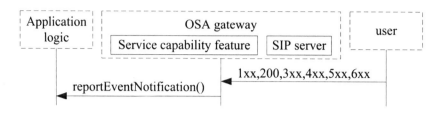

Fig. 10. Notification triggered by SIP responses

4   Formal Specification of Interoperable User Interaction Model

The formal specification of finite state machines as Labeled Transition Systems allows proving the behavioral equivalence and hence the interoperability of OSA user interaction control and IMS media service control. This may be used for automatic generation of test cases during the OSA gateway verification.

4.1   Labeled Transition Systems and Behavioral Equivalence

To prove behavioral equivalence between state machines formally, the notion of *Labeled Transition Systems* is used [13].

Definition 1. *A Labeled Transition System (LTS) is a quadruple* $(S, Act, \rightarrow, s_0)$, *where S is countable set of states, Act is a countable set of elementary actions,* $\rightarrow \subseteq S \times Act \times S$ *is a set of transitions, and* $s_0 \in S$ *is the set of initial states.*

We will use the following notations:

$s \xrightarrow{a} s'$ stands for the transition (s, a, s');

$s \xrightarrow{a}$ means that $\exists s' : s \xrightarrow{a} s'$;

$s \xRightarrow{\mu} s_n$ where $\mu = a_1, a_2, ..., a_n : \exists s, s_1, ..., s_n$ s.t. $s \xrightarrow{a_1} s_1 ... \xrightarrow{a_n} s_n$;

$s \xRightarrow{\mu}$ means that $\exists s' : s \xRightarrow{\mu} s'$;

$\xRightarrow{\hat{\mu}}$ means that $\Rightarrow$ if $\mu \equiv \tau$ or $\xRightarrow{\mu}$ otherwise

where τ is one or more internal (invisible) actions. More detailed notation description can be found in [13].

The concept of bisimulation [14] is used to prove that two LTS expose equivalent behavior. The strong bisimulation possesses strong conditions for equivalence which are not always required. For example, there may be internal activities that are not observable. The strong bisimulation ignores the internal transitions.

Definition 2. *[13] Two labeled transition systems* $T = (S, A, \rightarrow, s_0)$ *and* $T' = (S', A', \rightarrow', s'_0)$ *are weekly bisimilar if there is a binary relation* $U \subseteq S \times S'$ *such that if* $s_1 U t_1 : s_1 \subseteq S, t_1 \subseteq S'$ *then* $\forall a \in Act$:

$s_1 \xRightarrow{a} s_2$ *implies* $\exists t_2 : t_1 \xRightarrow{\hat{a}}' t_2$ *and* $s_2 U t_2$;

$t_1 \xRightarrow{a}' t_2$ *implies* $\exists s_2 : s_1 \xRightarrow{\hat{a}} s_2$ *and* $s_2 U t_2$.

4.2   Formal Description of OSA User Interaction

The application view on UI object is defined in [8]. The behavior of the UI object can be described by finite state machine. In *Null* state, the UI object does not exist. The UI object is created when the *createUI* method is invoked or a network event is reported by *reportEventNotification* method. In *Active* state, the UI object is available for requesting messages which have to be sent to the network. Both *sendInfoAndCollectReq* and *sendInfoReq* methods have a parameter indicating whether it is the final request and whether the UI object has to be released after the information has been presented to the user. In *Active* state, in case a fault is detected on the user interaction, an error is reported on all outstanding requests. A transition to *ReleasePending* state is made when the application has indicated that after a certain message no further messages need to be sent to the end-user. There are, however, still a number of messages that are not yet completed. When the last message is sent or when the last user interaction has been obtained, the UI object is destroyed. In *Finished* state, the user interaction has ended. The application can only release the UI object. A simplified state transition diagram for UI object is shown in Fig. 11.

By $T_{AppUI} = (S_{AppUI}, Act_{AppUI}, \rightarrow_{AppUI}, s'_0)$ we denote a LTS representing the OSA application view on UI object. Final and non-final attributes are shortly marked as X[f] and X[!f] respectively. Then:

S_{AppUI} = { *Null, Active, ReleasePending, Finished* };

Act_{AppUI} = { *createUI, sendInfoRes[!f], reportEventNotification,*
userInteractionAborted, sendInfoReq[!f], sendInfoErr[f],
sendInfoAndCollectReq[f], sendInfoErr[!f], sendInfoRes[f],
sendInfoAndCollectReq[!f], sendInfoReq[f], release,
sendInfoAndCollectRes[f], sendInfoAndCollectRes[!f],
sendInfoAndCollectErr[f], sendInfoAndCollectErr[!f] };

$\rightarrow_{AppUI}$ = { *Null createUI Active, Null reportEventNotification Active,*
Active   sendInfoReq[!f]   Active,   Active   sendInfoRes[!f]
Active,   Active   sendInfoAndCollectReq[!f]   Active,   Active
sendInfoAndCollectRes[!f]   Active,   Active   sendInfoErr[!f]
Active,   Active   sendInfoAndCollectErr[!f]   Active,   Ac-
tive release Null, Active sendInfoReq[f] ReleasePending,
Active   sendInfoRes[!f]   ReleasePending,   ReleasePending
sendInfoErr[f]   Active,   ReleasePending   sendInfoErr[!f]
ReleasePending,   ReleasePending sendInfoRes[f]   Finished,
ReleasePending   userInteractionAborted   Finished,   Re-
leasePending release Null, Finished release Null, Active
sendInfoAndCollectReq[f] ReleasePending, ReleasePending
sendInfoAndCollectErr[f] Active, ReleasePending sendIn-
foAndCollectRes[!f] ReleasePending, ReleasePending send-
InfoAndCollectErr[!f]   ReleasePending,   ReleasePending
sendInfoAndCollectRes[f] Finished, Active sendInfoReq[f]
Finished, Active userInteractionAborted Finished };

s'_0 = { *Null* }.

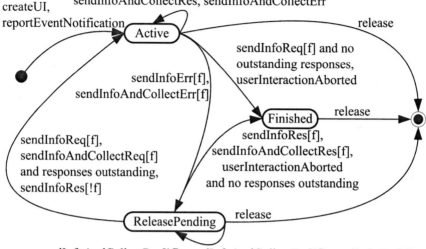

sendInfoReq, sendInfoRes, sendInfoErr, sendInfoAndCollectReq,
sendInfoAndCollectRes, sendInfoAndCollectErr

createUI,
reportEventNotification

Active

release

sendInfoReq[f] and no
outstanding responses,
userInteractionAborted

sendInfoErr[f],
sendInfoAndCollectErr[f]

Finished   release

sendInfoReq[f],
sendInfoAndCollectReq[f]
and responses outstanding,
sendInfoRes[!f]

sendInfoRes[f],
sendInfoAndCollectRes[f],
userInteractionAborted
and no responses outstanding

release

ReleasePending   release

sendInfoAndCollectRes[!f], sendInfoAndCollectErr[!f], sendInfotErr[!f]

Fig. 11. OSA application view on the UI object

4.3   Formal Description of SIP Session with MRFC

We formalize the SIP session with MRFC by $T_{SIP} = (S_{SIP}, Act_{SIP}, \rightarrow_{SIP}, s_0)$.
It is an LTS which represents a simplified SIP session state machine where:

S_{SIP} = { $Idle$, $Wait200_{INVITE}$, $Established$, $Wait200_{INFO}$,
$Wait200_{BYE}$ };

Act_{SIP} = { $INVITE$, 200_{INVITE}, $INFO$, 200_{INFO}, BYE,
200_{BYE} };

$\rightarrow_{SIP}$ = { $Idle\ INVITE\ Wait200_{INVITE}$,
$Wait200_{INVITE}\ 200_{INVITE}\ Established$,
$Established\ INFO\ Wait200_{INFO}$,
$Wait200_{INFO}\ 200_{INFO}\ Established$,
$Established\ BYE\ Wait200_{BYE}$,
$Wait200_{BYE}\ 200_{BYE}\ Idle$ };

s_0 = { $Null$ }.

4.4   Interoperability between OSA User Interactions and IMS Media Services

To prove the interoperability between user interaction models in OSA and IMS
we have to prove that the state machine representing the OSA user interactions
and the SIP state machine expose equivalent behavior. The behavioral equivalence is proved using the concept of weak bisimilarity.

Table 1. Bisimulation Relation between OSA User Interaction and SIP Session

Transition in T_{AppUI}	Transition in T_{SIP}
Null *createUI* Active	*Idle INVITE wait200$_{INVITE}$,* *wait200$_{INVITE}$ 200$_{INVITE}$ Established*
Null *reportEventNotification* Active	*Idle INVITE Wait200$_{INVITE}$,* *Wait200$_{INVITE}$ 200$_{INVITE}$ Established*
Active *sendInfoReq[!f]* Active	*Established INFO Wait200$_{INFO}$,* *Wait200$_{INFO}$ 200$_{INFO}$ Established*
Active *sendInfoRes[!f]* Active	*Established INFO Wait200$_{INFO}$,* *Wait200$_{INFO}$ 200$_{INFO}$ Established*
Active *sendInfoAndCollectReq[!f]* Active	*Established INFO Wait200$_{INFO}$,* *Wait200$_{INFO}$ 200$_{INFO}$ Established*
Active *sendInfoAndCollectRes[!f]* Active	*Established INFO Wait200$_{INFO}$,* *Wait200$_{INFO}$ 200$_{INFO}$ Established*
Active *sendInfoErr[!f]* Active	*Established INFO Wait200$_{INFO}$,* *Wait200$_{INFO}$ 200$_{INFO}$ Established*
Active *sendInfoAndCollectErr[!f]* Active	*Established INFO Wait200$_{INFO}$,* *Wait200$_{INFO}$ 200$_{INFO}$ Established*
Active *release* Null	*Established BYE Wait200$_{BYE}$,* *Wait200$_{BYE}$ 200$_{BYE}$ Idle*
Active *sendInfoReq[f]* ReleasePending	*Established INFO Wait200$_{INFO}$,* *Wait200$_{INFO}$ 200$_{INFO}$ Established*
Active *sendInfoRes[!f]* ReleasePending	*Established INFO Wait200$_{INFO}$,* *Wait200$_{INFO}$ 200$_{INFO}$ Established*
ReleasePending *sendInfoErr[f]* Active	*Established INFO Wait200$_{INFO}$,* *Wait200$_{INFO}$ 200$_{INFO}$ Established*
ReleasePending *sendInfoErr[!f]* ReleasePending	*Established INFO Wait200$_{INFO}$,* *Wait200$_{INFO}$ 200$_{INFO}$ Established*
ReleasePending *sendInfoRes[f]* Finished	*Established INFO Wait200$_{INFO}$,* *Wait200$_{INFO}$ 200$_{INFO}$ Established*
ReleasePending *userInteractionAborted* Finished	*Established INFO Wait200$_{INFO}$,* *Wait200$_{INFO}$ 200$_{INFO}$ Established*
ReleasePending *release* Null	*Established BYE Wait200$_{BYE}$,* *Wait200$_{BYE}$ 200$_{BYE}$ Idle*
Finished *release* Null	*Established BYE Wait200$_{BYE}$,* *Wait200$_{BYE}$ 200$_{BYE}$ Idle*

Table 1. (*continued*)

Transition in T_{AppUI}	Transition in T_{SIP}
Active *sendInfoAndCollectReq[f]*	*Established INFO Wait200$_{INFO}$*,
ReleasePending	*Wait200$_{INFO}$ 200$_{INFO}$ Established*
ReleasePending	*Established INFO Wait200$_{INFO}$*,
sendInfoAndCollectErr[f] Active	Wait200$_{INFO}$ 200$_{INFO}$ Established
ReleasePending	*Established INFO Wait200$_{INFO}$*,
sendInfoAndCollectRes[!f]	Wait200$_{INFO}$ 200$_{INFO}$ Established
ReleasePending	
ReleasePending	*Established INFO Wait200$_{INFO}$*,
sendInfoAndCollectErr[!f]	*Wait200$_{INFO}$ 200$_{INFO}$ Established*
ReleasePending	
ReleasePending	*Established INFO Wait200$_{INFO}$*,
sendInfoAndCollectRes[f] Finished	*Wait200$_{INFO}$ 200$_{INFO}$ Established*
ReleasePending *userInteractionAborted*	*Established INFO Wait200$_{INFO}$*,
Finished	*Wait200$_{INFO}$ 200$_{INFO}$ Established*
ReleasePending *release* Null	*Established BYE Wait200$_{BYE}$*,
	Wait200$_{BYE}$ 200$_{BYE}$ Idle
Finished *release* Null	*Established BYE Wait200$_{BYE}$*,
	Wait200$_{BYE}$ 200$_{BYE}$ Idle
Active *sendInfoReq[f]* Finished	*Established INFO Wait200$_{INFO}$*,
	Wait200$_{INFO}$ 200$_{INFO}$ Established
Finished *release* Null	*Established BYE Wait200$_{BYE}$*,
	Wait200$_{BYE}$ 200$_{BYE}$ Idle
Active *userInteractionAborted* Finished	*Established INFO Wait200$_{INFO}$*,
	Wait200$_{INFO}$ 200$_{INFO}$ Established
Finished *release* Null	*Established BYE Wait200$_{BYE}$*,
	Wait200$_{BYE}$ 200$_{BYE}$ Idle

Proposition 1. *The labeled transition systems T_{AppUI} and T_{SIP} are weakly bisimilar.*

Proof. To prove that bisimulation relation exists between two labeled transition systems, it has to be proved that there is a bisimulation relation between their states. By U it is denoted a relation between the states of T_{AppUI} and T_{SIP} where $U = \{(Null, Idle), (Active, Established)\}$. Table 1 presents the bisimulation relation between the states of T_{AppUI} and T_{SIP} which satisfies the Definition 2. The mapping between the OSA User Interaction interface methods and SIP messages defined in Section 3 shows the actions' similarity. Based on the bisimulation relation between the states of T_{AppUI} and T_{SIP} it is proved that both systems expose equivalent behavior.

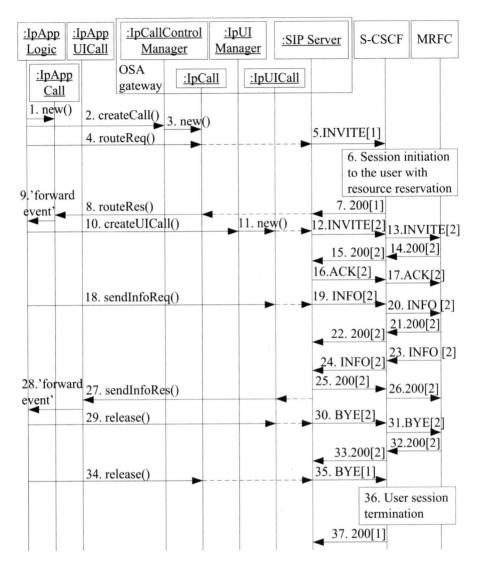

Fig. 12. Open access to media services in IMS

5 An Example of OSA Application Control on User Interaction in IMS

Let us consider an example application that sends greetings on occasion (e.g. on birthdays). The sequence diagram in Fig. 12 shows a 'greeting message', in the form of an announcement, being delivered to a user as a result of a trigger from an application. Typically, the application would be set to trigger at certain time, however, the application could also trigger on events. The application initiates a call to the user (steps 1-4), the call is setup in the network (steps 5-7) and the application is informed about the result of call setup (steps 8-9). Then the application logic determines to play an announcement to the user and creates a user interaction call (steps 10-11), the OSA gateway initiates a SIP session to the MRFC (steps 11-17). The application sends the greeting information to be sent to the user (step 18) and the OSA gateway sends instructions to the MRFC (steps 19-22). When the greeting is played the MRFC reports (steps 23-26) and the report is forwarded to the application (steps 27-28). At last the application releases the user interaction call (step 29) and the SIP session with the MRFC is released also (steps 30-33). The application releases the call to the user (step 34) and the call is released in the network.

6   Conclusion

OSA is seen by many mobile network equipment manufacturers as the successor of intelligent networks and CAMEL. That is why most service platform product lines now include an OSA gateway. By OSA interface deployment, operators can increase traffic on their networks, and hence revenue, by offering new services. Service providers can increase the number of users by offering attractive value-added services using connectivity with telecom networks. Users receive benefits through transparency and access to media services.

The paper investigates the interoperability of third party controlled user interactions and media services in managed all IP-based multimedia networks. The third party applications access user interaction functions in the network using APIs exposed by OSA gateway. The OSA gateway is responsible for transformation of API into network control protocol. We define a mapping between OSA User Interaction interface methods and SIP messages. Using a formal approach we prove behavioral equivalence between the third party application view on user interactions and the media resource control functions.

The approach is useful in testing the conformance of a black-box implementation of OSA gateway with respect to a specification, in the context of reactive systems.

Acknowledgments. The research is in the frame of Project DO-02-135/2008, funded by National Science Fund, Bulgarian Ministry of Education and Science.

References

1. Poikselka, M., Mayer, G., Khartabil, H., Niemi, A.: The IMS Multimedia Concepts and Services, 3rd edn. Wiley, Nokia (2009)
2. Gronbak, I.: NGN, IMS and Service Control - collected information, RI Research Note, Telenor (2006)
3. Crespi, N., Chadli, Y.: A Novel Mechanism For Media Resource Control in SIP Mobile Networks. In: World Wireless Congress 2004, San Francisco, USA (2004), http://www.it-sudparis.eu/dpt/rs2m/ncpub/2004/wwc

4. Burke, D., O'Flanagan, D.: An IMS Application Example Based on SIP Servlets and VoiceXML (2006),
   `http://dev2dev.bea.com/pub/a/2006/06/ims-sip-voicexml.html`
5. Burger, E., Van Dike, J., Spitzer, A.: Basic Network Media Services with SIP, RFC 4240 (2005)
6. Burke, D., Scott, M.: SIP Interface to VoiceXML Media Services, RFC 5552 (2009)
7. 3GPP TE 23.278 Customized Applications for Mobile network Enhanced Logic (CAMEL) Phase 4; stage 2; IM CN Interworking, Release 9, v9.0.0 (2009)
8. 3GPP TS 29.198-5 Open Service Access (OSA); Application Programming Interface (API); Part 5: User Interaction Service Capability Feature (SCF), v9.0.0 (2009)
9. 3GPP TR 29.998-05-1 Open Service Access; Application Programming Interface (API) Mapping for OSA: Part 5: User Interaction Service Mapping; Subpart 1: API to CAP Mapping, Release 9, v9.0.0 (2009)
10. 3GPP TR 29.998-05-5 Open Service Access; Application Programming Interface (API) Mapping for OSA: Part 5: User Interaction Service Mapping; Subpart 4: API to SMS Mapping, Release 9, v9.0.0 (2009)
11. 3GPP TS 24.229 IP multimedia call control protocol based on Session Initiation Protocol (SIP) and Session Description Protocol (SDP); Stage 3; Release 9, v9.0.0 (2009)
12. 3GPP TS 23.218 IP Multimedia (IM) session handling; IM call model; Stage 3; Release 9, v9.0.0 (2009)
13. Chena, X., Nicola, R.: Algebraic characterizations of trace and decorated trace equivalences over tree-like structures. Theoretical Computer Science, 337–361 (2001)
14. Panangaden, P.: Notes on Labelled Transition Systems and Bisimulation (2004), Retreived from
   `http://www.cs.mcgill.ca/~prakash/Courses/comp330/Notes/lts09.pdf`

A Process Interoperability Method for SMEs

Cuiling Liu, Chengwei Yang, Shijun Liu, Lei Wu, and Xiangxu Meng

School of Computer Science and Technology, Shandong University
Jinan, China
{sdling_0402,yangchengwei2006}@163.com,
{lsj,i_lily,mxx}@sdu.edu.cn

Abstract. This paper starting with the present status of enterprise interoperability, focuses on enterprise interoperability of SMEs (Small and Medium-sized Enterprises), and based on a SMEs oriented framework of enterprise interoperability proposes an approach of process level interoperability. The approach appropriate for SMEs mainly solves two types of interoperability involving processes' interior in the process level. Life cycle of process level interoperability is redesigned and reorganized. In each phase of the life cycle a comprehensive solution is given. In final, this paper gives a case study to describe and enhance the approach.

Keywords: Enterprise interoperability, SMEs, process interoperability.

1 Introduction

In modern enterprise computing environments, interoperability is a common issue caused by many factors such as heterogeneous systems, different organizational forms and diverse business processes. To gain more benefits and reach a common enterprise goal, enterprise interoperability has become a significant strategy for enterprises. In this context, many investigations concerning enterprise interoperability are done. The LISI (levels of information systems interoperability) approach with the goal of providing a maturity model and a process for detecting joint interoperability needs, evaluating the capability of the systems to meet those needs, and selecting pragmatic solutions and a transition path for achieving higher states of capability and interoperability for the US Department of Defense (DoD), was developed by C4ISR Architecture Working Group (AWG) during 1997 [1]. Other frameworks such as the IDEAS interoperability framework [2], the European Interoperability Framework (EIF) [3] and the ATHENA interoperability framework (AIF) [4] also have deep influence. But, a maturity framework particularly focusing on SMEs is still needed. All over the world, the proportion of SMEs in the whole enterprises is quite large. In this complex context, this paper reviews a SMEs oriented framework of enterprise interoperability. Based on the SMEs oriented framework, the main work of process level interoperability is elaborated, and an application about the traditional textile industry in China is given in this level as a case study.

The rest paper is organized as follows. Section 2 explains several related definitions and works about the thesis in this paper. Section 3 reviews the idea of a SMEs

M. van Sinderen and P. Johnson (Eds.): IWEI 2011, LNBIP 76, pp. 50–60, 2011.

oriented framework of enterprise interoperability. According to the framework and relationships between levels, an approach of SMEs oriented process level interoperability is proposed in section 4. Then, the process level interoperability is designed at the background of the SMEs cluster as a case study in section 5. Finally, section 6 concludes the whole paper and looks forward to the future work.

2 Related Works

Before entering the main topic, we have the need of interpreting some concepts and definitions about interoperability and process interoperability. Generally speaking, according to [5, 6], the ability of multiple system entities to understand each other and to use functionalities of each other by properly communicating and exchanging information is seen as interoperability. In the procedure of interoperability, the incompatible and heterogeneous features of multiple entities are covered, which becomes the goal of interoperability research. When interoperability is proposed in the enterprise computing environments, with the background of enterprise, it evolves enterprise interoperability.

Interoperability or the capability to interact and collaborate can be identified into three forms from [7, 8]. The three forms are respectively named as integrated, unified and federated interoperability, which depends on the location of the information used for reaching interoperability. In the integrated form, interoperability methods concern the internal implementation of software components. For the unified form of interoperability, a common meta-information entity is shared by each participant of interoperability. One kind of meta-information entity called standards has applied in the traditional industry for interoperability. However, the ambiguity and slow development of standardization make it unsuccessful in modern software engineering. The other kind of meta-information entity is explicitly shared meta-information which uses a specific modeling language to be defined and uses computing platform independent notations to illustrate components' features and interrelations. Compared with the previous two interoperability forms, federated interoperability form makes use of negotiation mechanisms, model verification and monitoring of service behavior referring on interoperability contract to work. The property of no common meta-information entity decides the necessity of a shared meta-model and meta-information management.

A process describes the collaboration of mutual or automated activities which have a common blueprint [9]. A process uses a meta-model to define the concepts and notations about process description and activities expression. Besides, a process model limits detailed process steps which a process instance relies on in execution. Process interoperability should contain control and synchronization to make sure that processes can interwork with other ones.

Considering process level interoperability for SMEs, an approach using E-mails communication to realize process interoperability is given in [10, 11]. In this approach, process interoperability is subdivided into one Build-Time component and four Run-Time components. The Build-Time component is a process of configuration, which requires that each SME must initialize its own processes based on the Reference Model Directory and store the processes in the Enterprise Process Repository. The four Run-Time components include detecting, tracking, assisting and advising. But, the approach uses a same process meta-model to define all the process models in SMEs and takes more attention to the composite application of processes. The authors in [12] propose a solution in interoperability of Process-Sensitive Systems (PSSs). The main idea of the solution is a virtual PSS independent of PSSs used to guarantee interoperability. The solution is efficient but costs much. In this paper, the sufficient use of existing resources and low cost are taken into consideration. Based on an integral SMEs oriented interoperability framework, a method of the process level taking more attention to interoperation involving processes' interior is proposed.

3   SMEs Oriented Interoperability Framework

As shown in Fig. 1, a five levels' framework of enterprise interoperability is proposed for SMEs. It contains data level, service level, process level, business level and presentation level. Based on the former fundamental interoperability forms, interoperability of each aspect in each level resorts to appropriate fundamental interoperability form, which we name as a mixed interoperability method used in the framework.

In the data level, interoperability commits to solving the incompatibility of different data models and query languages. Data from various heterogeneous data sources which may be established on different DBMS even OS will be used to exchange by the guarantee of data interoperability. Participants of interoperability can remain the

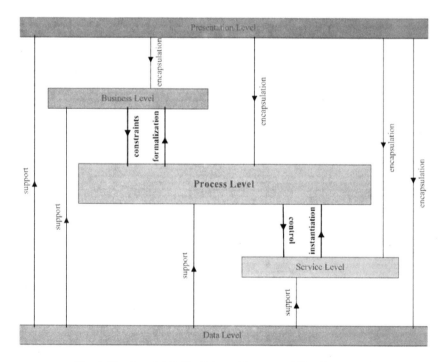

Fig. 1. Five Levels' SMEs Oriented Interoperability Framework

differences, but a shared meta-model is needed. Service Data Objects (SDO) [13, 14] is a specification for a programming model that unifies data programming across data source types, provides robust support for common application patterns, and enables applications, tools, and frameworks to more easily query, view, bind, update, and introspect data. In the procedure of implementing data interoperability, combination with SDO is a good selection in technology. Data interoperability is established with a mechanism supporting data transformation between senders and receivers, which provides convenience for other levels efficiently.

Service level interoperability refers to discover, composite different kinds of application functions or services for well collaborative work. SCA (Service Component Architecture) provides model for both service composition and service encapsulation, including reuse of existent function in SCA composite component [15, 16]. So, SCA can be selected as the service level interoperability technology.

The goal of interoperability in the process level is to make various processes work together. Interoperability of the process level is classified into two types in accordance with the interoperability scope. One is interoperability between processes independent of each other, which can be considered as interoperability between activity nodes not belonging to a common process. The other is interoperability between processes and their sub processes, and the interoperation points locate processes' abstract activity nodes which are related to the start and end activity nodes of sub processes. The details of process interoperability will be discussed in section 4.

Interoperability for the business level is on the standpoint of organization and company, and it deals with the interoperation barriers causing by diverse business rules, policies, strategies, legislation and culture. Business level interoperability is established by negotiation mechanism and monitoring facilities, which makes use of a federated analogous interoperability form. Considering interoperability of the business level, the circumstance of virtual enterprise and dynamic alliance can be considered. Due to the framework based on SMEs cluster, a domain ontology can be modeled by UML according to [17].

In interoperability, it needs flexibility, adaptability and agility in the presentation aspect to own well designed and harmonious presentation. In the light of the significance of presentation, interoperability of presentation is listed independently as the top level. Interoperability in this level emphasizes on integration more, especially a type of loosely coupled integration. Referring to [18], Widget Model can be used as a reference solution in technology. But Widget can't invoke remote resource. A modified Widget uses both local resource and remote resource in the process of across enterprise interoperability.

The process level's relationships with other levels will be explained explicitly. Firstly, the data level provides a comprehensive support for all the interoperation in the process level. Exchanging message meaningfully of processes is contributed to the incompatible data processing in the data level. Secondly, a process can be seen as a sequence of services. So processes have the ability of controlling multiple services work together for one common aim, and services are instantiation of process activities. In final, relationship with business level is discussed. Frankly speaking, the relationship is obvious. Business can directly impose constraints on process modeling. In this way, process models perform as business's formalization. Something still needing to be elaborated is that generally interoperability in any level or between any levels can't lack the support of the data level. So the data level can be seen as a basic level. However, the presentation level plays a role of showing all the understood information and can be considered as an encapsulation of other levels.

4 SMEs Oriented Process Interoperability

In this paper, we divide activity nodes of a process model into two types: abstract activity nodes and detailed activity nodes. Abstract activity nodes mean that they do not directly control activity services and they must be instantiated by other processes. In contrary to abstract activity nodes, detailed activity nodes must straightly invoke and control activity services.

To implement interoperability of the process level, a SMEs oriented process interoperability tool across enterprises is needed. It should contain process meta-model ontology, process activity analysis, interoperability point testing/sub process detecting and interoperability connection control. Here, the definition of interoperability point is limited to process activity nodes. Life cycle of SMEs oriented process interoperability includes two phases: Built-Time and Run-Time. In the Built-Time phase, the main task is finding interoperability points. Compared with the Built-Time phase, the Run-Time one mainly deals with establishing interoperation connection, interoperation and releasing interoperation. The following subsections will give a detailed description of the two phases.

4.1 Built-Time

Process meta-model ontology, process activity analysis and interoperability point testing/sub process detecting will perform in the phase. The information used in the whole process level generally can be divided into two types: requested information and responded information. Process activity analysis is used to identify requested and responded information for all the activity nodes including start and end of process models. For two activity nodes, if one's requested information is corresponding to the other's responded information partly or completely, interoperability point testing can decide that interoperability exists between them. Sub process detecting also makes use of relation about requested and responded information. If one abstract activity node's requested and responded information of a process are consistent with start node's requested information and end node' responded information of a common process, the latter process can be use as a sub process to instantiate the abstract activity node of the former process. Besides, decisions of information consistency need the semantic support of the data level. Process meta-model ontology is used in the mapping of process meta-models in diverse process definition languages and engines. With the help of process meta-model ontology, the quantity of nodes in interoperability points testing reduces largely, and the efficiency of interoperability points testing improves.

In interoperability between processes independent of each other, essentially finding interoperability point is a procedure of process activity analysis and interoperability point testing. Considering process interoperability with sub process, an abstract activity node using a sub process should detect, activate and monitor an appropriate sub process. When the selected sub process could not execute activities for the abstract activity node, the abstract activity node has the capability of finding a substitute solution. Sub process detecting is used in this kind of interoperability with respect to process activity analysis.

4.2 Run-Time

Interoperability connection control is used in the Run-Time phase for establishing interoperation connection, interoperation and releasing interoperation connection. In interoperability between processes independent of each other, two partners wanting to establish business relation respectively submit own process model to the process interoperability tool for interoperability point testing. After obtaining results, the two partners confirm the interoperability to establish a special interoperability connection. The meaning of the connection is to open process engine's certain function to each other for certain process instances in certain activity nodes. For example, in certain process instances A' (relying on process A) and B' (relying on process B) which belong to two different enterprises, activity A'.a of A' can use remote process engine function to signal an activity B'.b of B' in a special situation. Process instances end and the corresponding interoperability connection is released. Process interoperability with sub process is similar to the former one. Nevertheless, the abstract activity starts a certain instance of the selected sub process, and the instance's ending of the selected sub process signals the abstract activity.

The method of process interoperability for SMEs is illustrated by the Fig. 2. In Fig. 2, process A and process B in the top level denote the interoperability between processes independent of each other, and process A and process C in two diverse levels denote the interoperability between processes and sub processes. Finally, in order to improve efficiency, process activity analysis is done only one time before a new process model executing in process engine and the analysis results are saved for all the use.

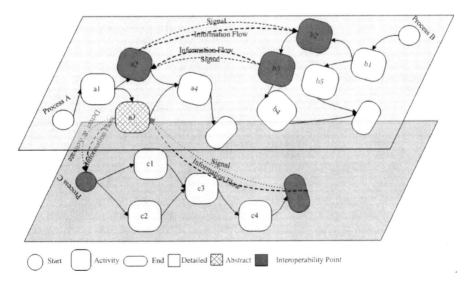

Fig. 2. Process Level Interoperability

5   Case Study and Analysis

Nowadays, there are many small and medium enterprises in the textile industry of China. These enterprises limited by scale and funds are still in the primary stage of information, which makes them at the disadvantage in the competition. The original purpose of this research is to help these enterprises in the textile industry of China improve efficiency in enterprise management and collaboration.

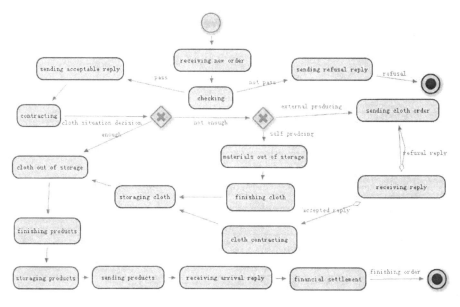

Fig. 3. Process Model of Enterprise A

A business scene is described as follows. When a textile enterprise A receives a new order, it firstly does a checkup for the new order. If the new order does not pass the checkup, the enterprise will send a refusal to the source of the order and the process is ended. Otherwise, the enterprise will send an acceptable reply to the order source and then contract with it. After the contract becomes effective, enterprise A begins to produce. Before producing products, the number of cloth in storage is checked. If cloth used in this order is enough, the cloth can be removed from the storage and be made into products. When the products are finished, they will be stored into the storage and then be sent. Later, enterprise A receives a goods arrival reply and goes into the phase of financial settlement. After financial settlement, the whole process comes to a finished end. There is also another situation that the cloth is not enough for the order. In this situation, enterprise A will decide to whether the cloth is produced by itself according to its own production capability and assignment quantity. If it can finish the cloth producing by itself, materials out of storage will be weaved into cloth. Then the cloth is stored in the storage for the use of producing products. If enterprise A can't finish the preparation of the cloth, it will send a cloth order to an enterprise B which is eager to producing cloth for A. After receiving an acceptable reply, enterprise A reaches a cloth agreement with enterprise B. When the

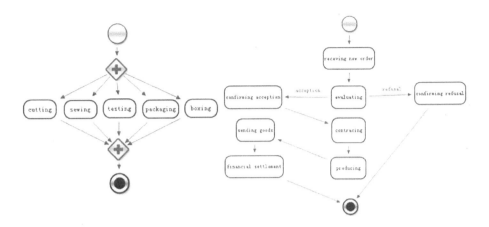

Fig. 4. Sub Process Model of Enterprise A (left) and Process Model of Enterprise B (right)

cloth produced by enterprise B arrives, the production will be continued. Besides, the procedure of producing products in enterprise A includes five phases: cutting, sewing, testing, packaging and boxing. Compared to enterprise A, enterprise B has a simple way of business. After contracts become effective, enterprise B will directly begin to produce and then send goods. Finally, enterprise B does financial settlements.

Based on the illustration of business scene, the global business of enterprise A can be modeled as a process model A shown in Fig. 3. In the same way, the business of producing product for enterprise A can be modeled as a sub process model A.1 shown in Fig. 4 (left), and the business of enterprise B can be modeled as a process model B shown in Fig. 4 (right). From the perspective of the process level, interoperability between process A' (relying on process model A) and process B' (relying on process model B) is interoperability between processes independent of each other; interoperability between process A' and sub process A.1' (relying on process model A.1) belongs to process interoperability with sub process used. The application implementation is based on a modified JBPM engine. Though a common process engine is used, process A', sub process A.1' and process B' use different versions to be modeled. After making process model A and B as input of process interoperability tool for interoperability point testing, confirm interoperability in certain instance A'-1 and B'-1. Then interoperability configuration in A' and B' can be showed like below.

```
<task g="503,88,160,52" name="sending cloth order" >
  <interoperability>
    <local-instance>A'-1</local-instance>
    <inter-instance>B'-1</inter-instance>
    <service>
      http://... /manageB/services/ProcessManger?wsdl
      <interface>signal</interface>
    </service>
    <activity>recerving new order</activity>
    <variable>cloth order<variable>
  </interoperability>
```

```
    <transition to="receiving reply"/>
  </task>
  <state g="673,210,169,52" name="receiving reply" >
    <transition name="accepted reply" to="cloth
    contracting" g="-43,-5"/>
    <transition name="refusal reply" to="sending cloth
    order" g="-9,-10"/>
  </state>
  ...
  <task g="117,177,133,52" name="confirming acception">
    <interoperability>
      <local-instance>B'-1</local-instance>
      <inter-instance>A'-1</inter-instance>
      <service>
        http://... /manageA/services/StateManger?wsdl
        <interface>complete</interface>
      </service>
      <activity>
        recerving reply
        <outcome>accepted reply</outcome>
      </activity>
    </interoperability>
    <transition to="contracing"/>
  </task>
  <task g="299,14,127,52" name="confirming refusal">
    <interoperability>
      <local-instance>B'-1</local-instance>
      <inter-instance>A'-1</inter-instance>
      <service>
        http://... /manageA/services/StateManger?wsdl
        <interface>complete</interface>
      </service>
      <activity>
        recerving reply
        <outcome>refusal reply</outcome>
      </activity>
    </interoperability>
    <transition to="end1"/>
  </task>
```

6 Conclusion

In this paper, we have reviewed a five levels SMEs oriented framework of enterprise interoperability. Interoperability of data level, service level, business level and presentation level is described in summary. Based on the whole framework, a process interoperability method for SMEs is proposed, and it focuses on two types of process interoperability. One is interoperability between processes independent of each other. The other is interoperability between processes and their sub processes. To cover the two type process interoperability, a SMEs oriented process interoperability tool across enterprises is designed and partly implemented. Moreover, an application of the textile industry in China is supported by the tool. However, both the approach and the application decrease the processing of semantic interoperability. So, in the future, we want to do some work about semantic interoperability for supporting SMEs oriented process level interoperability. Besides, the SMEs oriented process interoperability tool still have many disadvantages in design and implementation, which needs a long term hard work.

Acknowledgments. The authors would like to acknowledge the support provided for the project by the National Natural Science Foundation of China (60703027), the National High Technology Research and Development Program of China (2009AA043506), the China Postdoctoral Science Foundation (20090451313) and the Natural Science Foundation of Shandong Province (ZR2009GM028).

References

1. The C4ISR Architecture Working Group (AWG) (CAWG): Levels of Information Systems Interoperability, LISI (1998)
2. IDEAS: Interoperability Development for Enterprise Application and Software—Roadmaps, Annex 1—Description of Work (2002)
3. EIF: European Interoperability Framework, White Paper. Brussels (2004)
4. Guglielmina, C., Berre, A.: ATHENA, "Project A4" (Slide Presentation). In: ATHENA Intermediate Audit, Athens (2005)
5. Konstantas, D.: Object oriented interoperability. In: Wang, J. (ed.) ECOOP 1993. LNCS, vol. 707, pp. 80–102. Springer, Heidelberg (1993)
6. Chen, D., Vernadat, F.: Enterprise interoperability: a standardization view. In: Kosanke, K., et al. (eds.) Enterprise Inter-and-Intra Organizational Integration, pp. 273–282 (2002)
7. ISO: ISO 14258 – Concepts and rules for enterprise models. ISO TC184 SC5WG1 (1999)
8. Chen, D., Doumeingts, G., Vernadat, F.: Architectures for enterprise integration and interoperability: past, present and future. J. Computers in Industry 59, 647–659 (2008)
9. Conradi, R., Fernstrom, C., Fuggetta, A., Snowdown, B.: Towards a Reference Framework for Process Concepts. In: 2nd European Workshop on Software Process Technology, Trondheim (1992)
10. Burkhart, T., Werth, D., Loos, P.: Realizing process interoperability using E-Mail communication. In: 1st International Conference on the Applications of Digital Information and Web Technologies, pp. 579–583. IEEE Press, Ostrava (2008)
11. Burkhart, T., Werth, D., Loos, P.: Process interoperability through proactive e-mail annotations. In: 2nd International Conference on the Applications of Digital Information and Web Technologies, pp. 175–180. IEEE Press, London (2009)
12. Estublier, J., Barghouti, N.S.: Interoperability and distribution of process-sensitive systems. In: International Symposium on Software Engineering for Parallel and Distributed Systems, pp. 103–114. IEEE Press, Kyoto (1998)
13. Service Data Objects Specifications,
   http://www.osoa.org/display/Main/
   Service+Data+Objects+Specifications
14. SDO Resources, http://www.osoa.org/display/Main/SDO+Resources

15. Service Component Architecture Specifications,
    `http://www.osoa.org/display/Main/`
    `Service+Component+Architecture+Specifications`
16. SCA Resources, `http://www.osoa.org/display/Main/SCA+Resources`
17. Che, H., Mevius, M., Ju, Y., Stucky, W., Trunko, R.: A Method for Inter-organizational Business Process Management. In: IEEE International Conference on Automation and Logistics, pp. 354–358. IEEE Press, Jinan (2007)
18. Ma, Y., Chen, G., Thimm, G.: Change propagation algorithm in a unified feature modeling scheme. J. Computers in Industry 59, 110–118 (2008)

A Modeling Language for Interoperability Assessments

Johan Ullberg, Pontus Johnson, and Markus Buschle

Industrial Information and Control Systems, KTH Royal Institute of Technology,
Osquldas v. 12, SE-10044 Stockholm, Sweden
{johanu,pj101,markusb}@ics.kth.se

Abstract. Decision-making on issues related to interoperability can be furthered by the use of models of the organization or information system where interoperability is of concern. In order to provide decision-making support, the models should be amenable to analyses. This paper presents a modeling language specifically for interoperability issues where interoperability is defined as the probability that two more actors will be able to exchange information and use that information. The language is coupled with a probabilistic mechanism for automated interoperability assessments of the models created. The paper also presents an example of how the language can be applied.

Keywords: Interoperability, Modeling Language, Interoperability Assessment.

1 Introduction

Interoperability is a sought after quality for enterprises in today's competitive environment that has been approached from many different points of view and perspectives [1]. Several definitions of interoperability have been proposed, one of the most well known and the one employed in this article is that of IEEE, "the ability of two or more systems or components to exchange information and to use the information that has been exchanged" [2]. Based on this definition interoperability can be seen from the perspective of a decision maker as the problem of ensuring the satisfaction of a set of communication needs throughout the organization.

Enterprise architecture is an approach to enterprise information systems management that relies on models of the information systems and their environment. Instead of building the enterprise information system using trial and error, a set of models is proposed to predict the behavior and effects of changes to the system. The chosen architecture models must contain relevant information for the issue at hand. In the case of interoperability one important aspect is the information models, how messages are semantically and syntactically encoded. An architecture model describing how information is encoded, i.e. by containing relevant entities such as information models or protocols, is better suited for interoperability purposes than one lacking such information. Therefore there is a need of a tailored modeling language for representing the various aspects of interest for the decision maker. Most current enterprise architecture proposals, i.e. enterprise architecture frameworks, however lack such modeling languages that allow reasoning. In particular languages for describing architectures from an interoperability perspective are not available. [3]

M. van Sinderen and P. Johnson (Eds.): IWEI 2011, LNBIP 76, pp. 61–74, 2011.

Furthermore, the decision maker generally needs to decide on future (to-be) architectures and in order to facilitate this process there is a need for methods and tools that support the evaluation of interoperability in the enterprise. Such methods and tools are sparse in the field of enterprise architecture as well as in the field of interoperability [3]. Currently such analysis would generally have to be performed by a domain expert, a costly approach to analysis. Automating the analysis of architecture models would thus be of great benefit to the decision maker.

The contribution of this paper is twofold; firstly it defines a modeling language for describing architectures from an interoperability perspective. Secondly the modeling language is coupled with an assessment mechanism for interoperability, allowing the user, e.g. the decision maker of a large organization, to perform analysis of the created models without extensive knowledge of the interoperability domain. The modeling language is expressed in terms of a probabilistic relational model (PRM) [4] that, apart from constituting the modeling language, also specifies an analysis mechanism for the created models. This mechanism is however insufficient to express all types of interoperability concerns and is in this article augmented with statements written in the Probabilistic Object Constraint Language, P-OCL [5], see Fig. 1 below for an overview of how these concepts relate to each other.

2   Related Works

The related works can be divided into three main categories, although not completely mutually exclusive. The first category pertains to modeling in general and the second is concerned with interoperability frameworks. Finally work on assessing interoperability using maturity models or other approaches are of relevance.

There exists many architecture modeling frameworks and languages. The foremost software system modeling language is UML [6]. The language provides a very generic metamodel that can be used for system design and analysis. Apart from the basic language there also exists several extensions to UML, such as SysML. With such a general language as UML there is no, or only little, guidance in what to model and there is little support when it comes to interoperability analysis.

Furthermore a substantial number of enterprise architecture frameworks are available that, apart from the information system domain, also take business and the usage of systems into account. Examples are the Zachman framework [7], the Department of Defense Architecture Framework (DoDAF) [8] and Archimate [9]. These languages all provide more guidance for the modeler in what to model than for instance UML but are still not focused on interoperability and thus employing them as-is would likely result in a lack of several aspects important for understanding the interoperability issues.

Recently several initiatives on interoperability have proposed interoperability frameworks to structure issues and concerns in the domain. Examples include The European Interoperability Framework in the eGovernment domain [10], the e-Health interoperability framework [11] and the Framework for Enterprise Interoperability [12]. These frameworks generally provide means to classify the interoperability problems and solutions. At the same time they lack the ability to model interoperability situations and perform assessments of interoperability.

The ontology of interoperability (OoI) [13] is an approach towards a deeper under-standing of interoperability. OoI prescribes a set of metamodels to describe interop-erability from various viewpoints, including the communication metamodel aimed at describing interoperability situations. The language described in this article uses sev-eral of the concepts of OoI and additionally allows specific messaging situations to be modeled, something not offered by OoI. But foremost the OoI does not provide a means to assess the interoperability of the modeled scenario.

Several methods for assessing interoperability on a general scope have previously been suggested. The Levels of information Systems Interoperability (LISI) [14], Lev-els of Conceptual Interoperability Model (LCIM) [15] and i-Score [16]. Employing these methods would however require more domain knowledge in the field of inter-operability than the assessment method presented in this paper. These methods have the same goal as the work presented in this paper, to assess interoperability. Different from the work presented here these methods are often based on maturity models as apposed to this approach where an probability of successful communication is derived.

3 Architecture Analysis

For the sake of architecture analysis it would be of great benefit to have a modeling language that also contains an evaluation mechanism. Furthermore, the ability of expressing uncertainty, both in the assessment theory as such and regarding the con-tent of the model, would allow not only for an assessment to be performed, but also an indication of the precision in the analysis [17]. A *probabilistic relational model (PRM)* [4] specifies a template for a probability distribution over an architecture model. The template describes the metamodel *M* for the architecture model, and the probabilistic dependencies between attributes of the architecture objects. A PRM, together with an instantiated architecture model *I* of specific objects and relations, defines a probability distribution over the attributes of the objects. The probability distribution can be used to infer the values of unknown attributes. This inference can also take into account evidence on the state of observed attributes.

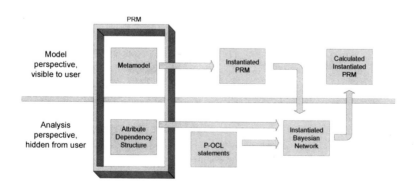

Fig. 1. Overview of the relationship between a PRM, P-OCL and Bayesian networks

A PRM *Π* specifies a probability distribution over all instantiations *I* of the meta-model *M*. As a Bayesian network it consists of a qualitative dependency structure, and associated quantitative parameters. The qualitative dependency structure is defined by associating attributes *A* of class *X (A.X)* with a set of parents *Pa(X.A)*, where each parent is an attribute, either from the same class or another class in the metamodel related to *X* through the relationships of the metamodel. For example, the attribute *satisfied* of the class *Communication Need* may have as parent *Communication-Need.associatedTo.communicatesOver.isAvailable*, meaning that the probability that a certain communication need is satisfied depends on the probability that an appropriate message passing system is available. Note that a parent of an attribute may reference a set of attributes rather than a single one. In these cases, we let *X.A* depend probabilistically on an *aggregated* property over those attributes constructed using operations such and *AND, OR, MEAN* etc.

Considering the quantitative part of the PRM, given a set of parents for an attribute, we can define a local probability model by associating a conditional probability distribution with the attribute, *P(X.A /Pa(X.A))*. For instance, *P(CommunicationNeed.satisfied=True/MessagePassingSystem.isAvailable=False)= 10%* specifies the probability that communication need is satisfied, given the availability of the message passing system.

3.1 P-OCL

PRMs do not, however, provide any concise means to query the models for structural information such as "given two actors with a need to communicate, do these actors have a common language (modeled as a separate object)?" The Object Constraint Language (OCL) is a formal language used to describe constraints on UML models. OCL expressions typically specify invariant conditions that must hold for the system being modeled or queries over objects described in a model. [18]

This ability to query models would be of great benefit to interoperability analysis, since many interoperability problems are due to structural factors. OCL is, however, a deterministic language and thus incapable of leveraging the benefits of a probabilistic analysis as described above. This section briefly describes how OCL is extended to *Probabilistic* OCL or P-OCL for short. For a more comprehensive treatment see [5]. For the sake of the P-OCL analysis it is necessary to introduce an existence attribute *E* in all classes and relationships corresponding to the probability that the class or relationship exists.

From a black box perspective P-OCL is used in the same way as OCL, the P-OCL statements are very similar to those of OCL. The difference is that the result of a P-OCL statement is always assigned back to an attribute in the model, something generally not done with an OCL statement. The modeler must also specify evidence on the values for the existence attributes of the classes and relationships in the model. Given for instance a model of a person's family and friends it is possible to evaluate whether a person's father is friends with any of the fathers of the person's friends with the following statement:

Self.parentalFriends := self.friend.father -> exist(self.father)

Using P-OCL, this evaluation will take into account the probability of the classes and relationships, i.e. does my friend really exist and, in this case more importantly, is he really my friend.

By combining the probability model of a PRM expressed in terms of parent attributes with P-OCL statements, cf. Fig. 1, it is possible to allow not only attributes to constitute the parents of an attribute but also various aspects pertaining to the structure of the model. This allows us to infer the probability that a certain attribute (e.g. *CommunicationNeed.satisfied*) assumes a specific value, given some evidence of the rest of the architecture instantiation. In this paper P-OCL statements are used for the main part of the analysis since many interoperability concerns are of the structural type. The general probability model of a PRM is instead used to aggregate attributes, e.g. the combination of the properties of a *CommunicationNeed* into the attribute *satisfied*.

4 A Probabilistic Relational Model for Interoperability Analysis

In this section a PRM for interoperability analysis is presented. The PRM is divided into two main parts, structural and conversation-specific, represented as white and shaded classes of Fig. 3 respectively.

☐ Structural aspects cover the basic infrastructure for interoperability. They detail for instance the parties that are to interoperate, the format with which the information is encoded and other similar aspects.

☐ Conversation-specific aspects are a more fine grained description of a particular conversation detailing the messages being sent between parties, the content of such conversation etc.

The classes related to the structural aspects can be used autonomously to create architecture models amenable to analysis whereas the conversation-specific classes are a refinement requiring the structural aspects as well and allow for a more in-depth description and an interoperability analysis of a particular messaging situation.

This chapter is the main contribution of the paper and is outlined as follows: First, a brief overview of the PRM is provided for orientation purposes. Then, the classes, reference slots and attributes are described in more detail as well as the requirements that are needed in order to achieve interoperability.

4.1 Overview of the PRM

Several definitions of interoperability have been proposed and one of the most widely adopted is "the ability of two or more systems or components to exchange information and to use the information that has been exchanged" [2]. Adopting this view these systems or components (corresponding to the concept Actor used in this paper) can be viewed as having a need for communication and the goal of the interoperability analysis is then to determine whether this need is satisfied. Actors can take various forms such as information systems, humans and whole enterprises but they all share the ability to actively operate on the information, e.g. interpreting or transforming information. To be able to exchange information, the actors need a medium for transmitting the information. Examples of such media, or Message-Passing Systems, are the Internet or Ethernet in computer communication, air in spoken communication between Actors of close distance or telephone lines when two parties use phones to communicate. Compared to Actors, the Message-Passing System is passive and can only transmit messages between Actors. Fig. 2 illustrates a simplified view of the PRM where the three concepts mentioned above correspond to the classes Communication Need, Actor and Message-Passing System respectively.

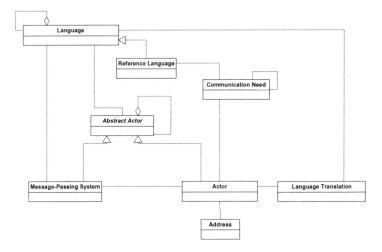

Fig. 2. Simplified PRM for the structural aspects of interoperability only showing the classes and slot chains

Actors need to identify other actors to interoperate with. This is done using an Address. Furthermore the actors need to encode the information in a format, or Language, that the other party also is able to use. Examples of such Languages could be XML to be transmitted over media such as the Internet or spoken English in human communication. Actors can use several languages for encoding the communication but need to share at least one to communicate. Actors can translate between different Languages through Language Translations (since Languages can be sub-languages to each other it is sufficient to speak a Language higher up in the hierarchy). Message-passing systems also use Languages for transporting information (i.e. the protocol), such as HTTP for the Message-Passing System Internet.

A special Language is the Reference Language, a language in which the communication need can be evaluated. Reality is one possible Reference Language that is used if the Communication Need is concerned with altering the reality, e.g. an enterprise receiving physical items from a supplier. Considering to Fig. 2, only the class Abstract Actor remains to be explained. Abstract actor is an abstraction of both Actor and Message-Passing System describing the common attributes and relationships of these classes. Most importantly, the reflexive aggregation relationship of the class Abstract Actor enables the modeler to describe the architecture on various levels of granularity, see the section Model Abstraction below.

In order to model specific conversations, four additional classes are needed. A Conversation Communication Need is the equivalent of the Communication Need and is shared by Actors. The goal of a Conversation Communication Need is to transmit a particular message between the actors, rather than expressing the probability that an unspecified message exchange will be successful as in the case for the previously described Communication Need. A Language can be detailed into its Constructs, defined as all valid symbols, words and sentences of the Language. A Conversation specifies a set of such constructs as the aim of the Actors to transmit. Constructs can be translated using Construct Translations and a set of such translations constitutes a Language Translation. Fig. 3 shows both the classes for structural and conversation-specific aspects and will be described in the remainder of this chapter.

4.2 Structural Aspects

The various model entities will now be described in greater detail. There are several requirements that need to be fulfilled so that a Communication Need can be *satisfied*. Firstly there must be a path between the Actors involved in a Communication Need. Furthermore, this path must be available; this is captured by the attributes *noPath* and *pathUnavailable* respectively. Requirements like these are expressed in P-OCL in order to be automatically assessed by an assessment tool. The definition of the *noPath* attribute is as follows in P-OCL:

> *context:* **Communication Need**
> *def: let*
>   ***getNeighbors(a : Actor) : Set(Actor)***
>   *= **a.MPS.Actor**->collect(**x : Actor** | **x**<>**a** and **getNeighbors(x))**-> asSet()->union(**a.MPS.Actor**)*
> ***self.noPath*** *:= not **self.Actor**->forAll(**a1** : Actor | **getNeighbors(self.Actor**->asSequence()->first())->exists(**a1**))*

where getNeighbours is a recursive support function needed in order to evaluate the *noPath* attribute in the latter part of the expression. In more detail, the Boolean *noPath* attribute is assigned the value False if all Actors of a Communication Need exist in the set returned by getNeighbors when called with one of the Actors of the Communication Need. The function getNeighbors receives one Actor as input and returns the union of all Actors related through the MPSs related to the input Actor and the recursive calls of the function which each of these Actors. Otherwise the attribute *noPath* is evaluated to True and this corresponds to evaluating if there is a communication path between the Actors. Furthermore, this evaluation of the structure of the model can be fully automated given an instantiated model. The remainder of this paper will only express the requirements in natural language due to space restrictions, the full set of P-OCL expressions needed for the analysis can be found in [19].

Returning to the requirements for satisfied communication needs, there must be a Language available that is spoken by all Actors which are related to this Communication Need, expressed through *noCommonLang*. Another requirement is that neither the syntax nor the semantics of the information which has been exchanged between the involved Actors has been modified so that it became unusable. This is modeled using the attributes *syntacticDistortion* and *semanticDistortion* respectively. It is also required that the addressing between the involved Actors is

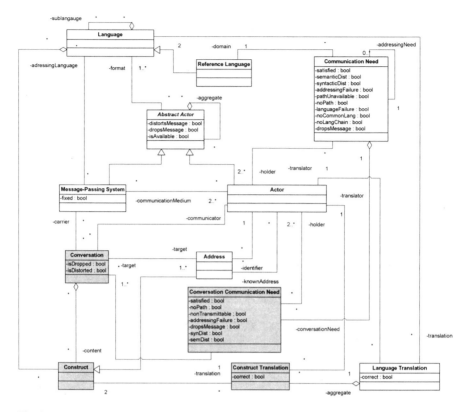

Fig. 3. The PRM for interoperability modeling and analysis containing the relevant classes and relationships for describing interoperability issues and performing interoperability assessments

performed without errors, corresponding to the property *addressingFailure*. Finally, for a Communication Need to be satisfied, no messages should be dropped on the route from the sender to the receiver, the corresponding attribute used within the model is *dropsMessage*. Only if all of these potential sources of error are cleared out, a Communication Need can be satisfied, which is reflected in the attribute with the same name. Evaluating the conditions described above is cumbersome but since they are defined in P-OCL [19] the evaluation can be automatically performed by a software tool.

The rest of the classes in the PRM will be described in four main groups. Firstly there are the classes that ensure a communication medium between the Actors sharing a Communication Need (the interoperation path). Secondly, classes related to language are described. This is followed by aspects covering addressing issues and finally the classes relating to a specific messaging situation, i.e. a conversation, are described.

4.2.1 Interoperation Path

Actors cannot be related directly to each other, there needs to be a transport medium that passes information between Actors. This medium is denoted Message Passing

System and is related to Actors via the *communicationMedium* reference slot of the Actor. The class MPS is associated to the class Language through two reference slots. The first, *uses*, indicates the languages used for message passing, i.e. the protocol according to which messages are formatted while transported by the MPS. Secondly the *addessingLanguage* reference slot expresses how valid addresses are encoded on the MPS. For a Local Area Network MPS, the addressing Language could be IP addresses. MPSs can be separated into two categories. Firstly, MPSs in which it is not necessary to take care of the addressing, as it can be solved unambiguously because the number of involved parties is fixed. Secondly MPSs where the involved parties are not fixed, indicated by the attribute *fixed*. For example, the MPS is fixed if it represents a cable connecting two Actors directly; in such case the involved parties can be identified unambiguously, otherwise, e.g. using a network for communication, addressing is necessary.

Actors and MPSs are specializations of the class Abstract Actor, which gathers common properties and relationships of Actors and MPS. There exist three scenarios in which an Abstract Actor might impede a communication. Either the Abstract Actor loses information, it modifies data so that it becomes unusable or it is unable to take part in a communication because it is occupied or defect. These three possibilities are reflected in the three Attributes *dropsMessage*, *distortsMessage*, and *isAvailable* of the Abstract Actor class. A key feature of the Abstract Actor is the reflexive aggregation relationship that allows for abstraction in the models and thus modeling on various levels of detail, see the Model Abstraction section below.

4.2.2 Language

The languages that are used within a scenario are modeled as Language entities. To format according to a Language, however, only means that the Actor can perceive and distinguish the Constructs (see conversation-specific aspects below) of the language. To understand those Constructs, the Actor needs a Construct Translation, or its aggregate the Language Translation, ultimately to a Reference Language.

A Language might consist of several sub-languages. Being a sub-language means that the language can be fully expressed by the corresponding super-language, either by being a subset of the super-language, e.g. HTML being a subset of XML with a set of specific tags, or by the super-language being a protocol for transmitting the sub-language, e.g. TCP being able to express, or rather transmit, XML (and thereby also HTML).

A Language can be mapped to other Languages, by the use of a Language Translation. This procedure needs to be performed by a translator, i.e. an Actor. As Language Translations might be performed incorrectly, the attribute *correct* of the Language Translation describes the quality of the translation. Language Translations are necessary, whenever two actors share a Communication Need, but lack a common Language to communicate in.

4.2.3 Addressing

Actors need to be identified, which is done using Addresses such as an IP address on the Internet. The Actor has two reference slots to Address, *identifier* and *knownAddress*. The former is used for identification of an Actor whereas the latter constitutes the set of such identifiers known by a specific Actor. The Actors that communicate over a certain Message Passing System must provide the Address to the Message Passing System for correct delivery of the messages. It is therefore important that Actors describe their Addresses in a Language that is compatible with the addressing Language of the Message Passing System.

If direct knowledge of the needed addresses is missing, this barrier can be mitigated of an address broker, e.g. a DNS or UDDI. Such situations can be expressed as a separate Communication Need between the Actor that is lacking information and other Actors corresponding to the address broker. In the model this is expressed in terms of a submodel for these address communication needs that describe how addressing in the original communication need is achieved.

4.3 Conversation-Specific Aspects

In addition to modeling the structural aspects described above it is also possible to model conversation-specific aspects. These aspects detail a particular message exchange between actors. Actors achieve ultimate communication success, i.e. interoperability, by transmitting the sought after conversation. For this purpose the classes Conversation, Conversation Communication Need, Construct and Construct Translation of Fig. 2 can be used for a more detailed scenario description.

A Language can be described in detail by its containing Constructs. Each possible message, which could be formulated in a language, is represented as a Construct. This is done to avoid the detailed modeling structure of the Language in terms of its grammar and thesaurus. During a message exchange Actors exchange several Constructs. This collection of transferred Constructs is called Conversation. As the modeling language is designed for static interoperability analysis, the order of the exchanged messages is not considered. A Conversation might be completely interrupted and not reach its destination. It might also be distorted reflecting that it has been unintentionally modified so that the original meaning is lost. These two characteristics are reflected in the properties *isDropped* and *isDistorted*. Conversations are sent through Message Passing Systems and are coupled with an Address, detailing the receiving Actor of a conversation.

For each specific conversation there is a Conversation Communication Need depicting the intension to exchange one instance of the Conversation class between a set of Actors. This class has a set of attributes similar to that of the Communication Need, as the requirements are similar for the two classes. There is one major difference, the attribute *nonTransmittable* ensuring that the Conversation is expressed in a language that can be passed between the Actors and over the Message Passing Systems employed in the scenario. Finally the class Construct Translation represents a mapping and transformation of one Construct of a Language to another one of another Language. A set of Construct Translations for constructs of a particular Language together form a Language Translation.

4.4 Model Abstraction

When performing assessments based on models there is often a tradeoff between the cost of modeling and predictive power of the analysis based on the model. In order to facilitate this tradeoff, the aggregation relationship of the abstract actor enables the system to be described on various levels of granularity. As previously described, Actors can take various forms such as whole enterprises, departments or information systems. A coarser-grained actor, such as an enterprise, generally contains several more fine-grained actors, such as information systems and employees. The most abstract instantiation of the PRM would be a model of the structural aspects with one communication need, two actors connected to one message passing system and the languages of the included parties. Although such a model would be easy to comprehend, the actors and message passing systems would in most cases be large and complex, consisting of several other actors. This in turn makes it harder to assess the probability of message dropping, availability etc., resulting in a less credible interoperability analysis, i.e. less predictive power. On the other end of the scale, a very thorough modeling of all details would require a larger modeling effort and make the resulting model harder to understand but it would also enable a detailed interoperability analysis with high predictive power.

5 Example Usage

To illustrate the use of the model, the setting of an electric utility company is chosen. In Sweden, electric utilities have recently been by law mandated to bill customers based on their actual monthly consumption rather than on an estimate that is adjusted once a year. This has led to the introduction of automated meter reading systems and a need for communication between these systems and the billing system.

In this example we have a Communication Need 'Get Meter Reading' between the Actors 'Billing System' and 'Meter Reading System'. These are connected using an 'ISDN' leased line of type Message Passing System that uses the protocol 'X.25' and the associated addressing language 'X.121'. The 'Meter Reading System' uses two Languages, the common information model ('CIM') and 'EDIEL' whereas the 'Billing System' only use 'EDIEL'. Fig 4 depicts a model of this coarse-grained scenario including the sublanguage relationships between the languages. On this model it is then possible to perform interoperability analysis once the modeler provides a scenario-specific parameterization of the existence attributes of classes and relationships as well as the descriptive attributes of the Actor and Message Passing System.

Returning to the requirements of the previous chapter, the P-OCL statements can be used to automate the analysis in a modeling tool and would for the current case show for instance: There is a path between the Actors of the Communication Need, these Actors do share a Language and this Language is transmittable on the MPS. It would however also show that the MPS requires addressing and at the same time the 'Meter Reading System' does not know the Address of the 'Billing System'. Furthermore the model does not indicate the existence of an address broker, so addressing will constitute a problem (i.e. GetMeterReading.*addressingFailure* will be true). Having evaluated all the P-OCL statements, the dependency model of the PRM will be used in order to combine the attributes into the *satisfied* attribute, which due to the addressing problems will indicate that the Communication Need will not be *satisfied*. For more information on this aggregation, see [19].

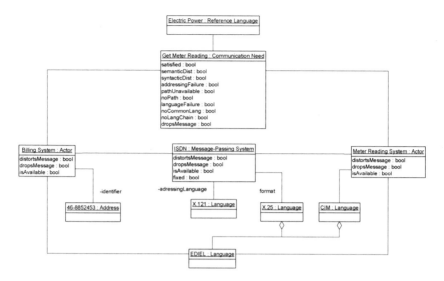

Fig. 4. Instantiated PRM for interoperability analysis of the communication need get meter reading. Reference slot names are only used when there is an ambiguity.

6 Conclusions and Further Works

This article has demonstrated how PRMs and P-OCL statements can be employed for interoperability assessment. The contribution of the article is twofold. Firstly, the language for modeling interoperability scenarios, expressed in a PRM, provides a means to describe interoperability problems and solutions in a generic fashion. Secondly, the P-OCL statements allow the modeler to assess the interoperability of the modeled scenario. A decision maker could employ this work for modeling various future scenarios and assess them with respect to interoperability.

The language was developed to be generic and capable of describing many different interoperability scenarios, not only in the information systems domain as outlined in the example above. A more specialized language would enable a more detailed analysis for that particular domain. Such specialization could be based on the language presented here and by PRM inheritance as described in [20]. At current, the language presented in this article is delimited to enabling factors for interoperability and does not cover directly preventive aspects such as various security measures. The versatility provided by the PRM formalism however allows such extensions to be added and it would be possible to create a new PRM covering both aspects.

Employing the language without tool support would be difficult for the decision makers it is intended for. In particular the evaluation of the P-OCL statements would be cumbersome. To aid in this, a software tool for enterprise architecture modeling and assessment based on PRMs [21] is currently being extended to handle P-OCL statements [22]. Using this tool, the decision maker can model current and future scenarios and automatically infer the degree of interoperability.

References

[1] Ullberg, J., Chen, D., Johnson, P.: Barriers to Enterprise Interoperability. In: Poler, R., van Sinderen, M., Sanchis, R. (eds.) IWEI 2009. LNBIP, vol. 38, pp. 13–24. Springer, Heidelberg (2009)

[2] IEEE: Standard Glossary of Software Engineering Terminology. Std 610.12. The Institute of Electrical and Electronics Engineers, New York (1990)

[3] Chen, D., Doumeingts, G., Vernadat, F.: Architectures for enterprise integration and interoperability: Past, present and future. Computers in Industry 59(7), 647–659 (2008), doi:10.1016/j.compind.2007.12.016

[4] Getoor, L., Friedman, N., Koller, D., Pfeffer, A., Taskar, B.: Probabilistic relational models. MIT Press, Cambridge (2007)

[5] Johnson, P., et al.: p-OCL – a language for probabilistic inference of the structure in relational models (2011) (to be submitted)

[6] Object Management Group (OMG). OMG Unified Modeling Language (OMG UML), Superstructure Version 2.2 (2009)

[7] Zachman, J.A.: A Framework for Information Systems Architecture. IBM Systems Journal 26(3), 454–470 (1987)

[8] Department of Defense Architecture Framework Working Group. DoD Architecture Framework, version 1.0. Department of Defense, USA (2004)

[9] Lankhorst, M., et al.: Enterprise Architecture At Work. Springer, Heidelberg (2005)

[10] IDABC, Enterprise and Industry DG. European interoperability framework for pan-European egovernment services. version 1.0, Brussels (2004)

[11] National E-Health Transition Authority (NEHTA). Interoperability Framework, Version 2.0. National E-Health Transition Authority, Sydney (2007)

[12] Chen, D., Daclin, N.: Framework for Enterprise Interoperability. In: EI2N, 2nd International Workshop on Enterprise Integration, Interoperability and Networking (2006)

[13] Ruokolainen, T., Naudet, Y., Latour, T.: An ontology of interoperability in inter-enterprise communities. In: Proceedings of Interoperability for Enterprise Software and Applications, I-ESA 2007 (2007)

[14] Kasunic, M., Anderson, W.: Measuring Systems Interoperability: Challenges and Opportunities. Technical Note, CMU/SEI-2004-TN-003, Pittsburgh: Software Engineering Institute, Carnegie Mellon University (2004)

[15] Tolk, A., Muguira, J.: The Levels of Conceptual Interoperability Model. In: Proceedings of the 2003 Fall Simulation Interoperability Workshop (2003)

[16] Ford, T., Colombi, J., Graham, S., Jacques, D.: The Interoperability Score. In: Proceedings of the Fifth Annual Conference on Systems Engineering Research (2007)

[17] Johnson, P., Lagerström, R., Närman, P., Simonsson, M.: Enterprise Architecture Analysis with Extended Influence Diagrams. Information Systems Frontiers 9(2) (2007)

[18] Object Management Group (OMG). Object Constraint Language specification, version 2.0 formal/06-05-01 (2006)

[19] Ullberg, J.: P-OCL expressions for interoperability analysis (2010), http://www.ics.kth.se/POCL/interoperability.html

[20] Sommestad, T., Ekstedt, M., Johnson, P.: A Probabilistic Relational Model for Security Risk Analysis. Computers & Security (2010)

[21] Buschle, M., Ullberg, J., Franke, U., Lagerström, R., Sommestad, T.: A tool for enterprise architecture analysis using the PRM formalism. In: Soffer, P., Proper, E. (eds.) CAiSE Forum 2010. LNBIP, vol. 72, pp. 108–121. Springer, Heidelberg (2011)

[22] Ullberg, J., Franke, U., Buschle, M., Johnson, P.: A Tool for Interoperability Analysis of Enterprise Architecture Models using Pi-OCL. In: Proceedings of the International Conference on Interoperability for Enterprise Software and Applications, I-ESA 2010 (2010)

Development of Innovative Services Enhancing Interoperability in Cross-Organizational Business Processes

Stefan Huber[1], Cyril Carrez[2], and Hannes Suttner[1]

[1] Siemens AG, Vienna, Austria
[2] SINTEF ICT, Oslo, Norway
{stefan.a.huber,hannes.suttner}@siemens.com,
Cyril.Carrez@sintef.no

Abstract. This paper presents the vision and ongoing results of the COIN (FP7-216256) European project for the development of collaborative and cross-organizational business process interoperability. Services for selectively publishing parts of private business processes are developed which enable the creation of a cross-organizational business process (CBP). Gap detection services provide analysis of the CBP with regards to interoperability gaps like potential deadlocks.

Keywords: Cross-organizational business processes, process interoperability, private-to-public transformation, interoperability gap detection, BPMN, SBVR.

1 Introduction

COIN (FP7-216256) is an integrated project in the European Commission Seventh Framework Program. According the COIN vision [1] by 2020 enterprise collaboration and interoperability services will become an invisible, pervasive and self-adaptive knowledge and business utility at disposal of the European networked enterprises from any industrial sector and domain in order to rapidly set-up, efficiently manage and effectively operate different forms of business collaborations, from the most traditional supply chains to the most advanced and dynamic business ecosystems.

The mission of the Coin IP is to study, design, develop and prototype an open, self-adaptive, generic ICT integrated solution to support the above 2020 vision. COIN is starting from existing research results in the field of Enterprise Collaboration and Enterprise Interoperability.

In this paper we present the vision and ongoing results for the definition and prototypic development of cross-organizational business process interoperability (CBPip) services in the course of the COIN project. The main objective of these services is to ensure a successful business process collaboration of participating enterprises. We concentrate on two main streams: rule-based transformation of private business processes into public processes, and detection of business process interoperability problems at design-time level. The transformation helps an enterprise to extract from its private processes the parts that can be of interest when collaborating with a partner.

M. van Sinderen and P. Johnson (Eds.): IWEI 2011, LNBIP 76, pp. 75–88, 2011.

The detection of interoperability problems helps the enterprises to design the cross-organizational business process and detect some problems at design time. Our previous work [4] is extended by providing more flexible transformations using business rules, and by analyzing the CBP for interoperability gaps.

This paper is structured as follows. The general approach of the CBPip services is depicted in section 2. The paper then presents the two services developed in this context: a service providing the private-to-public transformation of the involved business processes (section 3), and a verification service for finding gaps in the cross-organizational business process (section 4). Section 5 describes related work. Conclusions and future work are presented in section 6.

2 General Approach

In the scope of COIN it is important to distinguish "collaboration" from "interoperability".

According to COIN [1], *Enterprise Collaboration* comes from a business perspective and identifies the process of enterprises - mainly SMEs - to set-up and manage cross-enterprise win-win business relations in response to business opportunities. *Enterprise Interoperability* originates by the ICT world and identifies a capability of enterprise software and applications to exchange information and to mutually understand the information exchanged at the level of data, applications, processes and enterprise models involved. Enterprise Interoperability (EI) services provide functionality for applying IT solutions that overcome interoperability problems between two or more enterprises, and thus enabling them to set-up and run collaborations.

In this paper, we define *business interoperability* as the capability of two or more systems to cooperate using exchanged information, and an *interoperability gap* is a situation when interoperating business processes do not deliver the expected results while each of the business processes does. To be able to cooperate, a network of organizations needs to first define a Cross-Organizational Business Process and analyze it to find interoperability gaps.

Whereas other COIN services deal on collaboration issues, the services described in this paper are focused on interoperability issues only.

2.1 Creating a Cross Organizational Business Process (CBP)

Before showing how to create a CBP we first define some terms:

Process:
> A Process is any activity performed within a company or organization.

Cross-Organizational Business Process (CBP):
> A CBP describes a process involving two or more organizations.

Private Process:
> A Private Process is an internal process of a partner, and its functionality is invisible to any external entities. Making elements of a private process visible is the precondition of its "interoperability".

Public Process (View):
    A Public Process is a published process. It is a specific view on a Private Process of a partner. Via the Public Process, the collaborating partners may invoke specific functionality of the corresponding internal process.
Private2Public transformation:
    A Private2Public transformation is a model-to-model transformation, which generates public views for specific partners. It is based on Visibility Rules.
Visibility Rules:
    Visibility rules are business rules that define which process elements are shown to which partner. They are defined in SBVR (Semantics of Business Vocabulary and Business Rules [5]).

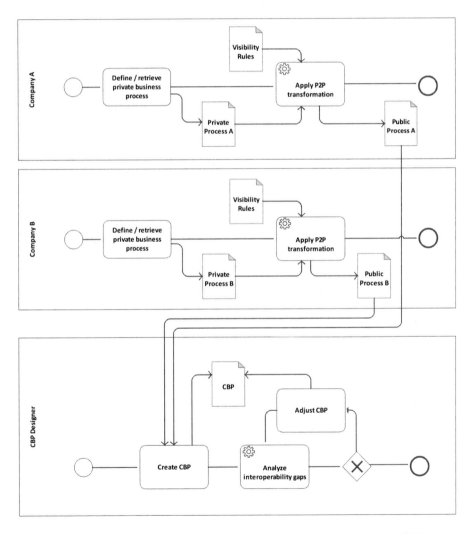

Fig. 1. Creating and Analyzing the Cross-Organizational Business Process (CBP)

Figure 1 shows the workflow for creating the CBP. The starting point is the business process model of a specific company, e.g. "Private Process A" for company A. The company A has already defined a set of "Visibility Rules" which specify the visibility rights to different elements of Private Process A, applied to different kinds of partners. The rules are applied to Private Process A for the company B, hence generating the Public Process A that can be used to model the CBP with company B. Similary, the Public Process B is generated. Under these prerequisites, the CBP can be modelled by using elements of the public processes of the involved companies.

2.2 Analyzing a CBP

Once the CBP has been specified, it needs to be analyzed for interoperability gaps.

A *Cross-Organizational Business Process Interoperability Gap* (CBPip gap) is a condition when two or more collaborating public processes don't deliver the expected business results, although they may work faultlessly under other conditions. In other words, an existing CBPip gap is a condition through which the CBP workflow process execution leads to unsuccessful business collaboration. Gaps can be deadlocks (i.e. the CBPip process possibly will not terminate) or interface mismatch (i.e. the formats of a sent document does not match the format being expected by the receiving organization).

In this paper, we address the potential business process collaboration problems at a technical level, and recognize them as CBPip gaps. Once the CBP is modelled, the CBPip gap detection is invoked and parses the CBP model to detect the CBPip gap patterns. The gap patterns are conceptually defined in classes and types. On detection, the known reason or an assumption of the CBPip gap will be displayed.

The following sections describe the Private2Public transformation and CBPip gaps.

3   Private-to-Public Transformation

This section presents the transformation from Private Processes to Public Processes and how Visibility Rules are used in such a transformation.

The aim of the Private2Public transformation is to produce a public process of a private process of a given company. This public process will hide all the private and critical data of the private process, resulting in a simplified process. Instead of annotating all activities and data with a public/private tag, we aim for the use of a business rule language in order to describe the visibility of different process elements of a private process. We chose SBVR (Semantics of Business Vocabulary and Business Rules [5]) for describing visibility rules. As a standard, SBVR offers a strong basis; it also allows a representation of rules in Structured English, and hence is more readable and usable for Business Analysts who will produce Visibility Rules. The main drawback of SBVR is the complexity of its meta-model and the production of a suitable vocabulary; however those drawbacks are taken care of by the technology experts who will develop tools to handle the complexity of the meta-model (end-users will see only the SBVR rules in Structured English) and who will create the vocabulary with the help of business experts.

3.1 Principles of the Private to Public Transformation

The SBVR for CBP allows describing how a public process should be produced from a private process, by way of business rules. This is achieved through three principles (Figure 2):

- The **SBVR rules are linked to specific elements of Processes**, so the transformation service knows which elements are described in the rules. This is done by two ways: First, the elements in a Process (Activities, Data, ...) can be annotated with an SBVR vocabulary which describes the purpose of those elements. However, as this may clutter the diagrams, a second possibility is to use the names of the elements in a Process (e.g.: an activity involving some Invoice contains the string "invoice" in its name).
- **A Vocabulary (in SBVR) which describes the semantic of Process elements, as well as the roles of partners in a CBP.** The vocabulary defines noun-concepts related to the modelling of Process elements (Activity, Data) or to their semantics (Sales Department, Customer, etc.), as well as verb-concepts to specify associations ("an *activity* *manipulates* some *invoice*"[1]). Notably a verb-concept "*is visible to*" associates elements in Processes with partners in the CBP.
- **Business rules which specify what should be public.** By default, nothing is shown to partners. The rules are then based on the RBAC principle (Rule-Based Access Control [6]). The business rules are based on the verb-concept "*is visible to*", and tell which element in the process should be visible to which kind of partner. For instance, "An *activity* that *is about* management *is visible to* some strategy department".

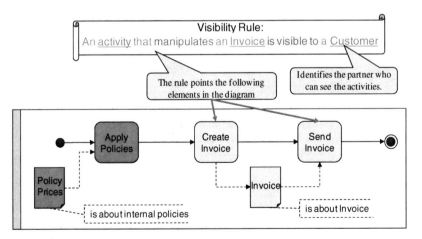

Fig. 2. Principles of visibility rules

---

[1] In this paper we show the Visibility Rules in Structured English, with four font styles for term, Name, *verb* and keyword, as documented in the SBVR specification [5, pp237-238].

Those principles are illustrated in Figure 2. The private process applies pricing policies in order to create and then send an invoice. The last two activities handle some data which is annotated with the SBVR expression "*is about* Invoice". A Visibility Rule can then use this information and specify: "An activity that *manipulates* an Invoice *is visible to* a Customer", which means that the activities "Create Invoice" and "Send Invoice", which send and receive some data that is about Invoice, are concerned by this rule and will be made visible to a Customer. The other activity "Apply Policies" and the critical data "Policy Prices" will be removed in the public view.

3.2 SBVR Vocabulary and Rules

In order to build the SBVR Vocabulary, we studied the COIN use case scenarios of healthcare and aeronautics clusters, and business examples which came along with the Enhydra Shark process execution environment[2]. This resulted in a vocabulary summarized in Figure 3. Facts and concepts related to process models identify abstract concepts that represent elements in BPMN, as well as the most important fact-types for visibility rules, "*is visible to*". Those terms are specialized with concepts related to roles, activities, control flow and data.

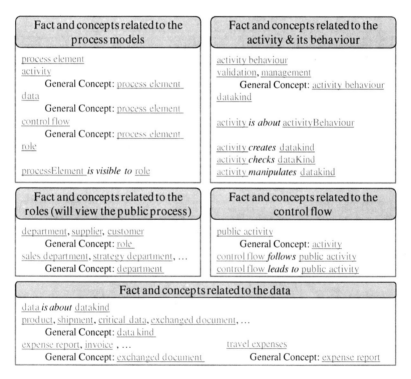

Fig. 3. Fact types and main concepts in the CBP Vocabulary

---

[2] http://www.together.at/prod/workflow/tws

3.3   Visibility Rules

Visibility Rules specify which elements in the model of the process are to be shown in the public view. They are specified as *Advices of Possibilty* in SBVR[3], and are based on the fact type "*is visible to*", which relates a Process Element with some Role. Visibility rules have two parts: the first one introduces the Process Element (Activity, Data, ControlFlow) in the private process; this Process Element is further characterized ("Activity *is about* management") in order to address a specific element in the private process. The second part of the rule specifies who is able to see the Process Element at stake ("*is visible to* some Customer").

Here are some examples of Visibility Rules:

It is possible that an activity that *is about* validation *is visible to* some strategy department.

It is possible that an activity that *manipulates* some feedback *is visible to* some customer.

It is possible that a data that *is about* some reclamation *is visible to* some sales department.

It is possible that a sequence flow that *follows* a public activity *is visible to* some role.

3.4   Principles of the Transformation

The principle of the transformation is shown in Figure 4: each public activity will be put in its own workflow, to allow an easy composition of the public views in the CBP. This is illustrated in the top part of the figure, where the activities "Request Invoice" and "Send Invoice" are public[4], and the private process is transformed into two Workflows, one for each activity. The lower part of the figure presents a special case in the transformation. In case the private process presents a sequence of public activities, then those activities are put in the same workflow. The sequence must be linear, meaning

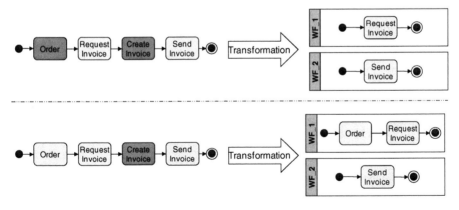

Fig. 4. Results of the transformation

---

[3] SBVR specifies *Rules*, which remove some freedom, and *Advices* which add some freedom. The transformation is such that everything is private (removes all freedom), and the Visibility Rule tells what should be shown (add some freedom), the choice of *Advice* was preferred.

[4] For the sake of clarity we removed the Visibility Rules and colored the activities instead (red/dark grey=private, green/light grey=public).

that no gateways (fork / join) between the activities are permitted, and only one transition is allowed between the activities. For instance, if "Order" and "Request Invoice" are public activities, they will be put in a single workflow, as shown in the figure.

4 Interoperability Gap Detection

Once the CBP has been created by using elements of the Public Processes of the involved organizations, the CBP can be analyzed for interoperability gaps.

Business process collaboration is seen as given, i.e. already agreed business collaboration between the partners of a specific CBP is a pre-condition for the CBPip. Although gaps on business collaboration level are not explicit subject of our considerations, we allocate them a unique gap class. CBPip considers gaps during design-time. Gaps at execution time (run time) are not considered in this paper; those gaps may arise during the CBP model execution as a result of common IP based network connectivity problems. Note that design-time is a phase where the process will be considered during its specification, e.g. during modelling in a business process modelling tool. Contrarily, run-time is a phase where a process or the automated parts of a process will be considered during its execution on a process execution engine.

We first give a short example of a CBPip Gap before describing the classification of those gaps. The detection service is presented in the end.

4.1 Description of an Exemplary CBPip Gap

As an introductory example a company A models a private business process $BP_{Travel\ reporting}$. Company A publishes activity "Create expense report" as a public process $VP_{Report\ Creation}$ (see upper left part of Figure 5). Company B does very much the like and publishes $VP_{Report\ Confirmation}$ (see upper right part of Figure 5). Both public processes are then used as parts of a Cross-organizational Business Process $CBP_{Travelmanagement}$ (grey activities in the bottom part of Figure 5).

Each company uses its own set of rules to transform (parts of) the private business process into public processes. In the example above, the transformation of activity "Create expense report" to $VP_{Report\ creation}$ works correctly. At company B the used rule-set implies that condition 2, which is attached to the activity "Confirm expenses", will not be published (take notice of the yellow note and the red highlighted arrow in Figure 5).

This transformation is also valid, but in the composed $CBP_{Travelmanagement}$ the missing condition might lead to a multiple source deadlock: when the upper part of the $CBP_{Travelmanagement}$ starts and follows the activity workflow, it might happen that this stream finishes before a "Send Report" message (from the activity $VP_{Report\ creation}$ in the lower part of the $CBP_{Travelmanagement}$) arrives at activity $VP_{Report\ confirmation}$. As a consequence this results in the following deadlock situation: when the lower part of the $CBP_{Travelmanagement}$ starts and reaches the activity $VP_{Report\ creation}$ the process will – due to the condition 1 "Do not continue before expenses are confirmed" – hold and wait until a "Confirm Report" message arrives. Because of the fact that the upper part of the $CBP_{Travelmanagement}$ has already finished, this waiting position will never be left and the final result is a multiple source deadlock, i.e. parts of the $CBP_{Travelmanagement}$ will never be executed (dashed activity in the $CBP_{Travelmanagement}$), and the process itself will starve and never finish.

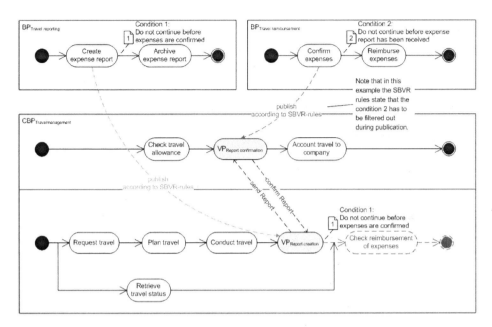

Fig. 5. Example: Erroneous Transformation leading to an Interoperability Gap (Multiple Source Deadlock)

The example above illustrates that although the transformation of each private process works correctly, interoperability gaps in a resulting CBP might occur. The challenge of scenarios as such lies in detecting interoperability gaps between partners and improving the support to bridge the gaps.

4.2 Classification of CBPip Gaps

The gap classes that have been identified so far on Business Level are:

- Deadlocks
- Interface Mismatches

Although this list is far from being exhaustive, the classification of CBPip-Gaps on Business Level, as well as the first set of identified CBPip Gap class types is depicted in Figure 6. Each class is further detailed hereafter.

Deadlocks
As stated in [7]: *A deadlock in a process model is given if a certain instance of the model (but not necessarily all) cannot continue working, while it has not yet reached its end.* The research by [8] also points out that CBPip deadlocks can be clustered in structural types such as:

- Loop Deadlock
- Multiple Source Deadlock and
- Improper Structuring Deadlock

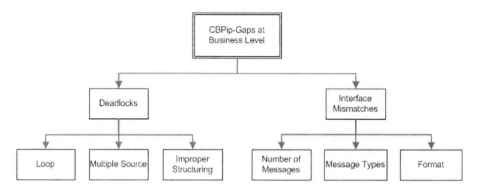

Fig. 6. Classification of CBPip Gaps

A **Loop Deadlock** occurs when there is an execution path from the output of an AND join back to a subset of its input points. If this path contains an XOR-split, deadlock occurs only when the branch leading to the loop is chosen. In case there is a path that does not contain XOR-splits deadlock occurrence is certain. See Figure 8 for an example.

A **Multiple Source Deadlock** occurs when an AND-join has input points which are at some point in the process up-stream originate from two different sources. Assuming that none of the source nodes is the AND-Join itself, we can see that the multiple-source pattern can occur (distinctly from other pattern) only when the process structure is one of the following:

- One of the two sources is an XOR-split.
- The process has multiple start points that are later on synchronized. In case of models specified in BPMN, multiple starts are permissible. Actually, multiple start points resemble an AND-split between the start events, hence we can deduce that there is reachability between two or more sources (start events) to the AND-join node. See Figure 8 for an example.

An **Improper Structuring Deadlock** occurs, when an AND-join receives input that early started from an XOR-split. See Figure 7 for an example.

Detection of deadlocks is done via path analysis considering flows and gateways in the BPMN model. [7] proposes queries to detect such deadlocks. Because of the prototypic nature of the gap detection service a straightforward approach based on those queries was chosen.

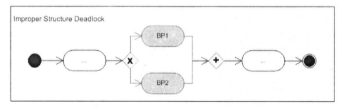

Fig. 7. Exemplary Improper Structure Deadlock at cross-organizational business process CBPc integrating public processes BP1 and BP2

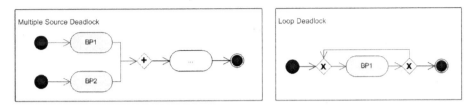

Fig. 8. Exemplary Multiple Source Deadlock and Loop Deadlock

Interface Mismatches

An interface mismatch in a CBP model is a serious impediment that prevents two separately-modelled business processes of successful interoperation due to different design assumptions.

A main difficulty of interoperable CBPs interacting with one another in ways not necessarily foreseen is to have interfaces that are generic enough so that they ensure easy and dynamic CBP interface adaption. It addresses a sub-problem of CBP mediation that arises when the interface that a CBP provides does not match the interface that it is expected to provide in a given interaction.

CBPip interface mismatches can be clustered in structural types such as:

- Number of Messages Interface Mismatch and
- Message Types Interface Mismatch

A **Number of Messages Mismatch** occurs when the number of messages provided differs from the number of messages expected. This gap applies to both directions:

- The business process provider provides a number of messages – the business process consumer expects a different amount of messages.
- The business process consumer provides a number of messages – the business process provider expects a different amount of messages.

A **Message Types Mismatch** occurs when the message format provided differs from the message format expected (e.g. the business process provider provides an e-mail – the business process consumer expects an SMS). This gap again applies to the consumption as well as to the provision scenario, like in the prior gap.

A **Format Mismatch** occurs when a message flow involves exchange of data or documents across organizations and the sending organization uses a different format than the receiving organization expects for this message flow.

4.3 CBPip Gap Detection Service

In general the process in providing innovative services that allow to bridge interoperability gaps falls into two steps: The first is to detect the CBPip Gaps, while the second is to eliminate CBPip Gaps – or at least to propose primitive courses of action to surmount the CBPip Gaps. Since each gap class has its own characteristics it was decided to follow a step by step strategy and start with the investigation on the basis of CBPip Gaps of type Deadlock.

The principal idea to detect deadlocks is to analyze the xPDL representation of a CBP model and to try to detect the deadlocks within the model. The approach described in [8] is adapted by COIN providing a web service relying on a set of so called deadlock patterns whose occurrence in process models usually leads to dead-locks. The WebService takes as request parameters the xPDL representation of a CBP model, and the name of the workflow to be verified. It delivers the number of detected deadlocks in the workflow with a short description for each deadlock as well as a suggestion for the deadlock elimination. The suggestion represents a primitive solu-tion to bridge each interoperability gap.

5   Related Work

As a predecessor of COIN, the ATHENA IP Project [2] proposed a CBP framework, with three levels of modelling: private, public ("view") and abstract process model-ling. Public and private processes are linked together at companies' sites, and are executable in a BPEL engine, in order to achieve collaborative processes between enterprises. Finally, the abstract process is an abstract view of the public process with only input/output operations. Abstract processes are not executable (or not meant to be), and are composed in the CBP. The CBP is also not executable, but can be used to monitor the choreography of public processes.

The business rule based private-to-public transformation is a very significant im-provement against the private-to-public transformation concept as described in ATHENA. We are using SBVR (Semantic Business Vocabulary Rules) [5] to define business collaboration rules. Note also that we can produce several public views from the private process, by changing only the Visibility Rules, as they specify what proc-ess elements are visible to which partner. Visibility Rules are specified in a separate file, and can apply to any number of private processes. The idea of annotating busi-ness process element to provide semantics has also been used by Rospocher et al. [8]: the authors provide mechanisms for semantically annotate business processes, using text-annotations (like we do) and ontologies.

Concerning deadlock detection in SOA protocols, several approaches exist. Seguel et al. [9] for instance describe approaches for creating protocol adaptors for service component integration. This work also covers some deadlock situations, but is merely based on SOA protocol and not at BPMN cross-organizational business process as-pects. Other work relating to gap detection exists based on Petri Nets. Dijkman et al. [10] try to map BPMN on Petri Nets (by the way finding some deficiencies in the BPMN definition) and then perform static checks on the resulting Petri Net like find-ing dead tasks or deadlocks. Anyway, this work does not put a focus on issues con-cerning mismatches occurring in cross-organizational business processes. Bonet et al. [11] do not consider BPMN directly, but provide some interesting static analysis ap-proaches on Petri Nets. In this work focus is more on performance issues, additionally covering some deadlock situations.

6   Conclusions and Future Work

We described a way of creating and analyzing a cross-organizational business process consisting of a model transformation of private to public business processes, creating a cross-organizational business process (CBP) by using the elements of the published process elements and analyzing the resulting CBP for interoperability gaps.

An eclectic diversification of interoperability gaps is currently not available in standard literature. Interoperability problems have been marginally addressed e.g. in the ATHENA project [2] or by Awad and Puhlmann [7]. But neither business process interoperability gaps within the enterprise, nor gaps of cross-organizational business processes have been the subject of a thorough analysis.

As the automated gap detection is based on the information being captured in BPMN and xPDL models, the degree automated gap detection is limited to information being captured in those models. Other gaps, like gaps in the quality of service required/offered in interactions between organizations cannot be detected in such models.

Future work will focus on extending the CBPip gap categorization and classification and improving the implementation of the business interoperability services. The number of identified CBPip Gap classes is far from being exhaustive. There is still room left to proceed with the initiated research to detect more gap problems, classify the gaps and describe them in more detail. Whereas currently all gaps are considered of same priority, defining different priorities for different gap kinds can also be part of future work.

Aiming at (semi-)automated resolution of CBP interoperability gaps is also a topic for further research, especially of the gap classes "interface mismatch" where a combination of other COIN services concerning ontology reconciliation can be leveraged.

The vocabulary for visibility rules we presented in this article is only a first version. We are currently working on an extension for health-care. The visibility rules we have presented should also not be overlapping, which is a shortcoming of the current implementation. We are planning to enhance the visibility rules with priorities (e.g. in case of conflicts, some rules will have precedence). Finally, as SBVR and ontologies are based on the Common Logic [12], it would be interesting to look for possible synergies with similar approaches for semantically annotating business processes using ontologies, like the shared workspace presented in [8].

References

1. COIN, COIN Home Page, COIN IP, http://www.coin-ip.eu/
2. ATHENA, Specification of a Cross-Organisational Business Process Model, Deliverable D.A2.2, Version 1.0 (June 2005)
3. BPMN12, Business Process Management Notation, version 1.2., OMG, http://www.omg.org/spec/BPMN/1.2/PDF/
4. Carrez, C., Del Grosso, E., Karacan, O., Taglino, F.: Towards cross-organizational innovative business process interoperability services. In: Poler, R., van Sinderen, M., Sanchis, R. (eds.) IWEI 2009. Lecture Notes in Business Information Processing, vol. 38, pp. 1–12. Springer, Heidelberg (2009)
5. OMG, Semantics of Business Vocabulary and Business Rules, version 1.0, http://www.omg.org/spec/SBVR/1.0/
6. Role Based Access Control, ANSI/INCITS 359-2004 (February 2004)
7. Awad, A., Puhlmann, F.: Structural Detection of Deadlocks in Business Process Models. In: BIS 2008. LNBIP, vol. 7, pp. 239–250. Springer, Heidelberg (2008)

8. Rospocher, M., Di Fransescomarino, C., Ghidini, C.: Collaborative Specification of Semantically Annotated Business Processes. In: BPM 2009. LNBIP, vol. 43, Springer, Heidelberg (2010)
9. Seguel, R., Eshuis, R., Grefen, P.: An Overview on Protocol Adaptors for Service Component Integration. Beta Research School Working Paper Series 265, Eindhoven University of Technology (December 2008)
10. Dijkman, R.M., Dumas, M., Ouyang, C.: Formal Semantics and Analysis of BPMN Process Models using Petri Nets (2010),
    http://eprints.qut.edu.au/7115/1/7115.pdf
11. Bonet, P., Llado, C.M., Puigjaner, R.: PIPE v2.5: a Petri Net Tool for Performance Modeling. In: 23rd Latin American Conference on Informatics (October 2007)
12. ISO/IEC 24707:2007 - Information technology — Common Logic (CL): a framework for a family of logic-based languages (2007)

An Approach for Interoperability Requirements Specification and Verification

Sihem Mallek, Nicolas Daclin, and Vincent Chapurlat

LGI2P - Laboratoire de Génie Informatique et d'Ingénierie de Production
site de l'Ecole des Mines d'Alès, Parc Scientifique Georges Besse,
F30035 Nîmes Cedex 5, France
{Sihem.Mallek,Nicolas.Daclin,
Vincent.Chapurlat}@mines-ales.fr

Abstract. Enterprises are today involved in collaborative processes with other partners sharing common economical interests in confidence. This allows these enterprises to focus on their core business, to optimize, and to be effective to respond to customers' needs. Implicitly, a partner that wishes to become involved in a partnership must demonstrate numerous qualities and enable to gain the confidence of other partners. Among other ones, demonstrate its ability to be interoperable is a major issue. This research work aims to define, to formalize and to analyze a set of interoperability requirements that each partner of a collaborative process have to satisfy prior to any collaboration. This paper focuses and illustrates how interoperability requirements related to the static and dynamic aspects of the collaboration may be formalized and verified by the use of a formal verification technique.

Keywords: interoperability, interoperability requirements, compatibility, interoperation, verification, model checker, conceptual graphs, collaborative process.

1 Introduction

A collaborative process can be defined as "*a process whose activities belong to different organizations*" [1]. It is a way allowing to formalize how partners (enterprises for inter organizational collaborative processes or team for intra-organizational processes) may work together regarding a common objective that is usually defined to provide - faster and efficiently - products and services (to design, to produce, to deliver...) to their stakeholders. However, before being involved with confidence in a collaborative structure, each partner may have to assume and, if needed, to demonstrate that it possesses relevant qualities and it respects needs regarding the type, the requested role and the nature of the collaboration. One of them is related to its ability to interoperate harmoniously and efficiently with other partners, in other words to be interoperable as defined in [2] as the "*ability of enterprises and entities within those enterprises to communicate and interact effectively*". Therefore, to help partners involved in a collaborative process to find their interoperability problems, this research work focuses on the detection from an anticipative manner – *i.e.* before the implementation of the collaborative process - of interoperability problems that can be induced

M. van Sinderen and P. Johnson (Eds.): IWEI 2011, LNBIP 76, pp. 89–102, 2011.

by characteristics or behaviors of partners. In this perspective, the anticipation of a problem requires to perform analysis on a model of the collaborative process. Then interoperability problems are extracted and characterized from interoperability needs of partners. Finally, to demonstrate that a need is satisfied or covered, several verification techniques can be implemented.

From these considerations, this research work aims, first, to define, to structure and to formalize interoperability needs that have to be satisfied by the partners. Second, it aims to promote and implement a set of formal verification techniques that can be used prior to any concretization of the collaborative process.

This paper focuses on the formalization and verification of interoperability requirements to be verified including static and dynamic aspects of the collaboration. It is structured as follows. Section 2 reminds the principles and classification of interoperability requirements. Section 3 introduces the proposed mechanisms used to analyze interoperability requirements. Section 4 presents the verification of static requirements using conceptual graphs. The verification of dynamic requirements using model checker is given section 5. To illustrate the verification of these kinds of requirements, an application case is given in section 6.

2   Interoperability Requirements Definition

A requirement is defined as "*a statement that specifies a function, ability or a characteristic that a product or a system must satisfy in a given context*" [3]. In other words, a requirement translates from an unambiguous manner any need. With regards to (1) the interoperability barriers and interoperability concerns proposed in the interoperability framework [4], (2) the maturity models [5] [6] [7] and several projects such as ATHENA [8] and, (3) an investigation made from enterprises to collect their interoperability needs, three classes of interoperability requirements have been defined such as:

–   **Compatibility requirements:** A compatibility requirement is defined as "*a statement that specifies a function, ability or a characteristic, independent of time and related to interoperability barriers (conceptual, organizational and technological) for each interoperability concerns (data, services, processes and business), that enterprise must satisfy before collaboration effectiveness*". Compatibility means to harmonize partners (method, organization, tool...) in order to be ready to collaborate. For instance, a compatibility requirement can be given as: "*A right access to shared data is allowed to external partners*". However, compatibility focuses on a static point of view of the collaboration and remains insufficient to determine if enterprises are interoperable during the execution of the collaborative process. It is necessary to consider the evolution of the context and of the situation of each partner.

–   **Interoperation requirements:** An interoperation requirement is defined as "a statement that specifies a function, ability or a characteristic, dependent of time and related to the performance of the interaction, that enterprise must satisfy during the collaboration". These requirements focus on the ability of the enterprise to be able to adapt its organization, its functioning modes and its behavior when it interacts. For example, an interoperation requirement can be described as: "For each data received, a receipt must be returned".

- **Reversibility requirements:** A reversibility requirement is defined as "a statement that specify functions, abilities or characteristics related to the capacity of enterprise to retrieve its autonomy and to back to its original state (in terms of its own performance) after collaboration, that enterprise must satisfy". Reversibility means that an enterprise may maintain or retrieve easily its autonomy and performance (including positive and/or negative variations that are accepted) at the end of any collaboration. For instance, a reversibility requirement for cost criterion at the level of service is described by: "the cost of a given service after the collaboration corresponds to the cost before collaboration including variations (e.g. admissible increase of cost)".

An interoperability requirement can be qualified as a static or not temporal requirement, *i.e.* independent of time, and has to be verified all along the process evolution. Conversely, it can be qualified as a dynamic or temporal requirement, *i.e.* dependent of temporal hypotheses and time evolution, and has to be verified only at some stages of the collaboration. Thus, compatibility requirements are static, interoperation requirements are dynamic and reversibility requirements can have both aspects. The description, formalization and understanding of a requirement can be difficult for many reasons: complexity, comprehensiveness, quantity of requirements, etc. To tackle this first obstacle, a requirement reference repository is proposed and is described as a causal tree, as illustrated in Fig. 1 (for more details, we refer the reader to [9]).

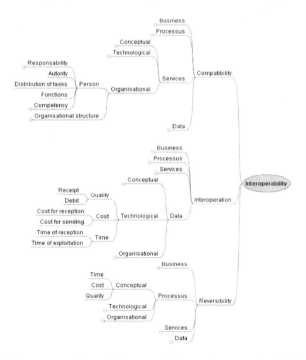

Fig. 1. Reference repository of interoperability requirements (partial view) [9]

A set of requirements represented as nodes in the causal tree and refinement relations from an abstract requirement (node) to a set of more precise requirements (subnodes) allows to obtain an oriented causal tree. The causal tree allows by successive refinement to reduce the ambiguity of requirements that may exist for each level.

Thereafter, to prove that each requirement is satisfied by the collaborative process model and, by the process itself in a formal manner, this research work proposes to apply verification activity. The objective is to ensure *"the confirmation by examination and proof that specified requirements have been satisfied"*[10]. Several verification techniques are presented in the next section.

3   Interoperability Requirements Verification

The objective of the verification is to demonstrate that a set of selected interoperability requirements is satisfied. Indeed the reference repository presented in [9] allows users to select relevant requirements to be checked. In order to be able to perform this verification before the runtime of the collaborative process, this one is done on a model of the collaborative process. Several verification techniques exist in the literature such as simulation, tests, or formal verification techniques [11] [12] [13].

The simulation is done on a theoretical model whose behavior is considered as similar to the behavior of the pointed out system. It is done before implementation of the system. However, simulation is unable to assume all behavioral scenarios of the system. It requires human expertise to analyze results and formulate the demonstration. Nevertheless, simulation is now a well known technique more and more developed and used in enterprise. A test is directly done on an existing system. It allows to check, for example, capacity and relevance to detect errors before system implementation.

On the other side, formal verification techniques allow to explore exhaustively a formal model *i.e.* a model obtained with a modeling language using a formal semantic. In this case, it is possible to provide a formal proof of the respect (or not) of a requirement independently from any human interpretation. In this way, it is proposed to use in a complementary way two formal verification techniques and to associate also a technical expertise as summarized in Fig. 2.

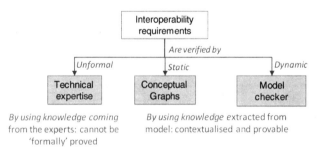

Fig. 2. Proposed verification techniques

The first verification technique is based on Conceptual Graphs [14] to verify static requirements. The advantage to use Conceptual Graphs is (1) to describe the collaborative process and interoperability requirements on the same formalism, (2) to dispose of a convenient graphical form to handle and, (3) to dispose of a mathematical foundation and mechanisms (projection, principles of rules and constraints principles) which are used to check static requirements.

The second one is based on model checking [15] for the dynamic requirements. The advantage to use model checker is (1) to include temporal aspect of the collaboration, (2) to consider all states of the collaborative process all along the collaboration and (3) to verify dynamic requirements exhaustively.

Applying these techniques requires to assume that the modeling language used to build the process model allows the description of interoperability requirements. The chosen modeling language is BPMN (Business Process Modeling Notation) [16]. It provides a standardized notation that is readily understandable by all actors involved in the design, development and monitoring of a collaborative process. However, it is necessary to enrich this modeling language to embed the interoperability requirements model. The proposed enrichments detailed in [17] include interoperability concepts such as the nature of the exchanged flow (information, energy, material and person), the availability of resources and their aptitudes.

Furthermore, the use of these verification techniques requires to translate the collaborative process model in enriched BPMN - thanks to model transformation rules - into an equivalent model upon which the formal verification techniques can be applied as shown Fig. 3. Indeed, the proposed enriched version of BPMN suffers yet from a lack of formalization and verification techniques cannot be applied directly, regarding to interoperability. The first equivalent model is obtained using a formal knowledge representation of Conceptual Graphs for static requirements proof as presented in [17] and [18]. In this case verification is performed with COGITANT tool [19]. The second equivalent model is obtained using a behavioral modeling language named Networks of Timed Automata for dynamic requirements proof. In this case, the model checker UPPAAL is used for various reasons: richness of TCTL temporal logic, open source, user friendly, and stand alone tool [15]. In both cases of target models, the required rules for model transformation are developed with ATL (Atlas Transformation Language) [20] in order to re-write the collaborative process model into Conceptual Graphs and Networks of Timed Automata. In the case of Conceptual Graphs, the transformation from enriched BPMN is of course not semantically preserved due to the rewriting hypothesis adopted. The objective is therefore to assume the coherence of the process model that is to say to prove that each BMPN modeling entity used and then instantiated in the process model is well and completely defined. In the case of Networks of Timed Automata, the transformation rules have been established respecting an equivalence between BPMN entities behavior and a standardized state model behavioral semantic. Therefore, under these equivalence hypothesis, these rules preserve the behavioral semantic of the enriched version of BPMN. Interoperability requirements are formalized to make their verification possible. Thus, static requirements are formalized with Conceptual Graphs and dynamic requirements are formalized with TCTL.

In other cases, if interoperability requirements highlight particular points of view of the process and cannot be described due to a limitation imposed by the modeling language, the technical expertise of the model is required. This aspect of checking is not considered in this work.

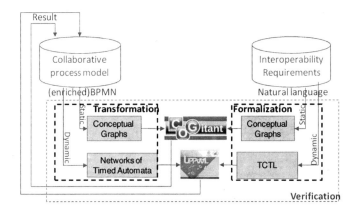

Fig. 3. Verification process for interoperability requirements

4   Verification Process for Static Requirements

A Conceptual Graph is defined as a graph with two kinds of nodes: concepts and oriented relations as shown in Fig. 4 with a conceptual graph that can be read as: *"Any activities* (concept) *begin* (relation) *at a beginning date* (concept)"*. Concepts and relations are described in hierarchical structures called concepts and relations lattices. Individual markers are added to obtain the model ("*" means generic concept on the following figure).

[Activity: *]———▸(Begin)———▸[Date: BeginningDate]

Fig. 4. Example of a conceptual graph

The tool COGITANT allows to handle Conceptual Graphs and to make formal graph transformations upon which the verification process of static requirements is based. The principle is to use a graph operation named projection in order to check if a constraint graph (*i.e.* a requirement) is really projected in the conceptual graph that describe the static model of the system. If projection operation fails the requirement is not verified and the causes can be highlighted by analyzing the resulting conceptual graph. To make verification with COGITANT, three types of files are necessary and known as: support, fact and constraint graph.

The "*Support*" represents all the concepts and relations from enriched BPMN metamodel and markers representing all the instances of these concepts and relations defined in the process model. The "*Fact*" contains the equivalent conceptual graph of the model obtained by applying ATL transformation rules and respecting the support. Finally, the "*requirements*" to verify are modeled in other conceptual graphs called "*constraints*". The verification is performed using the projection of a positive or a negative constraint on the conceptual graph that represents the model of studied process. A positive constraint is described with a cause and a conclusion and its projection is performed according to the following interpretation: "*If the cause is true, then the conclusion must be true as well*". A negative constraint is a single conceptual graph and its projection is interpreted as: *"If a negative constraint is not projected on the fact model, it is verified"*.

As mentioned the verification of a positive and negative constraint is made using the mechanism of projection. This mechanism involves to project a given property translated in conceptual graph on the obtained conceptual graph in the fact file that represents the translation of the model. If the projection fails, then the modeled constraint (*i.e.* requirement) is not verified and the causes are highlighted.

As a consequence, the transformation from process model to COGITANT requires to perform three ATL transformations. Hereafter, Fig. 5 represents the principle of the first transformation to get the support model (the two others transformations are based on the same principles and are not detailed here).

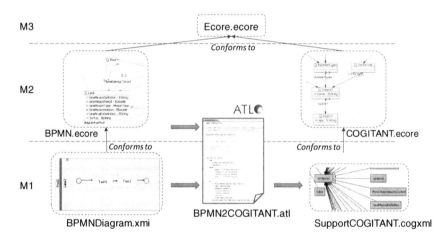

Fig. 5. Transformation from enriched version of BPMN to Support in COGITANT

The first transformation procedure to obtain the support file (level M1) starts with the consideration of the meta models (level M2) of the enriched BPMN language and COGITANT which are conform, as well, to the ecore model (level M3). Thus, each class (including its attributes) is translated into concept and each relation of the meta model is translated into relation in the support file. This transformation is made in order to provide all the needed concept and relations used and deployed, further, in the fact file.

The second transformation allows to obtain a representation into Conceptual Graph of the considered model (fact). Finally, the last transformation is performed to obtain constraints (representing the requirements) that have to be projected onto the equivalent graph model. In this case, the requirement is translated in a positive or negative conceptual graph constraint depending of the user intention.

For example, the compatibility requirement described as: *"Any task uses resources"* can be formalized into a positive constraint as shown Fig. 6. The verification of this constraint using the projection is performed with the projection of the cause (uncolored concept on left side) on the fact model. If the cause is projected on the fact model, the conclusion (colored concept and relation on right side) must be projected too in order to respect the requirement.

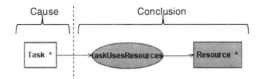

Fig. 6. Positive constraint representing a compatibility requirement

5 Verification Process for Dynamic Requirements

The principle of a model checker is to verify properties exhaustively with temporized and eventually constrained automata that describe the behavior of a system. Obviously, the system is here the collaborative process model.

Verification with model checkers requires two phases. The first phase consists to define a set of equivalent behavioral models of the collaborative process model and to define the collaborative process model transformation rules to be applied. The second phase consists to reformulate the dynamic requirements under the form of properties respecting the formal language adopted by the chosen model checker (in this study, a temporal logic) [21].

The chosen tool, UPPAAL, allows to handle a behavioral model defined as a set of templates, which communicates with synchronization (either on the form *Expression*! for sending or *Expression*? for receiving synchronization), using channels and syntax like sent/receive. Each template has locations and transitions to link a location source to a target source [15].

The enriched BPMN model must be transformed into Networks of Timed Automata to perform verification of dynamic requirements. In Fig. 7 the transformation procedure of models (level M1) starts with the consideration of the meta models (level M2) of the enriched BPMN language and UPPAAL which are conform, as well, to the ecore model (level M3). This transformation is made in order to provide all the needed concepts used and deployed in the Networks of Timed Automata. In this way, it is mandatory to consider all the modeling entities which will be used in the checking task. Thus, each class (including its attributes) of the meta model is translated into templates. Respecting this consideration, each BPMN element can be extracted from the collaborative process model in order to produce the corresponding template representing Networks of Timed Automata. Thus, these templates gather all the knowledge described in the model and represents the behavioral model of the collaborative process.

The proposed process model transformation is based on [22] which proposes the transformation of the few BPMN elements: start and end event, gateway (AND and XOR) and the Task. For instance, the task is transformed using four locations and two synchronizations as presented in Fig. 8 (a). In this figure, (b) and (c) consider the message flow between two tasks thus the single transformation proposed in the literature is extended. In the same manner, other own transformations such as resource, multi start/end event and so on, are fully developed in the frame of this research.

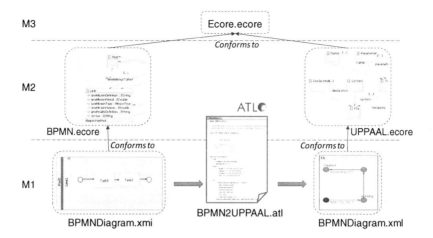

Fig. 7. Transformation from enriched version of BPMN to Networks of Timed Automata

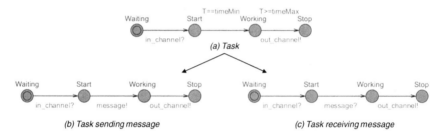

(b) Task sending message   *(c) Task receiving message*

Fig. 8. Single Task model template (a) extended to consider the BPMN message flow (b and c)

To enable the implementation of formal verification techniques, the dynamic requirements are formalized into TCTL properties (Timed Computation Tree Logic *i.e.* the UPPAAL property specification language) [23]. TCTL is an extension of CTL (Computational Tree Logic) which allows considering several possible futures from a state of a system. The model checker UPPAAL has four TCTL quantifiers (A: for all paths, E: it exists a path, []: all states in a path, <>: some states in a path) allowing to write a property p:

−   E<> p: reachability *i.e.* it is possible to reach a state in which p is satisfied.
−   A[] p: invariantly p *i.e.* p is true in all reachable states.
−   A<> p: inevitable p *i.e.* p will inevitable become true.
−   E[] p: potentially Always p *i.e.* p is potentially always true.
−   P → q: p leads to q *i.e.* if p becomes true, q will inevitably become true.

According to the templates defined above, the dynamic requirements written in natural language are manually re-written into properties using TCTL. Then the model checker UPPAAL verifies exhaustively properties in TCTL through all execution paths of the behavioral models that are reachable.

For instance, a requirement described as "*a task is working between T=5 time units and 10 time units*" can be formalized into a property using TCTL as:

"E<> Task.Working and T>5 and T<10"

This property indicates that a path can exists where a task is in the state Working between 5<T<10. This property can be verified on the template representing a task shown Fig. 8 (a).

To illustrate the proposed approach, an application case is given in next section to formally verify several static and dynamic interoperability requirements.

6 Application Case

To illustrate the proposed approach, an example of a collaborative process representing an European project called PABADIS'PROMISE is proposed [24]. This project extends the idea of distributed control to an innovative architecture which incorporates both resources and products. Furthermore, this project combines International forces to provide this architecture.

The project is composed of 8 work packages. A work package consists of several independent tasks which all together have to be performed in order to achieve the work package's goal. Each work package is under the authority of the Work Package Leader who will lead the work package team throughout the period of activity of all tasks involved in the work package. Each work package executes on its own control over internal tasks within the allocated resources. A task consists of a subset of activities within one work package.

Let us consider, a partner 1 that has to assume the work package 3 with three other partners (this application focuses only on the work package 3). This work package covers the development and implementation of the PABADIS'PROMISE manufacturing ontology, the manufacturing process and product description language based on it. To perform this work package, four tasks led by the four partners are highlighted. Each partner can be involved in all tasks. The task 1 titled "*development of manufacturing ontology*" is led by the partner 1. The task 2 "*Specification of product*", led by the partner 2, has to specify the PABADISE'PROMISE product and Production Process Description Language enabling the detailed description of products. The task 3 "*Implementation of product*", led by the partner 3, aims to implement the product and the process description and comparison systems. The last task "*Data protection and security aspect*", led by the partner 4, has to cover privacy, data protection, security and trust aspects related to technologies and organizational structures used on the PABADIS'PROMISE architecture. All interactions between tasks in this work package are presented Fig. 9 where the second and the last tasks work in parallel. The first task is triggered after receiving a message from a task of the work package 1. At the end of the work package 3, the work package 8 can start. The collaborative process shown Fig. 9 is a part of the full collaborative process between all work packages.

To illustrate the verification of the interoperability requirements using formal verification techniques previously presented, compatibility and interoperation requirements are effectively verified on this collaborative process.

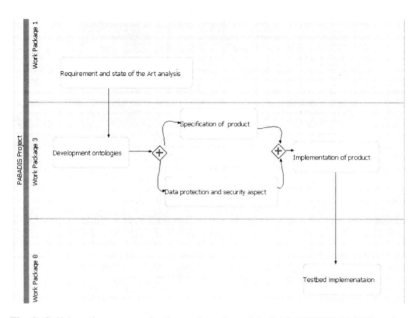

Fig. 9. Collaborative process for the work package 3 in PABADIS'PROMISE project

Before any collaboration between partners, each responsible or leader of each task must be clearly identified which can be typically a problem of interoperability. In fact, this identification is necessary to avoid loss of time to identify and to find the right responsible, that a non responsible person has access to confidential information... As a consequence, a compatibility requirement defined as: "*all tasks have an identified responsible*" must be verified using conceptual graphs thanks to COGITANT tool. This requirement is formalized into the positive constraint (a) as shown Fig. 10.

In PABADIS'PROMISE project, each leader has authority on the other partners. Therefore, another compatibility requirement defined as: "*each responsible of task has the authority on the other partners*" can be formalized into the positive constraint (b) shown Fig. 10 and verified on the fact model.

The verification of these compatibility requirements is performed using the projection of the cause (not colored concepts and relations) and the conclusion (colored concepts and relations) on the fact model. If causes are projected on the fact model and the conclusions are not projected, constraints are not verified which means that compatibility requirements are not satisfied. If these requirements are not satisfied on the fact model, it may dread mistakes during the transmission of orders that could lead to a deterioration of the collaboration performances (loss of time to convey the right order to the right person ...).

During the collaboration, partner 2 and partner 4 are involved in the two parallel tasks ("*specification of product*" (task 2) and "*Data production and security aspect*" (task 4)). The partner 2 is required on these two tasks simultaneously. As a consequence, it is necessary to verify if these two tasks do not use the partner 2 at the same time (*i.e.* to verify that a resource conflict does not exist on these tasks). The interoperation requirement described as: "*task 2 and task 4 uses the human resources of partner 2*" can be verified. If this requirement is verified as a static requirement using

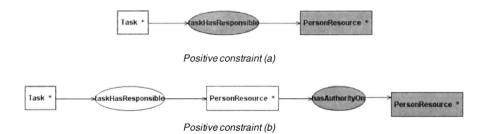

Positive constraint (a)

Positive constraint (b)

Fig. 10. Compatibility requirements formalized into properties as positive constraints

conceptual graph presented previously in section 4, it will be satisfied because conceptual graphs does not take into account the dynamic aspect of the collaboration. But if this requirement is verified using model checker, it will be not satisfied as demonstrated hereafter.

This requirement is verified on the dynamic model of the collaborative process presented by the task template and the resource template shown Fig. 11.

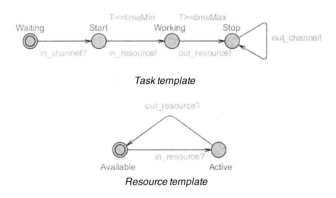

Task template

Resource template

Fig. 11. Task template and resource template

To verify this requirement on UPPAAL, it must be formalized into property using TCTL as:

E<> ResourcePartner2.Active and Task2.Working and Task4.Working

This property indicates that it exists a path where a resource is active when the two tasks are working. The verification of the property will go through all possible paths and answering true or false. In this case, the response of the model checker is false, because the resource cannot be used by the two tasks on the same time. Furthermore, if a time condition is added on the property, it is possible to use the same resource at different time. For instance if the partner 2 is involved in task 2 between 2 and 5 time units and after 6 time units on task 4, the requirement can be satisfied with the verification of two properties. Then, the properties to verify on the dynamic model will be given by:

E<> Resource Partner2.Active and T>2 and T<5 and Task2.Working

for the task 2 and by:

E<> Resource Partner2.Active and T>6 and Task4.Working

for the task 4 where T represents a clock. In this case, the properties are satisfied and the interoperation requirement is satisfied.

As a consequence, it is to note that the consideration of the temporal aspect of collaboration is a primordial aspect since it can changes the result of the verification.

7   Conclusion

In a collaborative context, interoperability takes a preponderant part. During the life cycle of any collaboration between partners, these partners aim to detect and to solve quickly interoperability problems. The proposed approach aims to verify static and dynamic interoperability requirements using different verification tools. In this way, formalization, and verification of interoperability requirements to help enterprises to find their interoperability problems can be a solution to improve collaboration.

This verification is performed using formal verification techniques. This paper focuses on the verification of static and dynamic interoperability requirements. Static interoperability requirements are verified using Conceptual Graphs. To make the verification of dynamic requirements, the verification technique used is model checking. In summary, two formal verification techniques are used. The usefulness of these verification techniques required to make transformation of models and to formalize interoperability requirements into properties using a formal language.

Future works are related first, to the verification of reversibility requirements using formal verification techniques. Second, it wills intent to define the link with a complementary simulation approach based on distributed multi agents systems [25] to improve interoperability problems detection.

References

1. Aubert, B., Dussart, A.: Système d'Information Inter-Organisationnel. Rapport Bourgogne, Groupe CIRANO (March 2002) (in French)
2. ISO/DIS 11345-1: Advanced automation technologies and their applications. Part 1: Framework for enterprise interoperability (2009)
3. Scucanec, S. J., Van Gaasbeek, J. R.: A day in the life of a verification requirement. U.S Air Force T&E Days, Los Angeles, California (February 2008)
4. INTEROP: Enterprise Interoperability-Framework and knowledge corpus - Final report. INTEROP NoE, FP6 – Contract n° 508011, Deliverable DI.3 (May 21, 2007)
5. Tolk, A., Muguira, J.A.: The Levels of Conceptual Interoperability Model. In: Proceedings of Fall Simulation Interoperability Workshop (SIW), Orlando, USA (2003)
6. C4ISR Architecture Working Group: Levels of Information Systems Interoperability (LISI). United States of America Department of Defense, Washington DC, USA (March 30, 1998)
7. Clark, T., Jones, R.: Organisational Interoperability Maturity Model for C2. In: Proc. of Command and Control Research & Techn. Symposium, Newport, USA (1999)

8. ATHENA Integrated Project : Requirement for interoperability framework, product-based and process-based interoperability infrastructures, interoperability life-cycle services, ATHENA deliverable A4.1 (2004)

9. Mallek, S., Daclin, N., Chapurlat, V.: Toward a conceptualisation of interoperability requirements. In: IESA 2010: Interoperability for Enterprise Software & Applications, April 14-15 (2010)

10. ISO 8402: Quality management and quality assurance. Vocabulary, Second edition 1994-04-01, International Standard Organization (1994)

11. Balci, O., Ornwsby, W.: Expanding our horizons in verification, validation and accreditation research and practice. In: Yücesan, E., Chen, C.-H., Snowdon, J.L., Charnes, J.M. (eds.) 2002 Winter Simulation Conference (2002)

12. Edmund, M., Clarke Jr., Grumbereg, O., Doron, A.P.: Model checking. The MIT Press, Cambridge (1999)

13. Bérard, B., Bidoit, M., Finkel, A., Laroussinie, F., Petit, A., Petrucci, L., Schnoebelen, P., McKenzie, P.: Systems and Software verification: model checking techniques and tools. Springer, Heidelberg (2001)

14. Sowa, J.F.: Conceptual Graphs. IBM Journal of Research and Development (1976)

15. Behrmann, G., David, A., Larsen, K. G.: A tutorial on Uppaal. Department of Computer Science, Aalborg University, Denmark (2004)

16. BPMN: Business Process Modeling Notation, V1.2 (2009), http://www.bpmn.org/

17. Roque, M., Chapurlat, V.: Interoperability in collaborative processes: Requirements characterisation and proof approach. In: Camarinha-Matos, L.M., Paraskakis, I., Afsarmanesh, H. (eds.) PRO-VE 2009. IFIP Advances in Information and Communication Technology, vol. 307, pp. 555–562. Springer, Heidelberg (2009)

18. Chein, M., Mugnier, M.-L.: Conceptual graphs: fundamental notions. Revue d'intelligence artificielle 6(4), 365–406 (1992)

19. Cogitant: CoGITaNT Version 5.2.0, Reference Manual (2009), http://cogitant.sourceforge.net

20. ATLAS Groupe INA & INRIA Nantes: ATL Atlas Transformation Language. Specification of the ATL Virtual Machine. Version 0.1 (2005)

21. Schnoebelen, P.: The Complexity of Temporal Logic Model Checking. In: Advances in Modal Logic, vol. 4, pp. 1–44 (2002)

22. Gruhn, V., Laue, R.: Using Timed Model Checking for Verifying Workflows. In: Computer Supported Activity Coordination 2005, pp. 75–88 (2005)

23. Alur, R., Courcoubetis, C., Dill, D.: Model-Checking in Dense Real-Time. Information and Computation 104(1), 2–34 (1993)

24. PABADIS'PROMISE STREP FP6: Plant Automation Based on DIStributed Systems (2008), http://www.pabadis.org/

25. Rebai, A.S., Chapurlat, V.: System interoperability analysis by mixing system modelling and MAS: an approach. Agent-based, Technologies and applications for enterprise interoperability (ATOP). In: Eighth International Joint Conference on Autonomous Agents & Multi-Agent Systems (AAMAS 2009), Budapest, Hungary (May 2009)

On the Move to Business-Driven Alignment of Service Monitoring Requirements

Patrício de Alencar Silva and Hans Weigand

Department of Information Management
Tilburg University, P.O. Box 90153
5000LE Tilburg, The Netherlands
{p.silva,h.weigand}@uvt.nl

Abstract. Current service monitoring capabilities have been not designed in alignment with business needs. We argue that service monitoring should be primarily thought of as an economic concern, with proper needs being elicited on the business strategy level and further drilled down to process and IT services management layers. Monitoring needs and capabilities should be designed independently from each other and exposed as abstract monitoring interfaces for matchmaking. This allows for treating monitoring as a service, with more flexibility and adaptability to fulfill specific business needs.

Keywords: Early Requirements Analysis, Monitoring as a Service, Value Models.

1 Introduction

Value modeling, as structured by the e^3value framework, builds upon a set of primitive economic concepts which allow for specifying how enterprises jointly satisfy a consumer's need, by exchange of valuable goods and services [1]. The rationale of a value model is to configure a value network such that its actors create a positive cash flow. By instantiating a value model (via running profitability sheets), it is possible to prospect the profit to be yielded by each actor, to whom it may represent a motivation to join the network or not. A value model, as a business case representation, can be used to configure business processes and IT services from an economic perspective [2].

A value model, nonetheless, states just "promises" made by business actors to create value in discourse. "Real" value delivery bounds to performance constraints of underlying business processes and IT services. As there are risks of sub-optimal value delivery by any of the actors engaged on a network, a research question that arises is *how value networks can be monitored*. This question further split into (1) *what monitoring requirements are critical for preserving a value network* and (2) *how these requirements can be realized by service monitoring mechanisms*. Answering these questions somewhat depend on a reality check on how service monitoring has been *designed* and *realized* nowadays.

An extensive literature overview has revealed that, in general, service monitoring *has not* been actually business-driven. Strategic business goals (e.g. to maximize value creation) and business process monitoring capabilities are rather disconnected.

M. van Sinderen and P. Johnson (Eds.): IWEI 2011, LNBIP 76, pp. 103–117, 2011.

Although process modelers may have knowledge on process monitoring aspects, typically they are not assigned to define enterprise-level service monitoring affairs. For instance, monitoring has a cost and can constitute a business in its own, with a proper rationale, roles, services and policies. From this point-of-view, it is worth to design service monitoring as a value-adding process, complementary to core businesses. Yet, without defining enterprise-level service performance metrics (a.k.a. Key Performance Indicators – KPIs) [3], "business" process monitoring is relegated to random Process Performance Metrics (PPMs), which may become meaningless to the business if not precisely connected to its strategic KPIs. Actually, such a practice leads to *overfitting* and *underfitting* of service monitoring requirements. When a KPI is more comprehensive than its potentially related PPMs, which in turn may not be computable from process execution data, KPIs *overfit* PPMs. In the opposite situation, KPIs *underfit* PPMs. In the last case, PPMs query too much from process execution data, therefore wasting service monitoring resources, and recursively turning monitoring into a system bottleneck. Our first research problem therefore is that *start thinking about monitoring on the "process" level gives no hint on what monitoring requirements are critical for a business case.*

This study has also revealed that, generally, service monitoring *has not* been designed in a service-oriented way. The initial WfMC vision [4] for process/service monitoring as a pluggable component to process execution environments is not a reality yet. Distinction between monitoring needs and capabilities is rather blurred. Tightly coupling of monitoring requirements specifications with monitoring services' capabilities reduces flexibility and adaptability on discovering, selecting and composing monitoring services and resources. This in turn affects negatively the economy of monitoring. Our second research problem thence comprises that *it is currently difficult to assert precisely how monitoring requirements can be fulfilled by service monitoring mechanisms, because "what-has-to-be" is still hardly-coupled with the "how-can-it-be" monitored.*

To start treating these problems, we propose two guidelines for designing service monitoring requirements on business collaborations: (1) start designing these requirements from the business strategic level, and further drill them down to the process and IT service layers, via Model Driven Engineering (MDE); and (2) decouple service monitoring "needs" from corresponding capabilities, treating *monitoring as a service* (MaaS). These two principles are integrated in a conceptual framework, whose architectural description is the first contribution of this paper. The framework grounds on the idea of using value models to configure business processes and IT services [2]. The concepts behind value models are extended with monitoring concepts, so as to enable an early service monitoring requirements analysis *from* and *for* the core business case. We therefore use *value models for monitoring value models*, which is the second contribution of this paper. Finally, we employ the framework on deriving service monitoring requirements of a real-world case study in electricity markets. The case brings about the specification of strategic service monitoring requirements for a value network of actors trading electricity production and consumption in a highly valued market of renewable energy resources, whose delivery of forecasted electricity amount depends on the stochastic nature of power generation.

This paper is structured as follows. In section 2, we present some of the current interoperability gaps in service monitoring based on surveying criteria derived from our research questions. In section 3, we introduce our framework for alignment of service monitoring requirements. In section 4, we pave the first layer of the framework by extending value models to specify service monitoring requirements. The extension is then applied on the electricity trading business case. Finally, we provide some discussions and outline for future research in section 5.

2 Currently Open Interoperability Issues in Service Monitoring

In this section, we present the results of a literature survey in business process monitoring. The objective is to position our research questions in the state-of-the-art in this field, so as to attest problem relevance. Based on those questions, we defined a set of evaluation criteria defined in terms of requirements. The six first ones relate to the specification of "what-has-to-be" monitored. The seventh one relates to the practical issue of how the "what-has-to-be" could be matched with the "how-can-it-be" specification. The evaluation requirements are detailed as follows:

RQ-1: *Business Rationale Definition* – this requirement answers *why* to monitor. It relates to business strategic goals behind monitoring strategies. For instance, the business rationale behind a value model is the shared goal of "maximizing profitability". This economic principle can be the same goal of monitoring, which ought to be configured to add value to the business. Other business rationales may be employed, though, grounded on different business management theories. This requirement requests on to what extent a strategic business goal has been considered as a primary driver for service monitoring configuration.

RQ-2: *Business Level Requirements Specification* – this requirement requests for the definition of *who*, *what* and *how* to monitor on the business level. These aspects refer to business monitoring *actors*, *objects* and *policies*, respectively, which can comprise the specification or an *abstract monitoring protocol*.

RQ-3: *Process Level Requirements Specification* – this requirement requests for the definition of the same elements stated in **RQ-2**, but referring to a set of processes, messages and process-level communication policies necessary to monitor process collaborations.

RQ-4: *IT Service Level Requirements Specification* – similar to **RQ-3**, but referring to the specification of IT services' inputs, outputs and access policies subject to monitoring from underpinning processes.

RQ-5: *Organizational Requirements Specification* – this requirement requests for the definition of role hierarchies and separation of duties (SoD) possibly maintained apart from monitoring policies. It constrains *who* can be involved in a monitoring. Such constraints should be initially defined on the business level and further refined in the IT services level.

RQ-6: *Monitoring Metrics Specification* – this requirement specializes how monitoring can be performed. Monitoring metrics are used to disclose verifiable information from monitored objects. They can be specified on the business strategy level (i.e. KPIs for measuring organizational performance), on the process level (i.e. PPMs for measuring process collaboration performance) and on the IT services level (i.e. for measuring network QoS).

RQ-7: *Monitoring Interfaces Specification* – this requirement requests for a clear separation of monitoring needs and capabilities. It assesses whether the principle of service orientation has been somewhat applied on the monitoring configuration.

The evaluation is summarized in Table 1. The analyzed works are ordered chronologically. Each a work is evaluated by considering each requirement explicitly, partially, or not considering. **RQ-7** is not applicable in some sparse cases. The works were selected from peer-reviewed publications in the field of business process monitoring, from 2004 to the current year.

Table 1. Comparison of approaches for business process monitoring

REFERENCE	RQ-1	RQ-2	RQ-3	RQ-4	RQ-5		RQ-6			RQ-7
					BUS.	IT	KPI	PPM	QoS	
Zur Muehlen [5]	No	No	Part.	No	Yes	Yes	No	No	No	Part.
Küng et al.[6]	No	No	No	No	No	No	Yes	Yes	No	No
Srinivasan et al.[7]	Part.	No	Part.	No	Yes	No	Yes	Yes	No	No
Yu, Jeng [8]	No	No	No	No	Part.	Part.	Yes	Yes	No	No
Alles et al [9]	Part.	No	No	No	Part.	Part.	No	No	No	No
Greiner et al [10]	Part.	Part.	No	No	No	No	No	No	No	No
Abe, Jeng [11]	No	No	No	No	Part.	Part.	Yes	No	No	Yes
Beeri et al.[12]	No	No	No	Part.	No	No	No	Yes	Yes	Yes
Kim et al.[13]	No	No	No	No	Yes	Yes	Yes	No	No	No
Strnadl [14]	Part.	No	Part.	No	Yes	Yes	No	No	No	Part.
Chen [15]	No	No	No	No	Part.	No	Yes	No	No	No
Ferro et al.[16]	No	No	No	No	No	No	No	Yes	Yes	No
Lamparter et al.[17]	No	No	No	Yes	No	No	No	No	Yes	-
Paschke, Bichler[18]	No	No	No	Yes	No	No	No	No	Yes	-
Pedrinaci et al.[19]	No	No	No	No	Part.	Part.	Yes	Yes	No	Part.
Rimini, Roberti[20]	No	Part.	No	No	Part.	No	Yes	Yes	No	No
Tsai et al.[21]	No	No	Yes	Part.	No	Part.	No	No	Yes	No
Unger et al.[22]	No	No	Yes	Yes	No	No	No	No	Yes	-
Vaculín, Sycara[23]	No	No	No	Yes	No	No	No	No	Yes	No
Bai et al.[24]	No	No	No	Yes	No	No	No	Yes	Yes	No
Comuzzi et al.[25]	No	No	Yes	Yes	No	No	No	No	Yes	Part.
Fugini, Siadat[26]	No	No	No	Yes	No	No	No	No	Yes	No
Kang et al.[27]	No	No	No	No	No	No	Yes	No	No	No
Momm et al.[28]	No	No	No	No	No	No	Yes	Yes	No	Yes
Pourshahid et al.[29]	No	No	No	No	Yes	No	Yes	Yes	No	No
Robinson, Purao[30]	No	Part.	Yes	No	Part.	Part.	No	Yes	No	Part.
Spillner et al[31]	Part.	Part.	No	Yes	No	No	No	No	Yes	Yes
Wang et al.[32]	No	No	No	Yes	No	No	No	No	Yes	No
Han et al.[33]	No	No	No	Yes	No	No	No	No	Yes	No
v. d. Aalst et al.[34]	No	No	No	Yes	Yes	No	No	Yes	Yes	Yes
Wetzstein et al.[35]	No	No	Yes	Yes	Part.	Part.	Yes	Yes	Yes	No

From Table 1 it can be inferred that most of the contributions have focused on SLAs and QoS metrics. KPIs and PPMs are the second most considered aspects, followed by organizational aspects, and business strategy and business level agreements at last. That is, current business process monitoring has been driven more by QoS related aspects than properly by business ones. Although this may indicate an increasing maturity of system-related monitoring capabilities, their effectiveness for businesses depend on how aligned they are with real business needs defined in terms of strategic business goals.

Specific findings include that: (1) with the exception of the work of Wetzstein et al. [35], correlations between KPIs, PPMs and QoS metrics were not fully considered; (2) few works have aligned organizational monitoring requirements in both business and IT service levels; (3) none of the works consider business, process and IT service monitoring requirements specifications as related by derivation; (4) even when partially considered, business monitoring requirements are not drilled down to the IT service layer; and (5) the concept of monitoring interface is seldom used.

The literature survey has revealed some critical research gaps in business process/service monitoring, which match with our research questions and attest their relevance. At a first instance, there is a problem of *design* of monitoring requirements on the business strategy level. Second, there is a problem of integration of cross-layered service monitoring requirements. In the next section we introduce our approach to start dealing with these problems.

3 Business-Driven Alignment of Service Monitoring Requirements

3.1 Value-Driven Service Monitoring Configuration Framework

Our framework is depicted in Fig. 1. We use architectural description guidelines provided by the IEEE Std 1471-2000 recommended practice [36]. The starting point is a 3-viewpoint service configuration framework which uses value models to derive business process and IT services models [2]. Each viewpoint comprises a service management layer. A value model represents a business case, with a proper system of economic actors and transactions. This system is derived from the concepts defined by the e^3value framework meta-model, which formalizes primitive economic concepts for service exchange. A value model derives business processes and IT services' descriptions, which can be

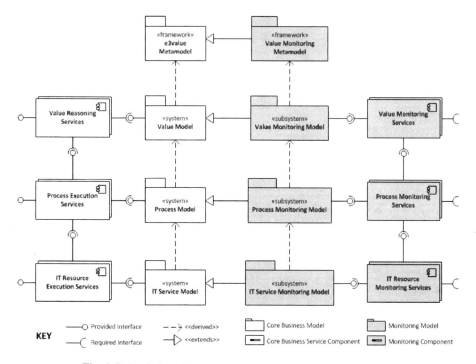

Fig. 1. Value-Driven Service Monitoring Configuration Framework

executed in different service execution platforms. For instance, a value model can be "executed" by running profitability sheets (a value-level reasoning service), whereby its concepts are instantiated for calculating an expected profit to be yielded by each actor within the collaboration, based on an estimation on the number of transactions to be performed. The configured process and IT service models can be executed on different execution services.

We extend this framework with a mirrored supporting one for seamlessly deriving service monitoring requirements *from* and *for* the core business case. The extension starts with a value monitoring meta-model, which extends the e^3value meta-model with a set of monitoring concepts for defining abstract monitoring protocols. The so-called value monitoring meta-model is used as a starting point to derive a 3-viewpoint set of monitoring models aligned with the core business. The monitoring models do not constitute a completely independent business, but consist on subsystems of the core business' ones. The internal separation of requirements, though, is aimed to enable cost assessment of different monitoring strategies and configurations. Truly, if monitoring aspects interleave the core business ones, it becomes difficult to assess monitoring as a value-adding process *per se*.

The generated monitoring models define monitoring needs *from* and *for* the underpinning business cases, and can be exposed as provided service interfaces. The same interface can be fulfilled by different monitoring services. For instance, by providing the monetary cost of economic objects traded on the value network, it is possible to perform a value-level monitoring via calculations provided from different investment theories (performed as reasoning services), such as the Discounted Net Present Cash Flow (DNPC) or Return on Total Assets (ROTA). If performed *ex-ante* the connection of the monitoring services to the (core) service execution environments, such calculations can provide just an *estimation* of value creation. If performed *ex-post*, i.e. in execution time via gathering monitoring data from BAM and/or PM engines, they can potentially reveal to what extent value creation is dependent on the performance of underlying processes and IT services. The *abstract state* of the framework, with its systems and subsystems is depicted in Fig. 1.

The framework *dynamics* is briefly described as follows. A business case is defined using a value model, from which process and IT service models are derived. These models are delivered to service execution platforms, enclosing the core business service configuration process, which for a detailed description we refer the reader to [2]. From the core business value model, monitoring requirements are elicited, which drive the specification of corresponding requirements on the process and IT service viewpoints. These requirements can be exposed as required monitoring interfaces. Service discovery, selection and composition mechanisms can be used to match monitoring needs with capabilities exposed by monitoring services. An example of monitoring capability is the set of monitoring metrics (e.g. KPIs, PPMs and QoS metrics) directly computable from service execution data. Being it part of the monitoring configuration, this matchmaking can define, in *design time*, what monitoring requirements are amenable to verification. By connecting the service monitoring services to the (core) business execution ones, monitoring metrics become amenable to verification in *execution time*. In short, the framework aims to integrate MDE and MaaS on service monitoring configuration.

3.2   Value Viewpoint on Service Monitoring

We start paving the vision of the framework by specifying the concepts of the value monitoring meta-model. As depicted in Fig. 2, all of its concepts are defined as stereotypes extending the meta-classes defined in the original e^3value meta-model (vide Fig. 2(a)). We describe each element as follows:

Monitoring Actor: an economically independent entity involved in a monitoring problem emerged from a business case. A monitoring problem starts with the typical scenario from the Agency Theory, where a *manager* (consumer) requests a service/good of value from an *agent* (provider) in exchange of an economically reciprocal one. As the agent may omit information about real value production and delivery, the manager may employ different strategies to get access to disclosure reliable information. Disclosure of internal value creation of enterprises is generally subject to regulation and may involve external parties. A monitoring actor, thence, can play different roles in a monitoring scenario, such as: (1) a *manager*, the active party who requests for monitoring; (2) an *agent* (the passive party subject to monitoring); (3) a *third-party*, who provides monitoring services, acting on behalf of the manager (e.g. accountants, auditors, expert witnesses, consultants, etc.); and (4) a *regulator* (who can grant access to verifiable information to any of the other parties [37]). Monitoring actors comprise the organizational view on the value monitoring viewpoint.

Monitoring Market Segment: consists of a set of monitoring actors involved in a same monitoring service, i.e. providing and/or consuming the same type of monitoring objects.

Monitoring Object: refers to the concept of monitoring *evidence* or reliable information about value creation, disclosed from and to a monitoring actor, in a document-based form. It can be of a *primary* type (i.e. raw information obtained directly from the agent) or a *secondary* one (e.g. reports and all kinds of information synthesized by third-parties). It can be subject to voluntary or mandatory disclosure [38].

Monitoring Port: used to request or to provide monitoring objects from and to its environment, which consist of other actors exchanging other objects.

Monitoring Interface: comprehends a logical container of monitoring ports, consisting of a channel whereby monitoring objects are offered from and to a monitoring actor. In e^3value, interfaces can be attached to internal value activities. However, as we are dealing with monitoring on the enterprise-level, we consider monitoring interfaces being attached only to actors.

Monitoring Exchange: comprises the communication act of transferring a monitoring object *from* and *to* a monitoring actor, through a monitoring interface.

Monitoring Transaction: a pair of economically reciprocal monitoring exchanges.

Monitoring Policy: a concept derived from the Role Based Access Control (RBAC) standard [39], which provides an abstract framework for promoting security administration on the business enterprise level. RBAC defines policies as *permissions*, which are referred to as functions that map a set of operations into a set of objects. Policy semantics depend on the abstraction level of the system in analysis. Here, policies are necessary to restrict access to private information about value creation. They define constraints over monitoring transactions, i.e. it defines *what* monitoring objects can be transferred from and to *whom*. Policies are attached to interfaces, which contains ports giving access to the monitoring objects. They can be derived from scenarios [40] and involve specific relations among monitoring roles,

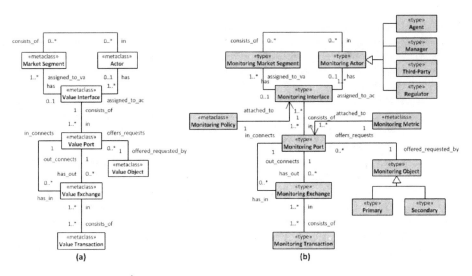

Fig. 2. (a) e^3value meta-model and (b) value monitoring meta-model

which for the sake of simplicity are not shown in Fig. 2(b), but will be further demonstrated in section 4, through the analysis of the business case study.

Monitoring Metric: refers to enterprise-level performance metrics, i.e. KPIs. In e^3value, a value port is used in profitability sheets to register the number of value objects produced/consumed by an actor. KPIs can cover different facets of organizational performance, such as the ones defined by the Balance Scorecard [3]. For instance, from a financial perspective, a KPI can be formulated declaratively on top of value ports as a composition of an *aggregation function*, a *value object*, a *time component* and a *location component*. An example of a simple KPI could be *"the average number of service units sold per day in region X"*. Complex KPIs can be formulated on top of simpler KPIs (e.g. *annual net profit*). More specific KPIs can be specified by using a qualitative aspect to define the way the value object is provided, defined elsewhere as "second-order" value [41]. Examples of second-order values are speed and reliability (defined separately on benchmarking standards). Although not explicitly defined in e^3value, KPIs can be used to measure enterprise-level performance, both on core and monitoring value networks.

The rationale behind this meta-model is to allow for treating monitoring as a business in its own, aimed to maximize value production of the (core) supported business case. In the next section, we demonstrate how these concepts can be used to derive business requirements for monitoring, by applying them on a real-world case study.

4   Early Service Monitoring Requirements Analysis via Value Models

In this section, we apply the value monitoring viewpoint on a case study in electricity trading markets. The case is provided by the Energy research Center of the Netherlands (ECN) and is concerned with the need for enterprise-level monitoring strategies to cope with the problem of reducing the imbalance between the amount of energy produced and consumed. We provide firstly a snapshot on the core business case. Following, we elaborate on the monitoring problems in the case, by providing guidelines to mitigate them using *value models to monitor value models*.

4.1 Business Case Description

The Electricity System is composed by two related subsystems: the *commodity subsystem* (for energy trading) and the *physical subsystem* (for energy generation, transmission and distribution). The Directive 2003/54/EC [42] provides a full description of attributions and legal responsibilities of the actors operating in the whole system. The Transmission System Operator (TSO) is on the intersection of these two systems, being responsible for matching overall production with demand for electricity. Energy suppliers accredited as Balance Resource Parties (BRPs) have the obligation to supply the TSO with energy programs, which posit the amount of electricity to be consumed and produced within a time interval of 15 minutes, based on forecast. This is necessary so as the TSO can prospect the full system capability to mitigate risks of surpluses or shortages.

High instance drivers, such as environmental issues, have pushed the inclusion of renewable energy resources so as to boost the energy mix (e.g. wind, solar, and biomass). However, even being effectively used to balance the system, intermittent sources such as wind and solar energy often create extra imbalances. When a wind turbine fails on delivering the expected electricity, it has to pay costs to the TSO. Two options are left to the supplier to cope with the failure: (1) to pay the balancing costs directly to the TSO, which may be high, for service transparency; or (2) use its own reserves to balance the system, which include either to freelance on the wholesale market to discover a bundle of Distributed Energy Resources (DER), or to use DERs from its own portfolio of reserves; in both cases, the DERs could fulfill the balance in aggregation. The second option has a high business value. In the best case, it can balance the system and yield profit. In the worst case, though, it can cause extra system imbalances.

A basic value model for this scenario is depicted in Fig. 3. It starts with the BRP's need for balancing its electricity production, which can be fulfilled by the DERs in two ways: the BRP can manage DERs directly, or can do it via intermediaries, so-called *aggregators*, which bundle DERs' individual capacities and offers to the BRP. This service has an aggregated value, as it hides from the BRPs the complexity of managing small-scale DERs. Low-capacity DERs increase their chances to sell energy to BRPs when included in an aggregators' portfolio. Aggregators constitute a new market segment, being subject of current research and future regulation. From this point, many monitoring scenarios can be identified. The electricity offered here is just an estimate. Risks of sub-optimal energy delivery threats value creation of all the actors. To mitigate these risks, actors can employ different monitoring strategies on one another, which can include the design of parallel monitoring sub-networks, with their corresponding set of actors and services, aimed to support value production on the core business scenario.

4.2 Value Monitoring Viewpoint on the Electricity Imbalance Reduction Case

We have followed five steps for developing a value viewpoint on defining monitoring strategies for a business case. They elaborate on the concepts defined in section 3 and are described as follows, interleaving examples from the case study:

Step 1 – Identify monitoring scenarios: as monitoring can be treated as a (business) need, we start by eliciting *who* wants to monitor *whom*. This can be done on a two-by-two actors' basis. From our business case, we take a snapshot on aggregators (as *managers*) which want to monitor DERs (as *agents*). Other scenarios would include BRPs and aggregators, and BRPs and DERs. From this point, the problem is to find alternative monitoring networks of *third-parties,* which could provide monitoring objects primarily produced *by* the agent *to* the manager.

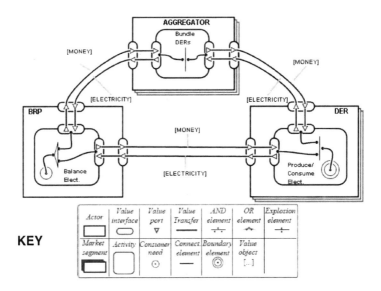

Fig. 3. Snapshot on the Imbalance Reduction Business Case

Step 2 – Define monitoring policies: these policies reduce the space of possible monitoring configurations to a set of law-compliant ones. Generally, they are defined by *regulators,* but can be subject of negotiation among the other actors. Consider our scenario of aggregators and DERs. A DER "promises" to deliver electricity to the aggregator, but the "real" electricity production can only be verified by duly authorized metering services. Recently, smart meters have been considered as a mean to collect more accurate information about electricity consumption and production [43]. Apart from its envisioned benefits, the introduction of smart meters in the electricity market has generated controversies on the disclosure of private verifiable information. Before the deregulation of the metering market segment, the Distribution Network Operator (DNO) was exclusively responsible for the management of collected consumption data. However, after the deregulation, BRPs can be granted with the responsibility for obtaining and validating measurement data from DERs [44]. Instead of being dependent on the DNO, an aggregator could therefore exercise control over this process, provided that either it enters into an agreement with an authorized Metering Responsible Party (MRP, *third-party*) or gets accredited as a MRP by the DNO. It is up to the monitored party to decide which parties, apart from the DNO, are to be given any additional access to the raw (*primary*) measurement data obtained via the meter.

We model this new situation for the metering scenario as a monitoring policy, depicted in Fig. 4. The starting point is the *manager's need* for monitoring the agent. This need can be fulfilled by monitoring objects provided by different monitoring actors, through different *traces*. A *trace* is a value creation path, starting at the manager's need and ending on the agent's boundary element, where the monitoring object is produced. The OR and AND-dependencies define policy *alternatives* and *duties*, respectively. These policies can be defined following a contract-first approach: a hierarchy of monitoring objects must be defined first, and then, they are attached to interfaces. The interfaces can further be attached to value activities and then to actors performing these activities. As we are defining an enterprise-level monitoring protocol, the internal activities are suppressed here, and we focus on monitoring objects rather than on the way they are produced. All the actors and monitoring objects are stereotyped using a UML-like graphical representation, according to the meta-model shown in section 3. The other objects are not typical monitoring ones, but are necessary to preserve the economical reciprocity. More complex policies can be defined by adding role hierarchies (e.g. hierarchies of regulators), separation of duties (for solving policy conflicts on role hierarchies) and time constraints (e.g. by setting different contractual times for the value transactions). Nonetheless, for the sake of tractability, we start from a *flat* RBAC strategy, which comprises basically defining policies and assigning them to stereotyped roles and further to actors [39].

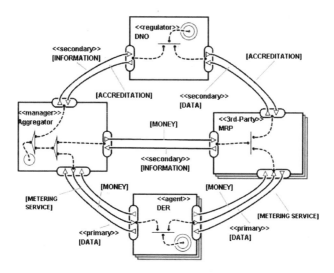

Fig. 4. Example of a monitoring policy expressed in a value model

Step 3 – Select a short-list of policy-compliant monitoring alternatives: from the example depicted in Fig. 4, it is possible to identify three alternative paths for the aggregator to monitor DERs: it can get *secondary* monitoring information from the MRPs, *primary* data from the DERs, or it can get both. In a more complex policy definition, a wider list of policies could be identified. Monitoring paths not specified in the policies are not allowed. That is why the monitoring policies reduce the monitoring configuration space. Selecting a pre-list of alternatives may depend on aspects such as the manager's internal assets to process data, or the need for more accurate data, in highly distrusted relationships. For instance, it could be sufficient for an aggregator to trust on the data provided by the MRP. For another one, however, it could be necessary to cross evidences from both primary data and secondary information. The last case can be particularly effective on mitigating fraud risks.

Step 4 – Derive KPIs to evaluate monitoring alternatives: KPIs can be defined to assess the pay-off of each monitoring strategy. According to our monitoring metamodel, these metrics are attached to value ports. If an actor wants to assess its *delivered* performance, the KPIs shall be attached to its *outgoing-points*. For assessing *received* performance, KPIs shall be attached to *ingoing-ports*. A KPI query can be formulated by concatenating an *aggregation function* (e.g. average, total, maximum, minimum) with a value *object discriminator* (e.g. units transferred), a *time unit* and a *locative unit* (not originally defined in e^3value, but important for this case study). For instance, a KPI for prospecting performance received from the aggregator could be the *average power delivered by the DERs per month in Noord-Brabant, NL*. This KPI is for assessing performance of the "monitoring" transaction. It has to be compared with the corresponding KPI from the core business, e.g. the *average power offered/promised by the DERs per month in Noord-Brabant, NL.* The difference between monitoring and core business KPIs can be used on incurring penalties and compensations for the parties involved. For generating reports, KPIs can appear on the model in form of annotations, or can be defined apart, in profitability sheets.

Step 5 – Calculate ROI for each monitoring alternative: finally, the return on investment of each monitoring strategy can be calculated. Thus, it is necessary to assess *investments* and *expenses* on monitoring. For instance, if an aggregator decides to process by itself the raw data gathered from the DERs, it has to cope with incurred investments on internal monitoring resources (e.g. metering information systems). If it decides to get data from a metering party, it has to cover the expenses with metering fees. Investments and expenses have to be subtracted from the expected return of the monitoring strategy (previously calculated via KPIs), for the sake of risk analysis. We can here identify two trade-off monitoring scenarios in this situation. If the DERs fail on delivering the electricity, the aggregator can use the penalty to cover the costs of monitoring and also to pay its own implied penalties to the BRP, in the macro business scenario depicted in Fig. 3. If the DERs deliver the promised amount of electricity, the costs of monitoring for the aggregator can be compensated by absenting from incurred penalties to the BRP, in the macro business scenario. Many other trade-offs can be identified, which can be used to select the (potentially) best pay-off monitoring configuration. The selected monitoring configuration can be attached to the core business scenario, as contractual terms and conditions expressed in terms of information disclosure policies.

These five steps produce a value viewpoint on service monitoring. Here we developed the monitoring rationale from the *manager's role* view, which in the electricity imbalance case, corresponds to the aggregator's role. Nevertheless, perspectives from the other monitoring actors may coexist, derived from the same core business case, which may not be necessarily convergent a priori. They can be used, however, for negotiating monitoring policies on enterprise-level business collaborations.

5 Discussion

In this paper we have demonstrated on a gap existing between the way business process/service monitoring is currently performed and critical business drivers (for monitoring). To start filling this gap, we have proposed a conceptual framework aimed to start configuring monitoring strategies from the business strategy layer. Assuming the use of value models on configuring business processes and services, we have demonstrated how to use them per se to reason about monitoring problems and alternative solutions from and for a business case. Proof-of-concept was provided via early monitoring requirement analysis from a real-world case study. We have primed for simplicity on the design of the value viewpoint on monitoring, as it is still unclear whether and how its most basic concepts can be drilled down to the process and IT service management layers. At this phase, complexity may introduce additional alignment problems across service management layers, which should be avoided.

Next steps of this research include: (1) the mapping of the value viewpoint on service monitoring on the process viewpoint one; and (2) formalization of the operations for discovery, selection and composition of monitoring services based on the abstract monitoring interfaces and protocols defined on these two viewpoints. A second real-world case study, on Intellectual Property Rights in the music industry is planned.

References

1. Gordijn, J., Akkermans, H.: Value based requirements engineering: Exploring innovative e-commerce idea. Requirements Eng. Journal 8(2), 114–134 (2003)
2. Gordijn, J., Weigand, H., Reichert, M., Wieringa, R.: Towards self-configuration and management of e-service provisioning in dynamic value constellations. In: Proc. of SAC 2008, pp. 566–571 (2008)
3. Parmenter, D.: Key Performance Indicators. Willey, Chichester (2007)
4. Hollingsworth, D.: Workflow Management Coalition (WfMC), The Workflow Reference Model, Document Number TC00-1003, Document Status - Issue 1.1 (1995)
5. Zur Mühlen, M.: Workflow-based Process Controlling. Foundation, Design, and Implementation of Workflow-driven Process Information Systems. In: Advances in Information Systems and Management Science, Logos, Berlin, vol. 6 (2004)
6. Küng, P., Hagen, C., Rodel, M., Seifert, S.: Business Process Monitoring & Measurement in a Large Bank: Challenges and Selected Approaches. In: Andersen, K.V., Debenham, J., Wagner, R. (eds.) DEXA 2005. LNCS, vol. 3588, pp. 955–961. Springer, Heidelberg (2005)
7. Srinivasan, S., Krishna, V., Holmes, S.: Web-Log-Driven Business Activity Monitoring. Computer 38(3), 61–68 (2005)
8. Yu, T., Jeng, J.-J.: Model Driven Development of Business Process Monitoring and Control Systems. In: Proc. ICEIS 2005, vol. 3, pp. 161–166 (2005)
9. Greiner, T., Düster, W., Pouatcha, F., von Ammon, R., Brandl, H., Guschakowski, D.: Business activity monitoring of norisbank taking the example of the application easyCredit and the future adoption of Complex Event Processing (CEP). In: Proc. PPPJ 2006, vol. 178, pp. 237–242 (2006)
10. Alles, M., Brennan, G., Kogan, A., Vasarhelyi, M.A.: Continuous Monitoring of Business Process Controls: A Pilot Implementation of a Continuous Auditing System at Siemens. Int. Jour. of Accounting Information Systems 7, 137–161 (2006)

11. Abe, M., Jeng, J., Li, Y.: A Tool Framework for KPI Application Development. In: Proc. ICEBE 2007, pp. 22–29 (2007)
12. Beeri, C., Eyal, A., Milo, T., Pilberg, A.: Monitoring business processes with queries. In: Proc. 33rd VLDB, pp. 603–614 (2007)
13. Kim, H., Lee, Y.-H., Yim, H., Cho, N.W.: Design and Implementation of a Personalized Business Activity Monitoring System. In: Jacko, J.A. (ed.) HCI 2007. LNCS, vol. 4553, pp. 581–590. Springer, Heidelberg (2007)
14. Chen, P.: Goal-Oriented Business Process Monitoring: An Approach based on User Requirements Notation Combined with Business Intelligence and Web Services, M. Sc. Thesis, Carleton University, Ottawa, Ontario, Canada (2007)
15. Ferro, D.N., Hoogendoorn, M., Jonker, C.M.: Ontology-Based Business Activity Monitoring Agent. In: Proc. WIC 2008, pp. 491–495 (2008)
16. Strnadl, C.F.: Bridging Architectural Boundaries Design and Implementation of a Semantic BPM and SOA Governance Tool. In: Krämer, B.J., Lin, K.-J., Narasimhan, P. (eds.) ICSOC 2007. LNCS, vol. 4749, pp. 518–529. Springer, Heidelberg (2007)
17. Pedrinaci, C., Lambert, D., Wetzstein, B., van Lessen, T., Cekov, L., Dimitrov, M.: SENTINEL: a semantic business process monitoring tool. In: Proc. OBI 2008, vol. 308, pp. 1–12 (2008)
18. Paschke, A., Bichler, M.: Knowledge representation concepts for automated SLA management. Decis. Support Syst. 46(1), 187–205 (2008)
19. Lamparter, S., Luckner, S., Mutschler, S.: Semi-Automated Management of Web Service Contracts. Int. Jour. of Service Sciences (IJSSci) 1(3/4) (2008)
20. Rimini, G., Roberti, P.: Business Process Monitoring: BT Italy case study. In: Mazzeo, A., Bellini, R., Motta, G. (eds.) IFIP Fed. for Inf. Processing: E-Government ICT Professionalism and Competences Service Science, vol. 280, pp. 227–234 (2008)
21. Tsai, W.T., Zhou, X., Wei, X.: A Policy Enforcement Framework for Verification and Control of Service Collaboration. ISeB 6, 83–107 (2008)
22. Unger, T., Leymann, F., Mauchart, S., Scheibler, T.: Aggregation of Service Level Agreements in the Context of Business Processes. In: Proc. EDOC 2008, pp. 43–52 (2008)
23. Vaculin, R., Sycara, K.: Semantic Web Services Monitoring: An OWL-S Based Approach. In: Proc. HICSS 2008, p. 313 (2008)
24. Comuzzi, M., Kotsokalis, C., Spanoudakis, G., Yahyapour, R.: Establishing and Monitoring SLAs in Complex Service Based Systems. In: Proc. ICWS 2009, pp. 783–790 (2009)
25. Bai, X., Liu, Y., Wang, L., Tsai, W., Zhong, P.: Model-Based Monitoring and Policy Enforcement of Services. In: Proc. SERVICES 2009, pp. 789–796 (2009)
26. Fugini, M., Siadat, H.: SLA Contract for Cross-Layer Monitoring and Adaptation. In: Ma, R., et al. (eds.) BPM 2009 International Workshops LNBIP, vol. 43, pp. 412–423 (2010)
27. Kang, B., Lee, S.K., Min, Y.-b., Kang, S.-H., Cho, N.W.: Real-time Process Quality Control for Business Activity Monitoring. In: ICCSA 2009, pp. 237–242 (2009)
28. Momm, C., Gebhart, M., Abeck, S.: A Model-Driven Approach for Monitoring Business Performance in Web Service Compositions. In: Proc. ICIW 2009, pp. 343–350 (2009)
29. Pourshahid, A., Amyot, D., Peyton, L., Ghanavati, S., Chen, P., Weiss, M., Forster, A.J.: Business process management with the user requirements notation. Electronic Commerce Research 9(4), 269–316 (2009)
30. Robinson, W.N., Purao, S.: Specifying and Monitoring Interactions and Commitments in Open Business Processes. IEEE Softw. 26(2), 72–79 (2009)
31. Spillner, J., Winkler, M., Reichert, S., Cardoso, J., Schill, A.: Distributed Contracting and Monitoring in the Internet of Services. In: Senivongse, T., Oliveira, R. (eds.) DAIS 2009. LNCS, vol. 5523, pp. 129–142. Springer, Heidelberg (2009)

32. Wang, Q., Shao, J., Deng, F., Liu, Y., Li, M., Han, J., Mei, H.: An Online Monitoring Approach for Web Service Requirements. IEEE Trans. Serv. Comput. 2(4), 338–351 (2009)
33. Han, K.H., Choi, S.H., Kang, J.G., Lee, G.: Performance-centric business activity monitoring framework for continuous process improvement. In: Zadeh, L.A., Kacprzyk, J., Mastorakis, N., Kuri-Morales, A., Borne, P., Kazovsky, L. (eds.) Proc. WSEAS 2010, Stevens Point, Wisconsin. Artificial Intelligence Series, pp. 40–45 (2010)
34. van der Aalst, W.M.P., Rubin, V., Verbeek, H.M.W., van Dongen, B.F., Kindler, E., Günther, C.W.: Process Mining: A Two-Step Approach to Balance Between Underfitting and Overfitting. In: SoSyM, vol. 9(1), pp. 87–111 (2010)
35. Wetzstein, B., Strauch, S., Leymann, F.: Measuring Performance Metrics of WS-BPEL Service Compositions. In: Proc. ICNS 2009, pp. 49–56 (2009)
36. IEEE Std 1471.: Recommended Practice for Architectural Description of Software-Intensive Systems (2000)
37. Cormier, D., Aerts, W., Ledoux, M.J., Magnan, M.: Web-Based Disclosure about Value Creation Processes: A Monitoring Perspective. Abacus 46, 320–347 (2010)
38. Dimitrako, T., Daskalopulu, A., Maibaum, T.: Evidence-based Electronic Contract Performance Monitoring. INFORMS Jour. Of Group Decision and Negotiation, Special Issue: forma Modeling of Electronic Commerce 11(6), 469–485 (2002)
39. Ferraiolo, D.F., Kuhn, D.R.: Role Based Access Control. In: Proc. 15th National Computer Security Conference, pp. 554–563 (1992)
40. Neumann, G., Strembeck, M.: A Scenario-driven Role Engineering Process for Functional RBAC Roles. In: Proc. SACMAT 2002, pp. 33–42 (2002)
41. Weigand, H., Johannesson, P., Andersson, B., Bergholtz, M., Edirisuriya, A., Ilayperuma, T.: Strategic Analysis using Value Modeling: The c^3value Approach. In: Proc. HICSS 2007, p. 175c (2007)
42. European Parliament and Council. Common Rules for the Internal Market in Electricity. EU Directive 2004/54/EC in: Official Journal of the European Union, July 15 (2003)
43. ESMA.: Annual Report on the Progress in Smart Metering 2009. Version 2.0. European Smart Metering Alliance (January 2010)
44. NMa/DTe.: Electricity Metering Code: Conditions within the meaning of Section 31, subsection 1b of the Electricity Act 1998, Informal Translation. Office of Energy Regulation (part of the Netherlands Competition Authority) (September 4, 2007)

A Trust Model for Services in Federated Platforms

Francisco Javier Nieto

ATOS Research and Innovation, Atos Origin, Capuchinos de Basurto 6,
48013 Bilbao, Spain
`Francisco.nieto@atosresearch.eu`

Abstract. Web services are a powerful tool for executing functionalities using third party applications and they are widely used in business processes. For this reason, it is necessary to complement traditional security solutions by adding soft security mechanisms, which take care of trust, in order to determine whether a web service and its provider are performing as they should. An extensible model for a trust evaluation system is presented for this purpose. It determines some parameters important in enterprise and Future Internet environments and it defines how to calculate the perceived trust by applying a three round algorithm with fuzzy logic. It exploits services semantics and it takes into account last updates about the service, consistency rules based on the semantic relationships between aspects and other specific calculations for each parameter. Semantics are used as well for sharing information with other platforms and federations for improving interoperability in distributed environments.

Keywords: trust; model; security; web services.

1 Introduction

Nowadays, web services are a powerful tool for accessing to functionalities offered by third parties, as a way to externalize the provision of certain operations which need to be integrated in complex systems.

Because of the importance of the functionalities to be used and the sensitive information exchanged in the process when several enterprises have to interoperate, those systems which perform an intensive use of external web services need to provide secure mechanisms which guarantee that the interactions are done as expected and that the information is exchanged in a secure way.

Analysis done about these kind of systems, like [1], reveal that there are hard security mechanisms (focused on encryption and access control) an soft security mechanisms (more focused on social aspects, such as trust and reputation).

There are not so many solutions for covering soft security mechanisms customized for SOA environments and which can be easily integrated with access control mechanisms to be applied in enterprise contexts. In addition, even if there are existing approaches related to reputation, it is hard to find solutions which cover more aspects related to the trust of web services and which are able to exploit services semantics for giving accurate results. The presented approach aims at exploiting the semantics

M. van Sinderen and P. Johnson (Eds.): IWEI 2011, LNBIP 76, pp. 118–131, 2011.
© IFIP International Federation for Information Processing 2011

and, at the same time, covering a lot of aspects which are related to trustworthiness in services while improving the robustness of the model by maintaining consistency of the data used.

In this context, according to this approach, it can be said that the trust on the service is seen as the belief in the reliability, truth and capability of the service.

The paper is structured as follows: section 2 provides a vision of the related work in the area, while Section 3 describes the main motivation and ideas in which the approach is based. Section 4 will describe the areas and aspects in the conceptual model and Section 5 presents how trust is evaluated. Finally, Section 6 presents a set of conclusions and future work.

2 State of the Art

There are several publications [1][2][3] which analyze the reputation topic and related approaches, They provide classification schemes and information about how to evaluate reputation and trust, but they are quite focused only in users' ratings.

They also include analysis of online traditional models for reputation (like eBay and Amazon) and other based on these ones with concrete improvements, such as NICE [4] or Sporas and Histos [5].

There are many ways to calculate the reputation associated to an agent or to a service, based on the ratings received from users. Approaches like [6] are focused on applying probabilistic theory by means of concrete distribution functions (as they are applied to data of the same nature), while other like RATEWeb [7] use weighted averages, but also predict the reputation of service providers by using a Hidden Markov Model when ratings are not readily available.

Most of the solutions proposed are focused only on a single rating obtained from users while only a few of them, like RATEWeb, take into account SLAs fulfillment and QoS, but also expressed as users' ratings and not measuring them directly or using other inputs for calculating a meaningful initial trust value.

In addition, only a few solutions, like REGRET [8], use ontologies as a way to identify derived aspects to be used when calculating reputation (for example, in the case of a seller, aspects like deliver date, price and product quality). The approach presented in [9] also exploits semantics, but it is focused on trust for actions performed by entities and it is not oriented to services.

There are some approaches which present fuzzy models, such as Afras [10]. They are quite useful for defining rules according to the fuzzy values and they increase the usability of the model, as users will understand the measures obtained much better without any reference for comparing. But robustness is delegated in the way to calculate trust and concrete filters, instead of controlling the data involved in a meaningful way, amending it when inconsistencies arise.

Finally, no approaches were found with the aim at solving sharing information with other platforms in a seamless way, taking into account federations as well.

3 Principles and Objectives

The work in [1] defines a set of requirements which should be covered by a trust model. The approach presented in this paper aims at fulfilling these requirements in the best way possible, providing a robust solution against attacks which calculates accurate values for long-term performance and which weights aspects in a fair way guaranteeing smoothness.

Moreover, the presented trust model goes beyond other existing approaches by looking for completeness, focusing not only on users' rating and its associated reputation, but also on general aspects and capabilities of the service, as a mean to evaluate service potential as well.

Since it may be necessary to customize the model, the presented approach offers the possibility to modify it, adding or modifying aspects and parameters. Besides, in a wide environment where enterprises are heterogeneous and are grouped in different ways, it is necessary to provide a mechanism which make possible to share information as a way to facilitate interoperability in scenarios where it is necessary to involve external platforms and services for executing business processes.

Finally, it is necessary to provide a mechanism which guarantees robustness of the model, not only based on the way to evaluate the trust, but based on controlling the most important asset of the model: the information on which everything is based.

For doing so, this solution aims at exploiting the full potential of the semantics associated to web services, as a mean to share information, evaluate the trust and avoid malicious attacks.

4 The Conceptual Model

The first step to create the model was to determine which concepts it should contain. For doing so, the SOA context and other trust models were analyzed, in order to know which aspects were meaningful for web services trust. In addition, an innovation game was carried out with some Atos Origin consultants. This game required adding notes to a picture of a big tree representing aspects which consultants take into account when thinking about the trustworthiness of software, indicating the importance of each aspect. At the end, some of these concepts were adapted to the SOA context and others were included in the model as defined originally.

The model was completed by adding some concepts related to trust, reputation and other SOA related concepts, such as Quality of Service (QoS) parameters.

The result is a model oriented to determine the trustworthiness of a web service which is divided in four main areas, as presented in Figure 1. The result obtained from applying the model is a value representing how much we can trust on a service, as a non-functional property, which can be used automatically together with other properties for ranking candidates when performing a service discovery, for instance.

The main aspects contained in each area are described in the following sections. Although some of them have to be obtained from the service provider and introduced manually, most of them can be obtained automatically by accessing to the service description and existing Service Level Agreements (SLAs), by requesting information to other platforms and federations or by monitoring the interactions with the service.

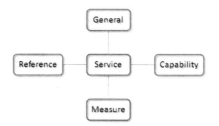

Fig. 1. High level view of the Conceptual Model

4.1 General Area

The General area is about a set of aspects which do not represent the behavior of the service itself, but those general characteristics of the service related to how it has been developed, its sustainability and how it is maintained, as shown in Figure 2.

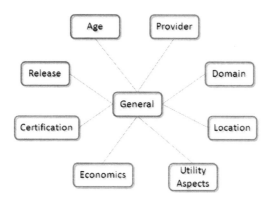

Fig. 2. General area of the Conceptual Model

These aspects are quite static, as it is not usual that they change, but some of them are important for determining whether the web service can guarantee a good operation, such as the aspect 'Provider' which represents the brand developing the service and evaluates as well the support to users when there is any problem.

Another aspect which is important is 'Certification' which evaluates whether there are any authority certifying that the development of the service is secure (such as the Common Criteria certification [11]) and that standardized processes are followed.

'Location' evaluates if the service is located in countries with specific regulation for protecting data and if the country provides good network infrastructures for accessing the service. The 'Release' aspect represents the effectiveness of the last version of the service and with which frequency it is updated. It gives an idea of the maintenance and improvement of the service, although it depends on other aspects for determining whether this is a positive or negative indication (e.g. too many bugs on previous releases).

The concept 'Utility Aspects' is interesting in the context of enterprise interoperability, as it evaluates the service with respect to its capacity to be used as a utility (for enterprise interoperability or enterprise collaboration) and to its usage in Virtual Organizations which carry out complex business processes.

While the 'Age' aspect gives an idea of how long the service has been working, 'Domain' determines the applicability of the service in different business domains, or its specialization in concrete domains only.

Finally, 'Economics' provide information about the revenue model and available payment methods, which may represent the sustainability of the service.

Most of this information will be introduced in the system by the system administrator (at least, for the first time). Even if for some aspects we need to rely on the information given by the service provider, most of that information can be validated, such as certifications, which can be validated with the corresponding authority, in order to guarantee the reliability on the model.

4.2 Capability Area

This area gathers information about WHAT the service can do and HOW it can do it. It represents what the service provider claims about the service. This information is expected not to vary too much during the service lifetime unless the service design and/or implementation changes. It is clearly divided in two main aspects: functionalities offered and non functional properties (NFP), as shown in Figure 3.

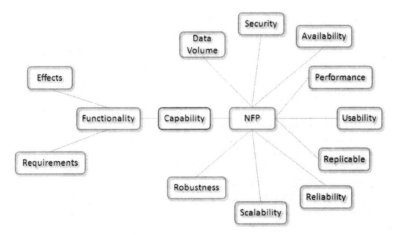

Fig. 3. Capability area of the Conceptual Model

The 'Functionality' aspect is divided in two aspects. While 'Requirements' represents the dependencies of the service (in the form of pre-conditions and assumptions) and the final requirements (the post-conditions of the service), 'Effects' represents the functionalities by what they do in the context where they are executed. This information is used for evaluating whether the web service may have too many requirements and whether it offers a lot of functionalities to users. As semantics of the web service are exploited in these aspects, it can be compared with other services which are similar or which belong to the same domain.

In the other hand, 'NFP' represents those aspects which are related to the claimed QoS. Some of these aspects can be compared later to the real QoS measures obtained from interactions with the service.

'Data Volume' refers to the amount of information exchanged between the service and the service consumer, for determining whether too much information is used or not, in comparison with other similar services. The aspect 'Availability' is focused in the percentage of time the service is available in comparison to other similar services.

The aspect 'Robustness' evaluates the percentage of failures expected from the service and its capability to react when there are problems (i.e. checking compliance with WS-Transaction [12]). Instead, 'Reliability' is more oriented to the trustworthiness in the delivery and reception of messages thanks to specifications such as WS-Reliability [13].

While 'Performance' evaluates if the service claims to offer good performance with respect to other services, 'Scalability' evaluates if the service maintain performance when requests and data volume increase, comparing with other services. 'Replicable' evaluates whether the service can be copied to several servers or if it can be executed in a distributed way, having a potential impact in performance, scalability, robustness and availability.

'Usability' evaluates whether it is simple or not to access to the web service. It is determined in terms of the signature complexity and the existence of semantic description for the operations, enabling automatic discovery and invocations.

Finally, 'Security' evaluates the kind of mechanisms offered by the service for guaranteeing a secure interaction. This covers aspects such as the existence of digital certificates and trust agreements, and the strength of encryption algorithms applied.

The service description (syntactical and semantic) and SLAs are the best sources of information for gathering data about the aspects presented here.

4.3 Measure Area

This area is the most dynamic one, as it evaluates the information which is continuously gathered about interactions with the service. Each time the service is invoked, it is monitored and analyzed according to the aspects presented in Figure 4.

Most of the aspects are directly related with those included in the 'NFP' aspect of the 'Capability' area. When evaluating these aspects, they are compared to the measured values for similar services as well as to any existing agreements (SLAs, etc.) for determining whether any agreement is violated.

'Response Time' represents the measure related to performance. It compares the real response time of the service with other services response time. Similarly, 'Data Volume' evaluates the amount of data exchanged between the service and service consumer, by comparing it to other similar services providing the same functionality.

The usage of the service is evaluated by means of 'Requests Number', so the interpretation is that good services are used by many users.

The aspect called 'Scalability' is measured in terms of response time variation when the number of requests increases and response time variation when the data volume grows, and then it is compared with other similar services.

While the 'Availability' aspect determines the percentage of errors because of failures accessing the service, 'Robustness' determines the percentage of errors because

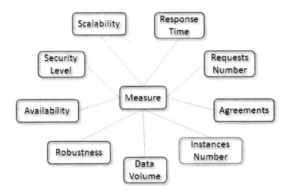

Fig. 4. Measure area of the Conceptual Model

of malfunctioning of the web service, and which could not be controlled (fault messages are controlled errors). While the first one is related to the hardware and network infrastructures, the second is directly related to the service design and implementation. They are also compared with the values measured for other services.

'Instances Number' represents the number of copies available of the service, so the calls received can be sent to different servers, balancing the load of the web service.

An important aspect is 'Security Level' which evaluates the mechanisms used for securing the message exchange. It includes the digital certificates used as well as the encryption mechanisms applied in comparison with other services and those mechanisms technically available but not used.

Finally, the aspect 'Agreements' evaluates whether the service is fulfilling its commitments by checking the measured values with existing SLAs and Trust Agreements (if any). It has a very important impact in trustworthiness.

All the aspects covered by this area can be evaluated by using the information which can be automatically gathered by monitoring the services, so it does not require manual provision of data.

4.4 Reference Area

This area represents the so called reputation of the web service. It aims at gathering external information about the service behavior and third parties' opinions about the service according to the aspects presented in Figure 5.

This information is used in order to determine the trust in the service as seen by others with their own experience and sources of information.

The 'News' aspect refers to those news published which are related somehow to the web service or the service provider, as they may be a source of information about the service behavior and, about the way the service provider manages its business.

'Forums' is another source of opinions about the service and the service provider. Users may use forums to report problems or to ask help about a service.

The aspect 'Trusted Feedback' represents the aggregation of users' opinions about the service. They can rate the web service according to their experience using it.

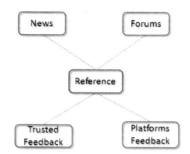

Fig. 5. Reference area of the Conceptual Model

It will also depend on how much a user is trusted and the level of expertise with services (as consumers without experience using services may have negative opinions because of their lack of knowledge instead of because real problems in the service).

Finally, 'Platforms Feedback' represents the reputation of the service obtained from the aggregation of experiences from other platforms which may provide their rating for the service or the concrete measurement of some of the aspects, usually as part of a federation. It depends on the level of trust in the platforms sharing their information for avoiding problems with malicious platforms and for giving preference to those platforms which collaborate actively with the one evaluating the service.

In this case, all the information depends on external sources. In the case of 'News' and 'Forums', an administrator should introduce the information in the system for its evaluation. In the case of 'Trusted Feedback', users have to rate the service and that rating can be obtained from a web-based form. For 'Platforms Feedback', next section presents an ontology used for sharing information between platforms.

4.5   The Model as an Ontology

As the presented approach wants to exploit semantics as much as possible, all the model is expressed as an ontology, defining all the main concepts (such as 'Area', 'Aspect' and 'Parameter) and instantiating them according to the aspects presented. It includes concepts for describing a 'Federation' and the entities related to it, focusing on the trust shared between them.

The ontology has been defined using WSML in order to facilitate its development, its usage with semantic services (as part of it could be used in services descriptions based on WSMO) and the creation of mediators whenever necessary. The ontology is presented in Figure 6, with the main concepts defined. Concrete aspects and parameters would be instances of the concepts presented in the ontology.

Those concepts related to Trust Concept represent areas, aspects and parameters which are taken into account when determining the trust of a service. They represent a hierarchy for organizing those aspects used. While some are atomic (such as Trust Parameter), others depend on the aggregation of more Trust Concepts (such as Trust Area and Trust Aspect). In its higher level, a group of Trust Concepts is a Trust Model, which will represent the way a Trust Provider evaluates trustworthiness.

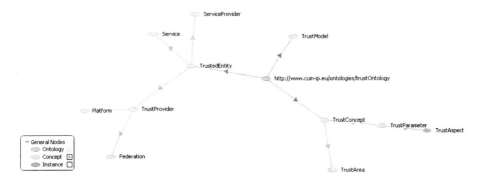

Fig. 6. Concepts of the Trust Ontology

On the other hand, concepts related to Trusted Entity represent entities which take part somehow in a Federation, a group where information about trust is shared. There are entities which will have a trust level assigned (Trusted Entities, which can be evaluated) and there will be entities which provide trust evaluations (Trust Providers).

One of the advantages obtained is that the information can be shared between different platforms and federations easily, even enabling the possibility to define mediators whenever necessary (in case of interactions between heterogeneous platforms). Each Trust Provider will generate a trust evaluation for those known Trusted Entities, publishing certain information for others, which can map Trust Models between platforms and re-evaluate trustworthiness when necessary or desired.

Another advantage is the possibility to extend and modify the model in an easy way. New parameters, aspects and areas can be defined, assigning to them a weight representing their importance where they are allocated, so the rest of weights can be adapted. This allows administrators to customize the way trust is calculated.

Finally, semantics will be used to relate those aspects with some kind of relationship, meaning that a change in the value of one aspect will affect another one or that their values change in a similar way at the same time. These relationships will be used for the trust evaluation, as explained in the next section. In the ontology, this is modeled as three slots in Trust Parameter, which represent parameters which affect to other parameter, parameters affected by the instantiated parameter and parameters whose value is just related with the value of other parameters.

5   Trust Evaluation

Once aspects and parameters are defined, it is necessary to determine how so much information can be aggregated in order to provide a result which represents how much a web service can be trusted.

As it is necessary a way to normalize somehow the value of each aspect (so all the results are expressed in the same metric) a set of linguistic terms (and their corresponding fuzzy sets) have been defined (see Figure 7), so all the values obtained will be based on those terms and their membership functions. This is appropriate, as users will understand easily the meaning of the trust evaluation and, moreover, it will be

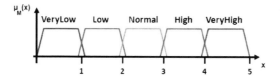

Fig. 7. Linguistic terms and their membership function

possible to apply fuzzy logic theory and aggregate aspects in a meaningful way. Besides, it facilitates statistical analysis of all the aspects and parameters in the model, in order to find relationships between them.

The idea is to allow users and other platforms to access to the evaluation of concrete aspects facilitating interoperability and, moreover, to use those values to improve the model robustness and analyze consistency between aspects.

Each time any aspect in the model is updated, the whole trust evaluation will be calculated. This is done in a three-round process, which first calculates aspects, then amends the results according to consistency rules and, finally, aggregates all the values with a weighted mean which adapts weights according to the context.

5.1 First Round – Evaluate Each Aspect in the Model

As explained before, each aspect is represented by a value between 0 and 5 which determines how good is the aspect but, how is this value obtained for each aspect?

The way to calculate each value will depend on its nature and in what we can do with it. Given the space limitations of this paper, only the general calculation types are presented with some examples, and not how each different aspect is calculated.

Some aspects, such as response time and data volume, allow predicting next values from previous ones, so techniques like **simple exponential smoothing** are applied for determining the future expected value, which are compared with the prediction for other services which are similar in order to see how good obtained predictions are.

Other aspects can be evaluated by analyzing the **tendency** with respect to some variables (such as with scalability, using response time and data volume). In this case, it is possible to 'virtually' generate a graphic representing the service behavior and determine the tendency by calculating the slope of the curve in a concrete time.

There are other aspects which may depend on a context which is out of the control of the platform. For instance, with 'Location', the quality and price of network infrastructures available, existing regulation about data protection and even resources spent for pursuing fraud are important inputs which are represented with **fuzzy sets** and combined with **fuzzy operations**.

Those aspects which are related to reputation using users' rating and other platforms as input are evaluated by applying the solution proposed in RATEWeb [7] because of its compatibility with the available information. Moreover, it can be used to predict reputation when users' feedback is not readily available, which is an expected situation when they have no good incentives.

Finally, whilst some aspects will be as simple as calculating a percentage and determine how good it is with respect to other services (such as in the case of robustness), others will be as complicated as determining the fuzzy set of a trust parameter by applying **statistical hypothesis tests**, like Student's t test for pair differences, which are combined later with fuzzy operators (such as in 'Release', where t test is used to evaluate the effectiveness of a new release by comparing old values of robustness and response time with new ones, obtained after updating the service).

5.2 Second Round – Amend Evaluations with Consistency Rules

As one of the key requirements for a trust model is to provide a mechanism guaranteeing robustness, the proposed model defines a way to check the information gathered for the evaluation in order to identify malicious manipulations of data.

This mechanism is built based on an analysis of the relationships between the aspects in the model. For example, the publication of new releases of the service may be good for the robustness of the service, as the number of errors is expected to decrease. But, it may happen that there are many releases in a short period of time because the service implementation is not good enough and the service experiences too many errors.

A fuzzy associative matrix is built according to the identified relationships, so a set of rules is defined. An example of rule, according to the previous example, would be: "*IF Robustness IS VeryLow THEN DecreaseRelease*". This way, it is possible to avoid that a malicious service provider tries to increase its trust level by publishing many releases without really doing meaningful modifications in the service.

There are two kinds of consistency rules for this purpose:

— *Basic rules*, as a result of the aspects analysis, especially for those relationships cataloged as cause-effect;
— *User defined rules*, as a customized configuration based on users' experience, requirements and desired constraints.

After the calculation of the value corresponding to each aspect in the model, the fuzzy rules are executed, in order to correct any incoherence in the aspects values. If one rule is activated because of an inconsistency, the value of one or more of the aspects will be amended, giving it an expected value defined in the rule.

5.3 Third Round – Aggregate Evaluations

Due to the heterogeneity of the aspects included in the model, probabilistic based approaches do not have too much sense. Since each aspect may be independent from others, that they measure different things and that they have different importance for the trust calculation, using a weighted average is the best solution. As aspects are grouped in areas, these areas are seen as blocks for calculating the trust, so each area is calculated first and, finally, the global value is calculated.

Equation (1) is used for calculating the trust level associated for each area and for the model in general, where factor k represents the weight to be applied, while T represents the trust level obtained for the aspect i in the model. The value of T will be always between 0 and 5 because the values are normalized with those fuzzy sets already mentioned.

$$T_B = \frac{\sum_{i=1}^{n} k_i * T_i}{\sum_{i=1}^{n} k_i} \qquad (1)$$

Although each aspect has a weight associated, there are certain cases where other aspects are somehow related to it, and thus need to be taken into account for refining that weight, so the factor k is not exactly the original weight assigned to each parameter.

One of the factors to take into account is when an aspect has been updated. Although it can be considered a cognitive bias, it is quite representative in a SOA context, as last updates of the service are the most representative of the service behavior. This is because good results in old requests do not guarantee good results during the next requests (for example, the availability and response time could decrease because of problems with the servers and networks). The conclusion is that it is necessary to increase the weight of those aspects which have been updated recently.

The other factor to have in mind is the effect of each aspect in the service behavior. Even if some aspects are not updated recently, they might have a lot of importance in the way the service behaves. 'Release' is a good example, as a good robustness is directly related to the last updates in the design and implementation. A service which was not updated recently may obtain a low rating in the 'Release' aspect but, if the service is performing fine, that value can be increased, as it was really important. In this case, we can say that 'Robustness' (in 'Measure' area) and 'Release' (in 'General' area) are closely related and so we annotate it semantically. The semantic distance between two aspects will determine how much they affect each other.

According to the described principles, factor k will be calculated by applying (2), where w represents the original weight for aspect i, t represents the factor related to time and D the factor related to the semantic distance with last aspects updated.

$$k_i = w_i * t_i * D_i \qquad (2)$$

The factor related to time (t) should give more importance to newest values and decrease the weight of old values smoothly. For calculating the effect of the time in the weight, all the aspects of the same block are ordered in a list according to the last time they were updated. Two aspects will be in the same position if they were updated at the same time, so the classification is some kind of grouping of aspects according to the time when they were updated. Then, (3) is applied, since the curve it produces is similar to an exponential smoothing, which is the effect to be produced in the weights of the parameters. In this equation p is the position of the aspect i in the list.

$$t_i = e^{1/p_i} - 1 \qquad (3)$$

Finally, the factor related to the importance of an aspect in the behavior of the service (D) should increase a bit the weight of those aspects which are more relevant, but should not penalize those aspects which may be more independent. For doing so, (4) is used, where $min(d)$ represents the minimum distance between an updated aspect and aspect i. The distance is obtained thanks to the semantic relationship declared in the instances of the ontology. The reason to apply equation (4) is that it performs an exponential smoothing as well, but its effect is softer and the difference between first values and next ones is not so pronounced.

$$D_i = \left(\frac{1}{\min(d_i) * Ln(10)} \right) + 1 \tag{4}$$

As recently updated aspects are rewarded when calculating the factor t, in this case, we will consider that $min(d)=1$ for most recently updated aspects and for those aspects which are directly related to them (as a cause, effect or normal relationship).

5.4 Initial Calculation

When a service is published in a platform, there is no information about the service behavior. The only information available is the service description and other information claimed by the service provider about its web service. This means that the first time the trust for a given service is calculated, it has to be a slightly different.

It is not possible to use information from 'Measure', as it will not be available (although it could be gathered with some invocations for testing purposes). For that reason, the calculation is focused mainly in the information gathered in 'General' and 'Capability' areas, which will give us a good idea about the potential of the service.

More information can be gathered by means of the 'Reference' area but, as it will not be possible to validate the information received (being weaker against malicious manipulations), its weight will be lower.

Having all these considerations in mind, the recommended weights to be used is 40 for 'Capability' and for 'General', while 20 for 'Reference' and 0 for 'Measure'.

6 Conclusions and Future Work

Given the importance of trust in those systems that perform an intensive use of web services, the presented approach provides a wide and complete conceptual model for determining the trust associated to a web service.

Although reputation is an important part for determining the trust level of a service, there are other aspects which may be even more important, such as the measures done during direct interaction with services and the service capabilities.

When determining the real weight of an aspect, its importance is not only determined by the weight provided by users, but also by when it was updated and by the effect it really has in the web service, which may not be visible at a first sight. It is also important to share information between platforms in an easy way (as it is used for determining reputation as well), always trying to guarantee a good level of robustness for the used model. For doing so, exploiting semantics is a very good tool, as they are becoming a widely used solution in the SOA context and allow modeling knowledge.

Future work will be focused in improving the model by analyzing all the relationships between the aspects defined in the model through deep statistical analysis, so they can be fully exploited.

After that, it will be possible to extend the approach in order to determine the trust level in Cloud Computing environments. Moreover it will be possible to determine the trust level which can be achieved by a business process (implemented as service compositions) by analyzing the trust related to the services which will be used. It will require mechanisms for analyzing the workflow and determining how the presented approach can be applied in this context.

Acknowledgments. This research was supported by the COIN project (http://www.coin-ip.eu/) and has been partly funded by the European Commission's IST priority of the 7th Framework Programme under contract number 216256.

References

1. Jøsang, A., Ismail, R., Boyd, C.: A survey of trust and reputation systems for online service provision. Decis. Support Syst. 43(2), 618–644 (2007)
2. Zhang, Q., Yu, T., Irwin, K.: A classification scheme for trust functions in reputation-based trust management. In: Proceedings of ISWC Workshop on Trust, Security, and Reputation on the Semantic Web (2004)
3. Sabater, J., Sierra, C.: Review on Computational Trust and Reputation Models. Artif. Intell. Rev. 24(1), 33–60 (2005)
4. Lee, S., Sherwood, R., Bhattacharjee, B.: Cooperative Peer Groups in NICE. In: IEEE Infocom, San Francisco, CA (April 2003)
5. Zacharia, G.: Collaborative Reputation Mechanisms for Online Communities. Master's thesis, Massachusetts Institute of Technology (1999)
6. Li, L., Wang, Y., Lim, E.: Trust-Oriented Composite Service Selection and Discovery. In: Baresi, L., Chi, C.-H., Suzuki, J. (eds.) ICSOC-ServiceWave 2009. LNCS, vol. 5900, pp. 50–67. Springer, Heidelberg (2009)
7. Malik, Z., Akbar, I., Bouguettaya, A.: Web Services Reputation Assessment Using a Hidden Markov Model. In: Baresi, L., Chi, C.-H., Suzuki, J. (eds.) ICSOC-ServiceWave 2009. LNCS, vol. 5900, pp. 576–591. Springer, Heidelberg (2009)
8. Sabater, J., Sierra, C.: REGRET: A reputation model for gregarious societies. In: Proceedings of the 4th Int. Workshop on Deception, Fraud and Trust in Agent Societies, in the 5th Int. Conference on Autonomous Agents (AGENTS 2001), Montreal, pp. 61–69 (2001)
9. Huang, J., Fox, M.S.: An ontology of trust: formal semantics and transitivity. In: Proceedings of the 8th International Conference on Electronic Commerce: The New e-Commerce: Innovations for Conquering Current Barriers, Obstacles and Limitations to Conducting Successful Business on the Internet (ICEC 2006), pp. 259–270. ACM, New York (2006)
10. Carbo, J., Molina, J., Davila, J.: Comparing predictions of SPORAS vs. a Fuzzy Reputation Agent System. In: 3rd International Conference on Fuzzy Sets and Fuzzy Systems, Interlaken, pp. 147–153 (2002)
11. Common Criteria for Information Technology Security Evaluation, Version 3.01 Revision 3, Final (July 2009), http://www.commoncriteriaportal.org/
12. OASIS: Web Services Transaction (WS-TX) Technical Committee, http://www.oasis-open.org/committees/tc_home.php?wg_abbrev=ws-tx
13. OASIS: Web Services Reliable Messaging TC WS-Reliability 1.1 (2004), http://docs.oasis-open.org/wsrm/wsreliability/v1.1/wsrm-ws_reliability-1.1-spec-os.pdf

Towards Pragmatic Interoperability in the New Enterprise — A Survey of Approaches

Camlon H. Asuncion and Marten van Sinderen

Center for Telematics and Information Technology (CTIT), University of Twente,
P.O. Box 217, 7500 AE Enschede, The Netherlands
{c.h.asuncion,m.j.vansinderen}@utwente.nl

Abstract. Pragmatic interoperability (PI) is the compatibility between the intended versus the actual effect of message exchange. This paper advances PI as a new research agenda within the gamut of enterprise interoperability research. PI is timely in today's new enterprises as it is increasingly important that organizations are able to collectively add value to their products and services through effective collaboration. When enterprise systems exchange information, PI goes beyond the compatibility between the structure and the meaning of shared information. It also considers the use of information in a given context as an equally important aspect. As PI is a relatively new domain, this paper attempts to elucidate its notion by identifying and relating its key concepts from proposed definitions, and by reviewing extant approaches to identify critical knowledge gaps in PI research.

Keywords: enterprise interoperability, pragmatic interoperability, survey of approaches.

1 Introduction

The International Organization for Standardization (ISO) defines an enterprise to be "one or more organizations sharing a definite mission, goals, and objectives to offer an output such as a product or service" [11]. This definition implies that either *one* or a *group* of organizations is involved. However, today's organizations remain competitive if they collaborate with other organizations with the objective of adding more value to their products and services (e.g. supply chain networks [7]). This cross-organizational nature of enterprises gave way to two types: a *virtual enterprise* (VE) and an *extended enterprise* (EE). While a VE temporarily exists between organizations to exploit an immediate market opportunity, an EE requires long-term trust and mutually dependent relationships [5]. These *new* enterprises have given rise to innovative business models that drive today's global economy [6].

Although today's enterprises want to leverage the benefits of their collaboration, interoperability problems between enterprise systems prevents them from doing so to the full extent [28]. Previous investments in equipment and software

M. van Sinderen and P. Johnson (Eds.): IWEI 2011, LNBIP 76, pp. 132–145, 2011.

cause incompatibilities between data representation and application methods. New acquisitions can cause impracticable integration with third party applications [12].

Vernadat [29] argues that interoperability in the enterprise: "provides two or more business entities [...] with the ability of *exchanging or sharing information* (wherever it is and at any time) and of using functionality of one another in a distributed and heterogeneous environment." Since organizations are not only composed of software but of people as well, achieving enterprise interoperability is multi-faceted [8]. Chen, et al. [5] argue that enterprise interoperability is ensured if there is interaction at least in the following layers: data, services, process and business.

In recent years, a number of researchers are also looking into the role of pragmatic interoperability (PI) as another layer in the general research of enterprise interoperability. They argue that while there is a need to agree on the structure and the meaning of the shared information, use of information is important as well. To provide a working definition of PI, we borrow Pokraev's [20] definition as being:

Definition 1. *The compatibility between the intended versus the actual effect of message exchange*

Various motivations from different domains have been put forward to advance PI as a new, timely and important research agenda. Among them, for example, is in the domain of collaborative enteprise computing where Kutvonen, et al. [13] argue that cross-organizational collaboration not only involves technology but social aspects of integration as well (i.e., pragmatics). In the domain of Web service discovery, Lee [14] argues that pragmatics can be used to select the most appropriate service from among a set of syntactically and semantically similar, yet competing, services. This view is shared by de Moor [17] where stakeholders interpret the appropriateness, suitability and applicability of a set of Web services, a process they call pragmatic selection in the domain of virtual communities. Singh, among others, proposes the notion of the Pragmatic Web [25], which entails that the meaning of information should be interpreted in the context of its use.

We recently conducted a systematic literature review to elucidate important concepts that can be derived from published definitions of PI [2] — essentially, we wanted to understand *what* PI currently means. The contribution of this paper, on the other hand, builds on previous work by investigating *how* current approaches propose to achieve PI. We do this by proposing a set of criteria whereby we can position the approaches accordingly.

The rest of this paper is structured as follows. Section 2 provides an elaboration on the notion of PI. Section 3 provides a framework to compare PI approaches. Section 4 compares extant approaches using the framework. Section 5 draws insights from the comparison. Finally, Section 6 presents conclusions and a brief research roadmap to further advance PI research.

2   Defining Pragmatic Interoperability

Our previous work focused on extracting dominant concepts from published definitions of PI as we have seen that there is a lack of canonical agreement as to how it is currently defined [2]. The following concepts from the proposed definitions of PI can be derived: *intention, exchange, use* and *context*.

A sender sends a message with some intention (also known as goal, need, preference, or intended effect). To realize this intention, the message must be delivered to the receiver, and hence, message exchange is part and parcel. On the receiver's end, message use deals with how the receiver acts to realize the intention of the message. However, a message must not be used arbitrarily but in a given context as its actual meaning varies according to the context in which it is used. Apart from this, context also changes over time which can affect the meaning of the message as well. Therefore, there must be a *shared* context which is *relevant* for the purpose of interoperation. Based on these concepts, we now propose a refinement of Definition 1 by stating PI as:

Definition 2. *The compatibility between the intended versus the actual use of received message within a relevant shared context.*

This is still consistent with Definition 1 in the sense that we relate *effect* to both *message use* and *context*. The notion of *message use* can be furthermore refined in terms of the *relevant subsequent use of information* and the *relevant subsequent actions using that information*. Essentially, we argue that the intended effect is achieved through a mutually dependent relationship between information, action, and context; i.e., *Actions on received information depend on context*.

- **Relevant subsequent use of information**: This denotes which relevant *information* (or part of the message) are to be used in a given context from the set of all data received during message exchange. We borrow this concept from Zeigler's notion of pragmatic frame [31].
- **Relevant subsequent actions**: This denotes which relevant subsequent *actions* the receiver can perform in a given context from the set of all possible actions. We borrow this from the Speech Act Theory (SAT) [23] and the Language/Action Perspective (LAP) [30], and from definitions given by such authors as Schade [22], Hofmann [10], Bazijanec [3], among others.

3   Criteria for Comparison

Seeing that the approaches are quite diverse in terms of their domain and implementation, a difficulty arises when they are compared with specific properties. Thus, we have resorted to devising a generalized set of criteria which is not too specific but still keeps the objective of this paper achievable. The approaches are compared in terms of the basic *architecture* it supports, the phase(s) of a development *life cycle* it contributes to, the role of *context*, the *adaptiveness* of its solution, how it realizes *compatibility*, and where the *scope* of the effect is achieved. We now briefly describe each criterion.

Architecture. This criterion positions an approach according to the support it has in terms of the types of relations participants have in the collaboration (e.g., one-to-one, one-to-many or many-to-many), the distributed computing model of the architecture (e.g., client-server, peer-to-peer, n-tier, or space-based), and how the intended effect can be achieved through message exchange (e.g., single request or dialogue).

Life cycle. This criterion positions the approach in terms of which phase of an information systems development life cycle it contributes or applies to. We use the phases of the Systems Development Life Cycle (SDLC) [9]: planning, analysis, design, development, testing, and implementation. Although more elaborate frameworks can be used (e.g. ISO/IEC 12207, ISO/IEC 15288), we deem it sufficient to make a simplified and generalized comparison of the approaches using SDLC. The *planning* phase defines a development plan (e.g., project definition, scope, documentation, etc.) of the proposed system. The *analysis* phase involves understanding and documenting system requirements. The *design* phase involves creating a "blueprint" of how the proposed system will work. The *development* phase involves building the actual system according to the design documents. The *testing* phase involves verifying if the actual system meets the requirements of the analysis phase. The *implementation* phase begins when the system becomes operational by the end users. Finally, the *maintenance* phase involves monitoring the actual system to ensure its compliance with business goals.

Context. Our previous work [2] showed that a number of approaches consider context to be important in PI. This criterion asks if an approach is dependent on the notion of context to achieve PI. If so, we classify the role of context using the two refinements of message use described in Section 2; i.e, message use as the relevant subsequent use of information, or the relevant subsequent actions using that information as means to achieve the intended effect, in a given context.

Adaptiveness. A pressing requirement in today's new enterprises is to be adaptive to change. Adaptation compels an enterprise to respond to changes because of the conditions of its environment in an effort to survive [4]. This imposes on the PI solution a high degree of flexibility. We use this criterion to position an approach as to whether it has some mechanisms that allow the solution to swiftly adapt to new situations and still remain interoperable.

Compatibility. Recalling Definition 2, the key relation between the intended versus the actual effect is compatibility, which can be achieved either absolutely or relatively. By relative, we mean that achieving the intended effect is approximate in that, for example, one sender may be satisfied at a different level from another sender. By absolute, we mean that the intended effect is either present entirely or not; i.e, either PI is there or isn't there.

Scope. This criterion positions the approach as to where the intended effect is ultimately realized. We propose in our previous work [2] that message exchange can create a intended effect either at the application level or business level. For each approach we ask: Does the intended effect remain at the digital world only (e.g., the update of a data item in a database column) or does the intended effect propagate to the business level to achieve a business objective; i.e, outside the digital world and into the real world?

4   Approaches to Pragmatic Interoperability

We now describe briefly and position accordingly each approach using the criteria. Of the 44 papers that were identified from our previous work [2], 9 are discussed here as they provide some level of detail as to how PI can be achieved; 24 papers, however, do not provide enough detail to warrant a comparison. The remaining 11 papers are in the domain of Multi-Agent Systems (MAS) which are deliberately excluded here.

Kutvonen et al. [13] The approach supports the collaboration of VEs, or eCommunities as the authors call them, where organizations can dynamically participate (i.e., they can join, leave, or be removed for various reasons) in global business environments based on open markets to achieve a certain business opportunity. An eCommunity is a venue for participants to be pragmatically interoperable as they can negotiate and agree on the compatibility of their business rules and policies.

The approach uses the concept of an eContract which not only encapsulates the rules and policies, but functional and non-functional properties of the collaboration as well. An eContract is implemented under an automated environment, called the webPilarcos B2B middleware, where facilities for finding, selecting and contracting relevant services are provided. The middleware is designed to follow a federated form of interoperation where services are developed independently by organizations and no meta-information is assumed to be shared allowing the approach to be adaptive. The middleware supports a many-to-many collaboration any organization can dynamically participate in the eCommunity, an n-tier distributed model is supported by the middleware, and dialogue is necessary during negotiation to agree on the eContract. The approach provides contribution to the analysis, design, and development of the eContract, and thereafter, maintenance and compliance monitoring using the eContract. It is oriented towards providing a PI solution at the business level achieving scope at that level. The role of context, however, is not explicitly explained.

Lee et al. [14] The approach proposes a solution for the automatic composition of Web services into a service workflow which combines simple services to form a complex one that meets user requirements. When a service requester is faced with a set of syntactically compatible, semantically equivalent, yet competing services, contextual knowledge can be used to select the most appropriate service. Pragmatic or contextual knowledge describes how and in what situations provided services can satisfy user requirements in a given context. Contextual knowledge is modelled using rule-annotated ontologies (e.g., RuleML and OWL).

An architecture uses a service composition agent to perform the necessary discovery and selection using pragmatic knowledge. We thus view interoperability in their approach to be one-to-many and n-tier; however, it appears that once the selection of the service is completed, achieving the intended effect occurs using a single service request only. The approach seems to focus more on the analysis, design, and development of the PI solution rather than with other phases. Context is used as the key component in selecting the most appropriate service; in particular, the composition agent uses contextual information of the service requester during the service selection process. The approach is adaptive in the sense that once the contextual information of the service requester changes, the most appropriate service can then be selected to compose a new service workflow. Compatibility seems to be absolute since if the composition agent cannot find an appropriate service based on the context of the service requester, the service workflow cannot be generated as well. Finally, the approach is largely oriented towards achieving PI at the application level.

Liu et al. [16] To design service-oriented applications, the approach leverages pragmatics (a component of the Theory of Semiotics [19]), which is concerned with the use of information in relation to its intended purpose in a given context. The approach proposes a Pragmatic Web Service Framework for service request decomposition and aggregation. Here, a service broker decomposes a request into finer sub-requests that specify requirements that a concrete Web service should satisfy. A sub-request is annotated with its own semantic and pragmatic (i.e., purpose and context, or a pragmatic frame) definitions which are then represented as Web service abstracts. A workflow is then designed using business process requirements and the Web service abstracts. To implement the workflow, the service broker uses pragmatic knowledge to find concrete Web services using the Web service abstract and the pragmatic frame. How a concrete Web service meets the requirements of an abstract Web service in terms of the pragmatic frame is measured as the pragmatic distance.

The interaction is one-to-many where one request can be satisfied by many providers, mediated by a service broker. Once an appropriate concrete Web service is selected, a single request seems to achieve the intended effect. The approach can be positioned in terms of the analysis, design, and development phases of the life cycle. Context is important, and the approach makes use of illocutionary acts from the SAT to achieve intended effect. The notion of pragmatic distance leads us to believe that compatibility can be achieved relatively; e.g., requesters may select concrete Web services with varying pragmatic distances. Since the approach is preliminary, we cannot sufficiently assess the adaptiveness of the solution. Finally, we view the scope of the approach to be at the application level.

de Moor et al. [17] The approach proposes a solution to Web service selection in virtual communities (VC) for the communication of their members using collaborative tools. Particularly challenging in VCs is that tacit knowledge cannot be completely and explicitly represented. In this respect, the authors leverage pragmatic concepts to provide a context-dependent mechanism so that service selection can be tied to the context of its intended use. This is important as VCs use services in novel and unique ways depending on their context. Guided by a methodology called RENISYS [18], relevant stakeholders of a VC interpret the usefulness of a set of syntactically and semantically compatible candidate Web services based on certain criteria. This is called as the process of pragmatic selection.

We cannot assess the architectural aspect of the solution as no architecture is used, but rather a methodology. RENISYS can be positioned mostly during the analysis stage when a VC selects the most pragmatically compatible set of Web services according to the VC's context of use. Context is critical as it will determine what sort of services a VC requires; however, it is not clear if context is described in terms of relevant information or relevant actions. Compatibility is relative as a virtual community may have different and unique requirements from another. Finally, the methodology is focused at achieving the intended effect ultimately at the business level.

Pokraev [20] The approach uses service-oriented and model-driven principles to provide solutions in the domain of Enterprise Application Integration (EAI) where multiple, heterogenous, autonomous and complex distributed systems need a flexible interoperability solution to collaborate effectively. It implements a service mediator that resolves data and process mismatches between collaborating systems with fixed service descriptions. A data mismatch occurs when systems have different denotations of the same message element in the real world. A process mismatch occurs when systems have a different understanding of message interaction protocols (i.e., the order of message exchange). PI is achieved when the sender and receiver of the message have the same expectation of the effect of message exchange which can be realized by ensuring that the proper order and execution of message invocations are followed.

We view the compatibility of the approach to be rather absolute as the specific order of service invocation must be observed. The approach proposes a five-step methodology for designing integration solutions which covers analysis, design, development, and testing. However, it does not explicitly consider the role of context in PI. As the approach leverages model-driven techniques, a key benefit is abstraction; i.e., with the same abstract solution depicted as platform-independent models, new implementations can be automatically generated, allowing adaptiveness. Furthermore, there is also work that extends the approach whereby business rules are used to separate the dynamic aspects of the requirements making the approach even more flexible [1]. We position the approach as having a business level scope.

Rukanova [21] The use of a standard can help organizations be interoperable. However, the challenge lies in determining if whether or not a standard is sufficient to meet the communication requirements of an organization's digital business transaction (DBT), where a DBT is an electronic exchange of products and/or services for some remuneration. Thus, when organizations choose to adopt a standard to perform DBTs with others, the "fit" or the capabilities of a standard vis-a-vis the requirements of a DBT should first be evaluated. To do this, the approach proposes a meta-model that can be used as basis for the evaluation, with an accompanying methodology for doing such evaluation. The theoretical foundations of the meta-model are derived from theories related to the pragmatics of communication, where context plays an important role. The approach argues that when a standard fits a DBT, PI is satisfied.

The architectural aspect of the approach cannot be positioned as no architecture is used, but rather a methodology. The methodology can be positioned at the analysis phase of the life cycle where it helps assess the fit of a standard for a given DBT. In terms of context, the meta-model uses the communicative acts of the SAT and LAP to describe the pragmatic aspect of the communication. Compatibility is therefore absolute as a selected standard should be able to address all communicative patterns of LAP; otherwise, pragmatic interoperability problems may occur. On the other hand, it is not clear how the methodology would allow the solution to be adaptive to business changes. Finally, we position the scope at the business level as the ultimate effect is realized through an effective DBT.

Tamani et al. [26] Motivated by the argument that collaborating parties use Web services differently according to their own context, the approach proposes a solution levaraging principles of the Pragmatic Web [25] for automated Web service discovery, where context is used to select the most appropriate service above and beyond semantically equivalent services. The approach uses XML to capture and XPath to query the personal, functional, and contextual information of collaborating parties stored in profile repositories. These XML profiles specify each requester's and provider's identity and role (the "who" part), the purpose and goal (the "why" part that specifies the context of the collaborating parties), the input and output parameters annotated by some ontology structure (the "what" part). A matching architecture is used to semantically match the "what" part of the request/offer XML and pragmatically match the "why" part of the request/offer XML. The Web service of the offer XML that is semantically and pragmatically closest to the request XML, through string tokenization algorithms, is selected.

Architecturally, the approach uses a one-to-many interaction as one requester may need to discover from one among many offers from the profile repository. A matcher sits in between the requester and provider that resolves semantic and pragmatic differences between the two. A single request, however, seems to be sufficient to achieve the intended effect. The approach falls within the design and development stages of the life cycle. Context is important by treating only the similar contextual information specified as "why" part of the request/offer XMLs. On the other hand, it is difficult to assess the adaptiveness of the approach as this criterion is not well described. Compatibility is rather absolute in the sense that if a matcher cannot find similarities between the "why" part of the request/offer XMLs, PI cannot be achieved. Finally, the intended effect is only realized at the application level through the successful matching of contextual information.

Tolk et al. [27] The approach proposes a framework for measuring the degree of conceptual representation between interoperable systems, known as the Levels of Conceptual Interoperability Model (LCIM), which is highly influenced by the Modelling and Simulation community. LCIM has seven levels of interoperability: no interoperability, technical, syntactic, semantic, pragmatic, dynamic, and conceptual. Focusing on the PI level, PI is reached when "when the interoperating systems are aware of each others methods and procedures. In other words, the use of the data — or the context of its application — is understood by the participating systems; the context in which the information is exchanged is unambiguously defined". LCIM takes two roles: descriptive and prescriptive, Descriptively, LCIM can be used as a documentation which serves as a maturity model whereby properties of an interoperating system is measured against an LCIM level. Prescriptively, LCIM has a set of methods for achieving a target interoperability level.

As LCIM is largely an assessment framework, no architecture is proposed. Furthermore, as LCIM can be used descriptively and prescriptively, we position it in terms of the analysis, design and testing phases of the life cycle. Context relates to how information is used in a given state and specification of the system. LCIM does not clearly discuss if reaching the PI level entails adaptiveness of the solution. We view compatibility as absolute because the meaning of information depends on the state and specification of the system. Finally, we view the scope as that which is confined only to the interactions of the systems.

Zeigler et al. [31][24] In the Modelling and Simulation domain, the approaches positions PI in one of three levels: syntactic, semantic, and pragmatic. At the pragmatic level, focus is on the receivers' interpretation of messages in the context of its application relative to the senders intent. Thus, at the pragmatic level, there is a shared agreement between the sender and receiver of a message as to how information is to be used; i.e, the receiver reacts to the communicated message in a manner that the sender originally anticipated (with the assumption that there is non-hostility in the collaboration).

The approach introduces the notion of a pragmatic frame. Information exchange involves reporting or requesting changes in the state of the world between a sender and a receiver. When a sender produces information by capturing the state of the world (through some form of ontology, derived from his own perspective of the world), the pragmatic frame characterizes how a receiver would use that information (which maybe the full or part of that ontology). Thus, the pragmatics of use describes how data will be subsequently processed.

Architecturally, the approach supports a one-to-many type of interaction, n-tier, and single request. We position the approach in terms of the analysis, design, development phases of the life cycle. Context is an important concept that emphasizes on the subsequent use of information. The approach is not clear as to whether adaptiveness is reached when PI is achieved. Compatibility is relative in the sense that the subsequent use of relevant information may depend on the receiver and its context. We position the scope to be at the business level as the ultimate effect is realized by the receiver of the message when it uses the acquired relevant information.

5   Discussion

A summary of the comparison among PI approaches with respect to the previously described criteria is given in Table 1. In this section, we first summarize and compare approaches per criterion to ascertain their differences and

Table 1. A summary of the comparison among pragmatic interoperability approaches

	Architecture[α]	Life cycle[φ]	Context[φ]	Adaptiveness	Compatibility[ξ]	Scope[δ]
Kutvonen et al. [13]	M2M/NT/D	A, Des, Dev, M	No	Yes	R	B
Lee et al. [14]	O2M/NT/S	A, Des, Dev	Yes, I	Yes	A	A
Liu et al. [16]	O2M/NT/S	A, Des, Dev	Yes, A	?	R	A
de Moor et al. [17]	none	A	Yes, ?	?	R	B
Pokraev [20]	O2M/NT/D	A, Des, Dev, T	No	Yes	A	B
Rukanova [21]	none	A	Yes, A	?	A	B
Tamani et al. [26]	O2M/NT/S	Des, Dev	Yes, I	?	A	A
Tolk et al. [27]	none	A, Des, T	Yes, I	?	A	A
Zeigler et al. [31]	O2M/NT/S	A, Des, Dev	Yes, I	?	R	B

[α] *O2O*: one-to-one, *O2M*: one-to-many, *M2M*: many to many / *P2P*: peer-to-peer, *NT*: *n*-tier, *CS*: client-server / *S*: single request, *D*: dialogue

[φ] *P*: planning, *A*: analysis, *Des*: design, *Dev*: development, *T*: testing, *I*: implementation, *M*: maintenance.

[φ] *I*: relevant subsequent use of information, *A*: relevant subsequent actions

[ξ] *A*: absolute, *R*: relative

[δ] *B*: business level, *A*: application level

similarities. Thereafter, we attempt to identify critical knowledge gaps in PI research based on this comparison. Summarizing the approaches per criterion:

Architecture. Although there are more architectural approaches to PI, either a methodology or an assessment framework is also used. Among the architecture-based approaches, a one-to-many type of relation is mostly supported. It is often the case that an intermediary software is used to coordinate participants in the collaboration (i.e., a middleware, mediator, matcher, or a Web service broker). Particularly, among service-oriented approaches, a single request is often the type of message exchange used to achieve the intended effect. We also notice that the "one-to-many : single request" pair occurs more frequently.

Life cycle. Most of the approaches can be positioned in terms of the analysis, design and development phases of the life cycle. No approach adequately supports the planning phase. Furthermore, there are very few approaches that support the testing and maintenance phases. Furthermore, it is interesting to note that non-architectural approaches contribute more to the analysis phase where the focus is on requirements elicitation; e.g., pragmatics is seen as a technique during service selection where the most appropriate service is chosen based on contextual information.

Context. A large number of approaches value context as an integral part of achieving PI. This is due to the fact that these approaches leverage pragmatic theories such as Semiotics, SAT, and LAP as foundations for designing their solutions. The difference lies, however, in their interpretation of context: either the focus is more on the relevant subsequent information use or relevant subsequent actions performed; we observe, however, that neither approach supports these types simultaneously. Approaches that do not use pragmatic theories are not explicit about their support for context.

Adaptiveness. Most of the approaches are not clear as to how adaptive their solutions are, and hence we cannot position them accordingly. For approaches which we have positioned as adaptive, we cannot directly attribute their adaptiveness to their use of pragmatics. An exception, however, is the one of Lee [14] where the change in context can be used to dynamically recreate a service workflow to meet the service requester's requirements by selecting the most appropriate service relative to the requester's context.

Compatibility. The approaches vary greatly in terms of achieving the intended effect either relatively or absolutely. There also seems to be a pattern: approaches whose scope is at the application level (i.e., that is the focus of the approach is rather technical, and, hence, the effect remains in the digital world) achieve PI absolutely. On the other hand, approaches whose scope is at the business level, achieving the intended effect is relative.

Scope. The approaches also vary in terms of scope. Some approaches, which are mostly technical (and, hence, the compatibility is absolute), achieve the intended effect at the application level; whereas, approaches with a relative compatibility achieve the intended effect at a business level scope. It is also interesting to note that single-request approaches have the scope of application level; whereas, dialogues are common in approaches whose scope is at the business level.

A number of critical knowledge gaps in PI research can be observed. We find that there is a need to bridge the gap among approaches that provide only architectural or methodological solutions to PI. We argue that to advance PI research, an architectural *and* methodological approach, which are both complementary, should be devised.

Currently, no approach seems available that supports the development of PI solutions in each phase of a software development life cycle (i.e., from planning to maintenance). Challenges are yet to be identified when pragmatic principles are considered in every phase of a system development life cycle specific to the goal of developing PI solutions. One promising approach is called MEASUR (Methods for Eliciting, Analysing and Specifying Users' Requirements)[15] that takes a semiotic approach to information systems development.

We still need to deepen our understanding in terms of which form of message exchange is necessary and sufficient to achieve the intended effect in PI: is it through a single request or through a dialogue? In human linguistics, pragmatic effects of communication are usually achieved through a dialogue that depends significantly on the prevailing context; how do we translate this when enterprise systems communicate pragmatically?

Our notion of context in PI needs further exploration as various approaches characterize context differently. This seems to be the most important aspect in PI, yet the most difficult to get to grips with. The two refinements of message use we described in Section 2 (i.e., relevant subsequent information use and relevant subsequent action in achieving PI) need consolidation as neither of the approaches treat both as important concerns together. Finally, it has been argued that not everything about context can be formalized [17]. Questions thus remain: how much of context can or should we automate for the purpose of PI? How do we handle context that is difficult to automate but is nevertheless important for achieving PI?

As we have mentioned, adaptiveness and flexibility are critical in today's new enterprises. There is a need to create approaches that are adaptive to change. Already we find that this has been one of the goals of more recent PI approaches; however, evidence is yet to be had to ascertain whether the adaptiveness of the solution can be directed attributed to its being pragmatic. Demonstrating adaptiveness may allow PI research rapid adoption in the industry.

PI is a new and still less-developed research area as evidenced by the lack of implementation and validation in real life scenarios and the diversity of the terminologies used. Application of pragmatics-based solution remains to be seen in real life settings. Already we find that PI has been applied in various domains, is it possible to conceptualize PI so that it becomes applicable in various domains, similar to how semantic interoperability is understood in whatever domain it is applied?

Finally, no approach offers a mature way to *measure* the intended effect especially in both cases when the compatibility is either absolute or relative, or the scope is either at the business level or application level. Measuring PI especially becomes difficult when the business level is considered. One promising measure is proposed by Liu [16] called the pragmatic distance at the application level; however, implementation details remain to be seen.

6 Conclusion and Future Work

Pragmatic interoperability (PI) is the compatibility between the intended versus the actual use of message exchange within a relevant shared context. The interest in PI has been increasing recently as more and more researchers argue that agreeing on the syntax and semantics during message exchange is not enough, how information is used in a given context is important as well to reap the benefits of a truly effective interoperability solution. The application of pragmatics in information system research, in general, and PI research, in particular, still remains preliminary. This paper attempts to advance this field by harmonizing different concepts related to the notion of PI from among currently diverse interpretations of its concept. We also position PI approaches according to a set of criteria so that critical gaps in knowledge, related to PI research, can be elucidated.

In summary, some of these knowledge gaps include developing an approach where both architectural and methodological aspects are considered, studying the impact when pragmatic principles are considered in every phase of a system development life cycle, exploring the role of context in PI, and validating approaches in real life settings.

As we have described earlier, there are several other approaches to PI specific to the MAS domain. We have not considered them in this paper deliberately as we believe that they deserve a separate review. We intend to do this in the future, and perhaps perform a further comparison between MAS and non-MAS approaches to PI. Finally, it is our aim to envision a future solution where service-oriented principles will be used to achieve PI particularly in the healthcare domain.

References

1. Asuncion, C.H., Iacob, M.E., van Sinderen, M.J.: Towards a Flexible Service Integration through Separation of Business Rules. In: 14th International Enterprise Computing Conference, Brazil, pp. 184–193. IEEE Computer Society, Los Alamitos (2010)
2. Asuncion, C.H., van Sinderen, M.J.: Pragmatic Interoperability: A Systematic Review of Published Definitions. In: Bernus, P., Doumeingts, G., Fox, M. (eds.) EAI2N 2010. IFIP Advances in Information and Communication Technology, vol. 326, pp. 164–175. Springer, Heidelberg (2010)
3. Bazijanec, B., Zaha, J.M., Albani, A., Turowski, K.: Establishing Interoperability of Coordination Protocols in Ad Hoc Inter-Organizational Collaborations. In: Interoperability of Enterprise Software and Applications, pp. 123–133. Springer, London (2006)
4. Chakravarthy, B.S.: Adaptation: A Promising Metaphor for Strategic Management. The Academy of Management Review 7(1), 35–44 (1982)
5. Chen, D., Doumeingts, G., Vernadat, F.: Architectures for Enterprise Integration and Interoperability: Past, Present and Future. Computers in Industry 59(7), 647–659 (2008)
6. Chung, W.W.C., Yam, A.Y.K., Chan, M.F.S.: Networked Enterprise: A New Business Model for Global Sourcing. International Journal of Production Economics 87(3), 267–280 (2004)
7. Davis, E., Spekman, R.: The Extended Enterprise: Gaining Competitive Advantage through Collaborative Supply Chains. Financial Times Prentice Hall Books, Englewood Cliffs (2004)
8. Doumeingts, G., Müller, J.P., Morel, G., Vallespir, B.: Enterprise Interoperability: New Challenges and Approaches. Springer, Heidelberg (2007)
9. Haag, S., Cummings, M., McCubbrey, D., Pinsonneault, A., Donovan, R.: Management Information Systems for the Information Age. McGraw-Hill, New York (2006)
10. Hofmann, M.: Challenges of Model Interoperation in Military Simulations. Simulation 80(12), 659 (2004)
11. ISO: ISO 15704: Industrial Automation Systems — Requirements for Enterprise Reference Architectures and Methodologies (1999),
http://www.mel.nist.gov/sc5wg1/gera-std/15704fds.htm
12. Jardim-Goncalves, R., Grilo, A., Steiger-Garcao, A.: Challenging the Interoperability between Computers in Industry with MDA and SOA. Computers in Industry 57(8-9), 679–689 (2006)

13. Kutvonen, L., Ruohomaa, S., Metso, J.: Automating Decisions for Inter-enterprise Collaboration Management. In: Pervasive Collaborative Networks, pp. 127–134. Springer, Boston (2008)
14. Lee, J., Lee, Y., Shah, S., Geller, J.: HIS-KCWater: Context-Aware Geospatial Data and Service Integration. In: 2007 ACM Symposium on Applied computing, pp. 24–29. ACM, Seoul (2007)
15. Liu, K.: Semiotics in Information Systems Engineering. Cambridge University Press, Cambridge (2000)
16. Liu, K.: Pragmatic Computing — A Semiotic Perspective to Web Services. Communications in Computer Information Science (CCIS), vol. 23, pp. 3–15. Springer, Heidelberg (2009)
17. de Moor, A., van den Heuvel, W.J.: Web Service Selection in Virtual Communities. In: 37th Annual Hawaii Int. Conf. on System Sciences, vol. 7, pp. 70–197 (2004)
18. de Moor, A., Jeusfeld, M.A.: Making Workflow Change Acceptable. Requirements Engineering 6, 75–96 (2001)
19. Morris, C.: Foundations of the Theory of Signs. University of Chicago Press, Chicago (1938)
20. Pokraev, S.V.: Model-Driven Semantic Integration of Service-Oriented Applications. Phd thesis, University of Twente (2009)
21. Rukanova, B.: Business Transactions and Standards: Towards a System of Concepts and a Method for Early Problem Identification in Standard Implementation Projects. Phd Thesis, University of Twente (2005)
22. Schade, U.: Towards the Edge and Beyond: The Role of Interoperability. In: 10th International Command and Control Research and Technology Symposium (2005)
23. Searle, J.: Speech Acts: An Essay in the Philosophy of Language. Cambridge University Press, Cambridge (1970)
24. Seo, C., Zeigler, B.: DEVS Namespace for Interoperable DEVS/SOA. In: 2009 Winter Simulation Conference (WSC), pp. 1311–1322 (2009)
25. Singh, M.P.: The Pragmatic Web. IEEE Internet Computing 6, 4–5 (2002)
26. Tamani, E., Evripidou, P.: A Pragmatic Methodology to Web Service Discovery. In: IEEE Int. Conf. on Web Services (ICWS), pp. 1168–1171 (2007)
27. Tolk, A., Diallo, S., King, R., Turnitsa, C.: A Layered Approach to Composition and Interoperation in Complex Systems. In: Complex Systems in Knowledge-based Environments: Theory, Models and Applications, vol. 168, pp. 41–74. Springer, Berlin (2009)
28. van Sinderen, M.J.: Challenges and Solutions in Enterprise Computing. Enterprise Information Systems 2(4), 341–346 (2008)
29. Vernadat, F.: Interoperable Enterprise Systems: Principles, Concepts, and Methods. Annual Reviews in Control 31(1), 137–145 (2007)
30. Weigand, H.: Two Decades of the Language-Action Perspective. Communications of the ACM 49(5), 45 (2006)
31. Zeigler, B.P., Hammonds, P.E.: Modeling & Simulation-Based Data Engineering: Introducing Pragmatics into Ontologies for Net-Centric Information Exchange. Academic Press, London (2007)

Contexts for Concepts:
Information Modeling for Semantic Interoperability

Paul Oude Luttighuis[1], Roel Stap[2], and Dick Quartel[1]

[1] Novay, P.O. Box 589, NL-7500 AN Enschede, The Netherlands
[2] TNO, Colosseum 27, NL-7521 PV Enschede, The Netherlands
{Paul.OudeLuttighuis,Dick.Quartel}@novay.nl, Roel.Stap@tno.nl

Abstract. Conceptual information modeling is a well-established practice, aimed at preparing the implementation of information systems, the specification of electronic message formats, and the design of information processes. Today's ever more connected world however poses new challenges for conceptual information models, as different models should enable mutual connection and reconciliation, even when developed in totally different situations. This paper argues that the 'vertical' bias of today's conceptual information modeling practice diverts models from meeting this new, 'horizontal' need. As an alternative, a conceptual information modeling approach is described that is simultaneously unconventional as well as interoperable with existing approaches. The key to this approach is conceptual context-awareness. It is based on ideas from the Metapattern work [31].

Keywords: enterprise interoperability, semantic interoperability, conceptual modeling, context-awareness, enterprise integration, information modeling.

1 Introduction

Conceptual information modeling practice has grown in the field of information systems design. Conceptual information models — CIMs, for short — mark the border between the worlds of the user (the problem domain) and the information system (the solution domain), or between what is called requirements engineering and systems engineering in information systems design [17]. Therefore, CIMs play a double-faced role in being both descriptive as well as prescriptive.

Figure 1 illustrates this view by positioning conceptual information modeling — CIMing, for short — in a design process chain. The vertical arrows do not imply a waterfall-type of process, but may involve iterative design cycles. This vertical positioning of CIMing is challenged by today's trend towards networked information processes and systems. In fields like organizational science and software engineering, these trends have led to the rise of new paradigms, such as network organizations [7] and service-oriented architecture (SOA) [10]. These paradigms share a shift from 'hierarchical' towards 'networked' thinking. In SOA, services are not part of other services, but linked through contracts. And, participants in a network organization are not casted in a classical hierarchy, but involved in peer-to-peer or market-type relations.

M. van Sinderen and P. Johnson (Eds.): IWEI 2011, LNBIP 76, pp. 146–162, 2011.
© IFIP International Federation for Information Processing 2011

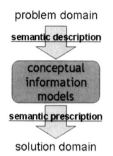

Fig. 1. Design roles of CIMs

Somehow though, these developments have not led to the adoption of new or evolved paradigms in the CIMing realm, although at least one is available [31]. Such situation may suggest that this realm has been ready for large-scale information networking. This paper argues otherwise. Although some of the current CIMing approaches do have the required relational ingredients at hand, these approaches are generally used to establish CIMs with predominant hierarchical structure. With regard to SOA, this may seem surprising, because major service characteristics such as self-containment, loose coupling and reusability are not primarily technical but semantic. No service will be more reusable than the information it deals with.

A naive approach to deal with the trend towards networked systems and processes would be to enlarge the modeling scope. This approach however assumes the fundamental possibility of grasping all possible domains into a single object of design. It also assumes the fundamental possibility of an absolute, objective, context-independent perception of the world. Even for those who think this is theoretically possible, it will still prove to be practically unfeasible.

Therefore, one is left with the challenge to connect and reconcile CIMs from different sources and circumstances. CIMs in practice, though, vary considerably in the extent to which they allow for mutual connection and reconciliation. Semantic reconciliation is already subject of research in the ontology engineering field [1].

This paper describes a context-aware approach to CIMing. The approach is inherently networked and horizontal, in contrast to common approaches that are predominantly hierarchical and vertical.

Rather than working up from a philosophy or formal semantics, the paper introduces the approach by letting it materialize from a set of confrontations between pairs of CIMs. Each of these confrontations represents a typical semantic interoperability problem. Sections 2 and 3 start with basic notions. Section 4 presents the conceptual confrontations. Section 5 explains the approach – Contextual CIMing – in terms of a semi-formal definition and some basic principles. Section 6 compares and combines Contextual CIMing with a range of other approaches, viz. UML, ERM, ORM, OWL, MERODE, relational database modeling, and large-scale e-business standardization. Section 7 discusses the business rationale behind this work. And section 8 ends with conclusions and ideas for further work.

2 Modeling Options

Experienced conceptual information modelers will acknowledge that the same real-world phenomenon may be modeled in alternative ways ([29], Ch. 9; [25], Ch. 7, 8). Should enrollment be modeled as an action (to enroll) or as an entity (enrollment)? Should a property be modeled as an attribute or as a relation? Should a specialized type be modeled as a subtype or as a role type? Should a relation have its own lifecycle? Such dilemmas are typically settled by a modeler's professional experience, sometimes using explicit modeling patterns ([11]; [15]). Often, they are settled with a claim that one alternative is more natural or more concise than the other.

Naturalness. A claim of naturalness suggests that one modeling alternative is somehow closer to the real world than the other. Yet, the assumption that the only connection between the CIM and the real world is via the interpreters of the model, makes any such claim relative to the specific interpreters. The only way to let such a claim extend beyond a single interpreter is by confrontation with models of others. Then, establishing a CIM is not merely a matter of objective problem analysis, it is primarily a matter of communication about the problem with stakeholders and subjective confrontations of their views.

This also sheds a light on the use of natural language as a basis for CIMs. For instance, NIAM/ORM [12] is well-known for the use of natural language for information analysis. Yet, although natural language may be seen as a powerful and flexible means of human communication, there is little reason to assume that the structure of any specific natural language utterance, articulated by a specific writer or speaker in a specific context, would be any more natural than another. In fact, comparable real-world phenomena may be expressed by a wide variety of different natural language sentences, the choice between which may be guided by criteria considered important in the particular context at hand, such as efficiency, bias, perspective, or habit.

Conciseness. As for conciseness claims, two types may be distinguished, referring to the two roles of CIMs depicted in Figure 1. First, *prescriptive conciseness* is the quality of leading to more efficient implementations in targeted software platforms. Clearly, modeling decisions based on such considerations carry the risks of implementation bias. Second, *descriptive conciseness* is the conciseness of the problem description, i.e., of the CIM itself. Modeling decisions may lead to smaller or less complex models. For example, one might say that in a given problem domain, no country will ever have multiple capitals. This may lead to a model with the *capital* type subordinate to the *country* type. This however is a context-specific decision. It excludes contexts in which countries may have multiple capitals.

In general, conciseness counteracts variation and distinction in CIMs, and thus their expressivity. Should CIMs be prepared for semantic interoperability, and hence for variable contexts, they should strive to refrain from prescriptive and descriptive conciseness for specific contexts. Especially for descriptive conciseness, this will not be easy, as users, business people, and project clients will generally accept CIMs only if they address their own specific contexts concisely.

3 Context

This paper presents an approach to CIMing, called *Contextual CIMing*, that uses context-aware CIMs. A CIM is considered context-aware if it models the linguistic context of each of its concepts explicitly, i.e., the concepts on which the concept semantically depends. Context-awareness improves the openness of CIMs, i.e., its receptivity to change and reconciliation, and thus its interoperability. The approach is not meant to substitute other CIMing approaches, but to enhance and prepare them for the confrontation, connection, and reconciliation with other CIMs. Our aim is to preserve a formal relation with other approaches, so that transformations are possible both ways.

As Figure 2 shows, Contextual CIMing involves context-aware CIMs that provide a common context at which connection and reconciliation is feasible. It should be said however, that there is no a priori stringent separation between context-aware and context-unaware models. Rather, context-awareness is a quality that CIMs may have in different grades. The only way to experience a model's level of context-awareness is by confronting it with other models. And even then, the revealed level only holds with respect to the other models encountered.

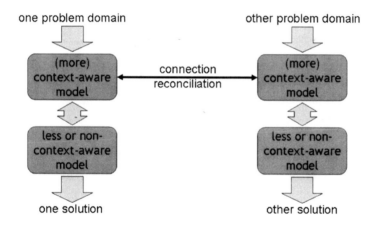

Fig. 2. Reconciliation requires context-aware CIMs

As a consequence, context-awareness should be included in the CIM itself, rather than a separate model extension. In other words, there should not be an a priori distinction between information and meta-information, as such distinction would produce its own bias. This approach is the basis for a model-based semantic interoperability process, depicted in Figure 3. In this process, CIMs of parties participating in the interoperability problem are first made (more) context-aware and then connected or reconciled, leading to a shared CIM. This shared model retains its relation with the particular models of the participants, and is the basis for the realization of an intermediate information process or system ([9]; [22]). If such intermediation is not wished for, the shared model may at least be the basis for communication formats.

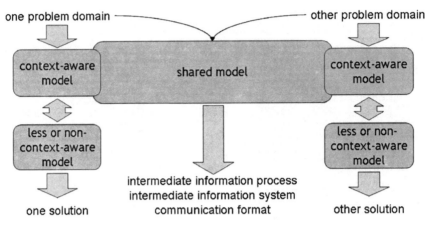

Fig. 3. Semantic interoperability process map

The map of Figure 3 allows for different semantic interoperability routes. On either side, such route may comprise:

- the tabula rasa composition of a context-aware model from the outset; in the map, this corresponds to a route from the problem domain down;
- the transformation of an existing non- or less context-aware CIM to a context-aware CIM, in order to prepare for reconciliation; in the map, this corresponds to a route from the non- or less context-aware model upwards;
- in case a solution is in place, but no CIM to go with it, the reverse engineering of a CIM out of the solution; in the map, this corresponds to a route from the solution upwards.

Concluding, rather than two, as depicted in Figure 1, CIMs should play at least four roles, as illustrated in Figure 4: semantic description of the problem, semantic prescription for the solution, semantic interoperability with other models, and semantic adjustability for future models.

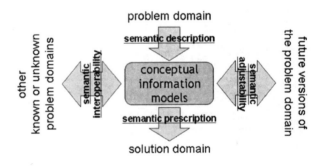

Fig. 4. Four roles of CIMs

4 Conceptual Confrontations

It is worthwhile to revisit how different types of semantic interoperability are often conceived. Pokraev ([22], Section 2.3) gives a classification of seven types of semantic interoperability problems: "*Different systems use ...*":

1. "*the same symbol to represent concepts with disjoint meanings.*"
2. "*the same symbol to represent concepts with overlapping meanings.*"
3. "*the same symbol to represent concepts with more general/specific meanings.*"
4. "*different symbols to represent the same concept.*"
5. "*different symbols to represent concepts with overlapping meanings.*"
6. "*different symbols to represent concepts with more general/specific meanings.*"
7. "*different definitions of the same concept.*"

For the purpose of this paper, interoperability problem types 1 and 4 pose little problems. Confusion about symbols (syntax) can in principle be dealt with easily by changing names or using name spaces. In terms of the well-known semiotic triangle [21], this problem can be dealt with in the symbolic corner. Using the same argument, we do not distinguish between types 2 and 5, nor between types 3 and 6. Furthermore, type 7 can also be dealt with in the symbolic corner, because if parties agree that the same concept is at stake, they can simply use either definition, or both.

This leaves us with two specifically semantic interoperability problems:

a) "*Different systems use concepts with overlapping meanings.*"
b) "*Different systems use concepts with more general/specific meanings.*"

These two distinguish conceptual overlap from conceptual generalization/specialization. The latter though, can be seen as a special case of the former. Just like *woman* and *president* may be seen as having overlapping meanings, *dog* and *Great Dane* can be seen so. Hence, for this paper, a semantic interoperability problem occurs when *two parties use different concepts with related meanings*. Notice that this statement swapped *system* for *party*, in order to avoid the idea that only software agents are at stake, and *overlapping* for *related*, in order to avoid the pre-assumption of a first-order set-theoretic formal semantics, where *overlap* implies conjoint instance sets.

Obviously, the parties use different concepts, as there would be no semantic problem otherwise, except for the symbolic problems mentioned before. Equally obviously, these different concepts should be related, as otherwise there would be no sense in interoperating. The interoperability challenge is precisely to find that relation. The conceptual differences might be large, but the shared context should reveal a relation, even if it would take a range of intermediate concepts to bridge the gap. So, semantic interoperability is about conceptual reconciliation and hence, in model-based approaches, about the confrontation of different CIMs. This requires context-awareness.

The following paragraphs will address four typical types of interoperability problems that arise when concepts from different CIMs are related. Each of these confrontations leads to reconciliation using the same modeling construct. This modeling construct is the basis for Contextual CIMing.

4.1 First Confrontation: Static and Dynamic

The distinction between static structure and dynamic structure is felt as very intuitive by many. Conceptual modeling approaches embed such a distinction in their modeling language, or even use it to scope their language or diagramming technique. For example, business process modeling [23] is dedicated to dynamic phenomena, and data modeling to static phenomena. Some methodologies [25] involve both, but separate them a priori. Apparently, this distinction is felt to be very fundamental. This also causes many to see semantic interoperability as a data issue (see e.g. [16]), whereas semantics in fact applies to processes as much as it does to data.

In Contextual CIMing therefore, classifying a phenomenon as either static or dynamic is a matter of perspective. One CIM might see *to enroll* as a business activity, where the other sees *enrollment* as a business object. Natural language does not settle the dispute. Even though many modern natural languages have a subject-verb-object-type of grammar, they generally offer a grammatical construct for switching between the verb and the noun for the same phenomenon. In English, for instance, this is called *gerund* [4]. So, any reconciliation of two CIMs that have, given their contexts, made different modeling choices in this respect, requires the ability to match *to enroll* with *enrollment*, assuming they have agreed to address the same phenomenon.

So, rather than objects or entities on the one hand, and events or actions on the other, one needs a notion that transcends this distinction. This is possible by first having all dynamic phenomena materialize into concepts themselves and, second, awarding any concept its dynamic aspect. This is convenient, as many would agree that virtually no concept is entirely static. Dynamics are an aspect of concepts, not a separate category.

4.2 Second Confrontation: Properties

It is a well-known transformation in information modeling to release an attribute type from the object type that contains it. Instead of saying that a *person* has an attribute called *birth country* that always carries a value drawn from a *country* type, one might also model *persons* to be related to *countries* by a *birth country* type.

There may be several reasons for choosing the attributive variant in this case. One is that it allows for more efficient implementations (prescriptive efficiency). Another is that a birth country is often felt to be attributive to the person, rather than to the country (naturalness). But, why would any of the two be more natural than the other?

The attributive variant of modeling properties can be seen as a special case of the relational variant, because the relational variant enables the property to have properties itself, whereas the attributive variant doesn't. So, the reconciliation of the two variants is found in the relational variant itself.

4.3 Third Confrontation: Roles

Suppose an organization wants to have their employee information system interoperate with their knowledge management system. In the first, *engineer* occurs in the CIM as a subtype of *employee*. In the second, *engineer* occurs in the CIM as a subtype of *professional*. Now, suppose also that both occurrences of *engineer* would be found to address the same real-world phenomenon, but *employee* and *professional* don't. Still, both the *employee*-perspective as well as the *professional*-perspective on engineers should be retained. See the leftmost model fragment in Figure 5.

In case subtyping would involve inheritance — that is, the proliferation of any properties from the supertype to the subtype ([25], Section 8.2) — the shared *engineer* type might inherit the properties from both sides. However, proliferation is awkward here, because the context-specific properties of *engineer* should remain local. The shared engineer type should be the semantic intersection of the *engineer-as-an-employee* and the *engineer-as-a-professional*. Property proliferation would make *engineer* the semantic composition of both and propagate context-specific properties.

Contextual CIMing therefore refrains from any property proliferation and looks at subtyping as a one-to-one relationship between the subtype and the supertype. This one-to-one relationship can be identified as an existence dependency relationship ([25], Section 4.2). Rather than saying that an instance of a subtype always is also an instance of the supertype, both types are taken to have disjoint instance sets, mutually tied by existence dependence.

This is a well-known transformation used in object-relational mapping [2]. In the example, the context-specific *engineer* types at both ends are made context-aware: they can be seen as replaced by *"engineer-as-an-employee"* and *"engineer-as-a-professional"*. In addition, both are existence dependent on the shared *engineer* type.

In this model, *engineer*, *engineer-as-an-employee* and *engineer-as-a-professionals* all have their own set of instances. They have become role types that tie the shared fragment of the conceptual model to the private fragments of the model. Even if some might object that these types still address the same "real-world" person, they are different linguistic categories and therefore span different linguistic instance sets. These sets are tied by existence dependency, instead of by property proliferation.

This may be depicted by the rightmost model fragment in Figure 5. The *engineer-as-an-employee* type is existence dependent on both the *employee* and the *engineer* type. For brevity, the labels on the existence dependency relations are omitted, as well as the multiplicity of the existence dependency, which is single everywhere in this example. Figure 5 uses a notation that is also used in our case studies (see below), but other notations might be used instead, such as UML association classes or ERD associations. For a comparison with these and other approaches, we refer to section 6.

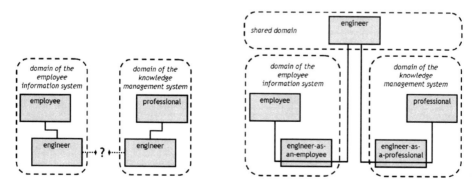

Fig. 5. Before (left) and after (right) reconciliation with role types

Every type is represented by a rectangle. A line that runs through a rectangle represents that the existence of the instance of the represented type depends on the instances of the connected types. This example uses two-way associations, but one-way or more-way associations may be used as well.

In this way, Contextual CIMing enables loose coupling between shared and private information types, which is a much wished-for quality in interoperability. The adoption of property proliferation would imply tighter semantic coupling.

The choice between role types and subtypes is also discussed by [24] (Section 4.10.4). They state that "*the role entity class is usually the neatest solution [...] when there are significant differences [...]*". Given that preparation for interoperability involves uncertainty about new contexts, there will probably always be significant differences, so that the role type is to be preferred. They however see "*a danger [...] of blurring the distinction between subtypes and [...] relationships*". But, in Contextual CIMing, subtypes are contextually restrained role types. They represent a model optimization that can only be justified within restrained contexts.

4.4 Fourth Confrontation: Higher Context

Above, the confrontation between subtypes in different contexts made them become role types, which relate the shared semantic domain to the private semantic domains. Now, this is taken a step further to show that this can be done for any type.

Suppose that two government agencies in a given country operate different information systems. On the one hand, municipalities operate a citizen registration system that involves a type *person*. On the other, the tax department operates a CRM system, involving a type *person* as well. The parties agree that there is ample reason to communicate about these persons, but discover that the populations addressed by each of their registrations are different. These differences are not accidental, they reflect the context (in particular, the business process) for which the registrations were designed originally. See the leftmost model fragment in Figure 6.

To start, the parties notice that their *person* types are semantically different, by the bare fact that they represent different populations. Only persons that are residents of the country are represented in the citizen registration. And, only persons that are taxable persons with respect to some legal taxation system are recognized to be represented in the CRM system.

The next step should be *not* to stress that some persons may be both taxable and residents. Instead, *residents* and *taxable persons* should be considered as different, but related. These types are both found to be specializations of *natural person*. From there, the same approach as with subtypes can be used: resident and taxable person are seen as relations, connecting specific contexts (the citizen registration and the CRM system) with the shared type *natural person*. Looking back at the original CIMs of each system apart, their original *person* types appear to have been context-specific.

Again, in Contextual CIMing, the resulting *resident* and *taxable person* types do not have overlapping instance sets. Rather, specific pairs of *residents* and *taxable persons* may be existence dependent to the same *natural person*. The real-world counterpart of such a *natural person* may henceforth have at least three linguistic manifestations: one for each linguistic category present in the reconciled CIM.

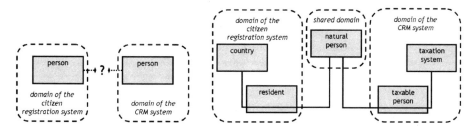

Fig. 6. Before (left) and after (right) reconciliation with context

This may be depicted as in the rightmost model fragment in Figure 6. Notice the resemblance with Figure 5. There is also an important difference though: the particular models at both ends have grown: they have become more context-aware. This is because the predecessors-before-reconciliation of the *resident* and *taxable person* types where "top types", who were assumed to "simply exist". Reconciliation though has revealed that their semantics is context-dependent. The context categories should be introduced into the CIM, so that the model gains context-awareness. This example chose to model a *resident* as a *natural person* with respect to a *country*, and a taxable person as a natural person with respect to a legal system for taxation.

5 Contextual CIMing

Even though there may be many more types of confrontation than those addressed above, out of every confrontation came the same modeling construct as the one best prepared for reconciliation. It is an association-oriented type that has its own set of instances, but at the same time relates instances of other types. It therefore always has object-like as well as relational characteristics. Every type is existence dependent to the other types it relates. Furthermore, the type may represent any real-world phenomenon, be it felt as static or dynamic.

The Contextual CIMing language involves only this one single construct, called *contextual specialization*. Contextual specialization connects any type to the one or more other types that constitute its context. There is no type without context, i.e., any type is a contextual specialization of one or more other types [31].

In order to enable finiteness of models, the modeler may close or conclude the model with a special type, called the *contextual horizon* ([32], Paragraph 31). This type has no context, that is, not one that is represented in the given model. Adjustment or confrontation with other models may make this horizon shift, because confrontation of models leads to the widening of context. So, the contextual horizon shows that any model is blinkered, but is aware of that.

As a semiformal definition of a contextual model in Contextual CIMing, the following may serve. A Contextual CIM is a set C of concepts, a special $\perp \notin C$ (the horizon) and the context function $c:C \rightarrow (C \cup \{\perp\})^+$. The context function labels each contextual connection, so that they may be told apart.

Quality before quantity. A crucial principle of Contextual CIMing is that concepts are firstly defined qualitatively, that is, as a feature-as-such, without their "sets of instances". Such sets constitute the quantitative aspect of a concept, which is seen as a refinement of the qualitative aspect. Hence, contextual specialization does not include cardinality restrictions, for instance. These, though, can be added when the modeler decides to refine a model to the quantitative level.

So, contextual specialization is a qualitative relation between concepts. As such, it can guide conceptual model reconciliation and evolution.

This implies that Conceptual CIMing needs a formal semantics beyond classical set-theoretic semantics, that associates a set of instances with each concept. Instead, the concepts-as-such (and their contextual specialization relations) should be the backbone of the formal semantics.

Still, at the quantitative level, each concept is awarded its set of instances. Yet, each two of these sets (for different concepts) are disjoint. Rather than overlapping, instances may be related, but only if their concepts are involved in a contextual specialization relation at the qualitative level. These quantitative relations may be governed by cardinality restrictions. So, again, quality enables quantity, not reversely.

Intensional, not extensional. Second, Contextual CIMing involves the arrangement of concepts, where each concept simultaneously relates other concepts, and adds its own (qualitative) substance to the model. In a geometrical analogy, concepts would simultaneously be points and lines. This implies that Contextual CIMing requires more than a first-order formal semantics. It requires a more recursive semantics.

Even stronger, Contextual CIMing does not contain a fixed first layer, in which concepts can be defined extensionally, that is, by referring to a set of "real world" objects, thought to be collectively represented by the concept. The model horizon is only a temporary break in a contextual generalization process, that may asymptotically converge, but will never end definitely.

Instead, all concepts are defined intensionally, that is, by identifying the contexts from which they take meaning. These contexts are themselves conceptualized, so that they are easily included in the model.

Synthetic, not analytic. By rigorously pointing out that any concept only takes meaning from its context, any absolute objectivity of concept definitions is abandoned. There is no a priori real-world structure, no "semantic coordinate system", on which a conceptual model can be projected. This implies that conceptual models become in fact synthetic, rather than analytic, because there is no natural structure against which any analysis can be carried out.

So, if one would continue to use the term *information analysis* for the process that leads to conceptual information models, it would not be information itself that is being analyzed. Instead, the objects of analysis would be the perspectives of the stakeholders on their domains. Information itself, or at least the conceptual models used to represent it, would be synthesized, not analyzed.

Structuralism and atomism. These principles can be seen as to arise from a philosophical choice. Contextual CIMing appeals to linguistic structuralism of De Saussure, more than to Russell's and Wittgenstein's logical atomism. Logical atomism teaches that language (hence CIMs) is built from primitive elements (types, facts, terms), that carry meaning in themselves. Contrarily ([14]), "*[...] a crucial feature of Saussurean structuralism is the idea that structure itself creates the units and their relations to one another. [...] Linguistic structure is not an assemblage: it is not built up piecemeal.*" In structuralist thinking, information takes the structure of the language (hence, the CIM) used to express it, rather than "the structure of the real world". The only way to approach "real-world structure" is socially, in communication — by having interpreters reconcile their models. In philosophy, structuralism enjoys more appreciation than in CIMing, probably because the latter is dominated by technology-oriented professionals.

6 Related Approaches

This paper describes an approach to CIMing that is simultaneously unconventional as well as familiar. It is unconventional because it positions quality over quantity, it reconciles modeling options that, for many, are intuitively felt as irreconcilable. It reconciles the static and dynamic natures attributed to real-world phenomena, it reconciles subtyping and relations, as well as objects and relations. In the end, it is the (objectified) relation that comes out as the most important, or even only, modeling construct. This may come as no surprise, as it has been driven by the demand for semantic *inter*operability, rather than the design of a single information system or process.

At the same time though, relational modeling is not new in itself. Virtually any information modeling approach used in practice has at least some notion of relation types. Often though, relations are seen as second- or third-class citizens in information modeling.

Sometimes, the subordination of relations is embedded in the modeling language itself. Sometimes, as the remainder of this paper will show, the language itself essentially enables the predominant use of relations. But then, these languages are often so rich — they supply so many modeling constructs — that, in practice, one hardly sees predominantly relational CIMs. In fact, modeling tools for these languages may even decide to not support the entire relational capabilities of the language and hence disable contextual CIMing. It is important to notice, though, that the reuse of existing modeling languages for the purpose of Contextual CIMing is only possible as far as these languages allow for structuralist semantics.

ERM and UML. In ERM [3], entity types are the first-class citizens, but relation types are of course also included. In order to use ERM for contextual CIMing, the associative relation, or associative entity, should be promoted to the first class. This is unconventional, as general practice only uses this modeling construct in case a many-to-many relation appears. For UML class diagrams, the exact same points can be made. Here, one needs the promotion of UML's *association class* [19] to first class or even to the only construct used. So, ERM and UML can both be used for contextual CIMing, provided that a very restricted part of the language is used. This part can then be given a structuralist semantics.

ORM. Object Role Modeling (ORM) [12] does not include the attributive variant of property modeling, but uses the relational variant only, as Contextual CIMing would do. Yet, ORM has a built-in distinction between entities and relations. Relations are called *predicates* and may relate any number (one or more) of other types. Still, ORM includes an associative relation type, much like ERM and UML. It is called *objectification*, which conveniently expresses the reconciliation between object (entities) and relations. It is also called *nesting*, suggesting that a relation is nested in an object. This is a less convenient term for contextual purposes, as it suggests the subordination of relations to objects. In contextual modeling, there is no such subordination. Any type simultaneously has objective features (that is, it has a set of instances) as well as relational features (that is, it is existence dependent on the types in its context).

OWL. The DL (Description Logic) variant of OWL [27] does not allow quantifying over predicates, because of its first-order restriction. Since relations translate to predicates, this implies that relations cannot have their own set of instances. The first-order restriction would enable only one level of context in CIMs, which is too restrictive for Contextual CIMing. In contrast, OWL Full supports higher order constructs that are needed for Contextual CIMing, but at the (probable) cost of loss of convenient computational properties.

MERODE. MERODE [25] is a CIMing approach from the object-oriented modeling world. The first step of MERODE's enterprise modeling phase involves: (i) an existence dependency graph (EDG) expressing existence dependency relations among so-called object types, and (ii) the identification of business events and the construction of an object-event table (OET).

Additional structure may be added to the EDG through the distinction between object types and attribute types, and through generalization and specialization (subtyping). MERODE provides guidelines for deciding whether to model a given phenomenon as an object type or an attribute type and whether as a subtype relationship or a so-called role type. It appears that, if these guidelines would be used from the perspective of keeping the model as open as possible, all modeling decisions are taken in favor of object types, rather than attribute types, and in favor of role types, rather than subtyping. So, if one would parameterize MERODE with the requirement to keep the enterprise model as context-aware as possible, the EDG would approximate contextual models. It is approximation, not equality, because MERODE would never decide to turn all object types into role types.

In MERODE, the difference between event types and object types is defined with reference to the real world. Contextual CIMing denies that mere inspection of the real world can settle any dispute about whether some phenomenon should be represented by an object type or an event type. From the perspective of Contextual CIMing, MERODE's object types and event types are specializations of phenomenon types. The participation of object types in event types is specified in the OET. This participation relationship can be seen as a specialization of existence dependency.

Most differences between MERODE and Contextual CIMing can be explained by the object-oriented oriented philosophy of MERODE vis-à-vis the association-oriented background of Contextual CIMing. Despite these differences, the approaches may be used in combination.

Relational database modeling. There is a straightforward structure-preserving transformation of conceptual CIMs into relational database schemes [5]. In this transformation, basically, every type t is given its own table, with its own unique primary key and an attribute — that is, table column — for reference to the key of the table of each type in $c(t)$. This transformation is also semantics-preserving, simply because the relational database itself constitutes the context within which all of its data should be interpreted. The database itself can be seen as the implementation of the contextual horizon in the contextual CIM. So, a switch from a structuralist view to an atomist view is not needed. Much like a map does not equal the area it is meant to describe, the database does not equal the real world it is meant to describe.

E-business standardization. One of the ebXML specifications [26] includes a notion of context in order to allow for some degree of variation. It consists of a set of eight context categories — such as business process, product classification, and industry classification — with which context-specific selection and composition of data components, called core components, can be made. This is very different from Contextual CIMing, because it presumes that core components have context-independent meaning, context is separated from the information model, the context categories themselves are assumed to have context-independent meaning.

XBRL has another way of dealing with context. The base specification [35] allows for a set of three separate context categories: reporting period, reporting entity and reporting scenario. For this, the same can be said as for the ebXML notion of context. In a separate specification, the context notion is generalized with so-called *hypercubes* [8]. At first sight, hypercubes resembles the context function in Contextual CIMing, but to comply to the higher-order character of Contextual CIMing one would need nested or stacked hypercubes. In XBRL, these are not provided, though. This makes XBRL contextually flat, much like the first-order approaches discussed above.

In contrast to e-business standardization approaches, Contextual CIMing starts with the recognition of *variation*, and then looks for common semantic ground, hence for candidates for standardization. E-business standardization approaches tend to go the other way and look at variation as an (unwelcomed) exception on variation.

Structuralist (re)use of other approaches. Most uses of existing CIMing approaches are used — explicitly or implicitly — in an atomist way, whereas Contextual CIMing builds on structuralist views. This might imply an unbridgeable gap between the two groups. Yet, there is a bridge. Such a bridge uses the fact that many CIMing languages contain a sublanguage that allows for structuralist use. This then only helps if the language does not inextricably come with a first-order formalization that excludes the language, and any of its sublanguages, from being used in a structuralist sense. This paper found such sublanguages:

- UML class diagrams, in which all types are association classes;
- ERM diagrams, in which all types are associations;
- ORM (assuming that standard first-order formalization is let loose) diagrams, in which all types are objectified relations;
- MERODE, restricted to EDG's in which all types are separate object types.

7 Business Rationale

In this paper, the business value of, and business need for, interoperability within and between organizations (enterprise interoperability) is taken for granted. The semantic aspect of the problem however often does not get the business attention it should. Semantics is regularly seen as a data issue, in contrast with process interoperability, which is seen as a business issue. This is a flaw, because not only data, but also processes and services need semantics in order to be meaningful and valuable. It is no coincidence that the words *meaningful* and *valuable* have closely related meanings. The semantics of enterprise information, rules, processes, and services is about the (operational) core of the organization. Semantics are indispensable for business IT alignment.

The business value of using Contextual CIMing is about whether and how the fruits of enterprise interoperability are harvested at all. Enterprise interoperability can only be *effective* if all involved are able to meaningfully and valuably engage in the information exchange at hand. This requires the information exchange solution to respect all relevant contexts and, at the same time, seize their common ground as well as relate to particularities. Only when enterprise interoperability solutions are effective, they can bring about *efficiency*, by yielding reuse of enterprise data, processes, services, events, and the like.

In a number of case studies, we found support for these claims. In one case study [33], two government agencies experienced difficulties in reusing each others data about employers, their employees and their wages. The ambition to reuse these data stemmed from an efficiency goal: to reduce the administrative burden for the companies involved. However, at first, neglect of the semantic differences concerning, for instance, the term *employer*, threatened the effectiveness of reuse, since the data was not sufficiently meaningful to all involved. Standardization may seem to be an efficiency measure, but without appreciating necessary variation, efficiency quickly evaporates by lacking effectiveness. In the case study, we reconciled the two party's models about employers, following a reconciliation process as sketched in Section 3. According to the domain experts involved, this reconciliation process led to a model in which both parties simultaneously recognized their own context, as well as their shared universe of discourse.

In a second case study, we again set out to reconcile two information models under the requirement to leave both unchanged, but nevertheless find maximum options for mutual reuse. A semantic bridge (or hinge) between the two was found, thanks to the loose coupling among terms in Contextual CIMing: it keeps semantics local to terms, rather than having properties proliferate through the model.

In both cases, it was welcomed that Contextual CIMing brought in a new and valuable perspective in information modeling, while retaining the connection with many (not all) popular modeling languages in use.

Yet, even though these case studies were successful, there have been too few of them, so far, to substantiate our claim on what may be the most important business value of Contextual CIMing, in relation to other approaches: the added value of Contextual CIMing increases if the semantic scale grows. The more domains, contexts, or perspectives at hand, the less one can neglect variability, and the less one can continue without context-awareness. The same points can be made with regard to semantic changes through time (that is consecutive contexts, rather than simultaneous ones). Only by increasing the scale of our case studies (in time or space), we will be able to prove that Contextual CIMing also yields:

- *agility,* as it postpones premature semantic structures that may hinder change;
- *durability,* as it enables the discovery of shared contexts, which may be called semantic infrastructure, and are more stable than specific contexts;
- *scalability,* as it takes a rigorously networked approach instead of a hierarchical approach.

Again, there is a parallel with SOA in this respect. It is with the ambition to enlarge the scale of our attempts, that we recently started a consortium project with market players and user organizations (www.essence-project.nl).

8 Conclusions

This paper introduced an approach to conceptual information modeling that makes it applicable to large-scale semantic interoperability across domains. The approach is at the same time unconventional as well as related to existing conceptual modeling practice. The unconventional aspect is probably rooted in its structuralist nature, where in information technology surroundings, atomist views generally prevail.

Contextual CIMing postpones distinctions, and hence CIM structure, that other approaches fix a priori in their metamodel. Such distinctions include: static versus dynamic phenomena, attributes versus relations, subtypes versus role types, objects versus relations, information versus meta-information, information versus context. Each of these distinctions hampers large-scale interoperability, because different contexts will apply them in different ways. The real world, nor natural language, can be the ultimate judge when such differences occur. Still, the point is not to deny such distinctions, but to apply them at the appropriate moment.

In parallel, new research lines are investigated. One of them concerns the use of Contextual CIMing for reconciling metamodels of existing CIMing approaches, from the relational, the object-oriented, the business-process, and the service modeling field. Another is the relation between Contextual CIMing and (role- and rule-based) authentication approaches. Yet another concerns the formal specification of a structuralist semantics for the approach.

References

1. Abels, S., Haak, L., Hahn, A.: Identification of common methods used for ontology integration tasks. In: Proceedings of the First International Workshop on Interoperability of Heterogeneous Information Systems (Bremen, Germany), pp. 75–78 (2005)
2. Bashir, K.: Inheritance in O/R Mapping (2010),
   http://www.alachisoft.com/articles/inheritance_mapping.html
3. Chen, P.P.S.: The Entity-Relationship Model: Toward a Unified View of Data. ACM TODS 1(1), 9–36 (1976)
4. Chen, P.P.S.: English sentence structure and entity-relationship diagrams. Information Sciences 29(2-3), 127–149 (1983)
5. Codd, E.F.: A relational model for large shared data banks. CACM 13(6), 377–387 (1970)
6. Cover, T.M., Thomas, J.A.: Elements of information theory. John Wiley & Sons, Hoboken (2006)
7. Daft, R.L.: Organization Theory and Design, 10th edn., Cengage Learning, Florence (2009)
8. Debreceny, R., Felden, C., Ochocki, B., Piechocki, M., Piechocki, M.: XBRL for Interactive Data: Engineering the Information Value Chain. Springer, Heidelberg (2009)
9. Del Grosso, E., Missikoff, M., Smith, F., Taglino, F.: Semantic Services for Business Documents Reconciliation. In: Proceedings of Workshop ISDSI 2009 (2009)
10. Erl, T.: SOA: principles of service design. Prentice Hall, Upper Saddle River (2007)
11. Fowler, M.: Analysis patterns: reusable object models. Addison-Wesley, Reading (1997)
12. Halpin, T.: Object-Role Modeling (ORM/NIAM). In: Berners, P., Mertins, K., Schmidt, G. (eds.) Handbook on Architectures of Information Systems, pp. 88–103. Springer, Heidelberg (2006)

13. Halpin, T., Morgan, A.J., Morgan, T.: Information Modelling and Relational databases, 2nd edn. Morgan Kaufmann, Burlington (2008)
14. Harris, R., Taylor, T.J., Love, N., Versteegh, C.H.M.: Landmarks in linguistic thought, 2nd edn. Routledge, New York (1997)
15. Hay, D.C.: Data Model Patterns: Conventions of Thought. Dorset House, New York (1996)
16. IDA: European Interoperability Framework for Pan-European eGovernment Services. Version 1.0. European Commission, Brussels (2004)
17. Insfrán, E., Pastor, O., Wieringa, R.J.: Requirements Engineering-Based Conceptual Modelling. Requirements Engineering 7(2), 61–72 (2002)
18. Kent, W.: A Simple Guide to Five Normal Forms in Relational Database Theory. CACM 26(2), 120–125 (1983)
19. Object Management Group: OMG Unified Modeling Language (OMG UML), Superstructure. (version 2.3) (2003a),
    `http://www.omg.org/spec/UML/2.3/Superstructure`
20. Object Management Group: MDA Guide (version 1.0.1) (2003b),
    `http://www.omg.org/cgi-bin/doc?omg/03-06-01.pdf`
21. Ogden, C.K., Richards, I.A.: The Meaning of Meaning: A Study of the Influence of Language Upon Thought and of the Science of Symbolism. Routledge & Kegan Paul, London (1923)
22. Pokraev, S.V.: Model-Driven Semantic Integration of Service-Oriented Applications. Ph.D. Thesis. Novay PhD Research Series No. 25. Novay, Enschede (2009)
23. Sharp, A., McDermott, P.: Workflow modeling: tools for process improvement and applications development. Artech House, Norwood (2009)
24. Simsion, G.C., Witt, G.C.: Data Modeling Essentials, 3rd edn. Morgan Kaufmann, San Francisco (2005)
25. Snoeck, M., Dedene, G., Verhelst, M., Depuydt, A.M.: Object-Oriented Enterprise Modelling with MERODE. Leuven University Press, Leuven (1999)
26. UN/CEFACT: Core Components Technical Specification. Part 8 of the ebXML Framework (version 2.01) (2003),
    `http://www.unece.org/cefact/ebxml/CCTS_V2-01_Final.pdf`
27. W3C: OWL Web Ontology Language Guide. W3C Recommendation (February 10, 2004),
    `http://www.w3.org/TR/owl-guide/`
28. Wand, Y., Storey, V.C., Weber, R.: An Ontological Analysis of the Relationship Construct in Conceptual Modeling. ACM TODS 24(4), 494–528 (1999)
29. Wieringa, R.J.: Design methods for reactive systems. Morgan Kaufmann, San Francisco (2003)
30. Wikipedia: Associative Entities (2010),
    `http://en.wikipedia.org/wiki/Associative_Entities`
31. Wisse, P.E.: Metapattern: Context and Time in Information Models. Addison-Wesley Professional, Boston (2000)
32. Wisse, P.E.: Ontology for interdependency: steps to an ecology of information management. PrimaVera Working Paper 2007-05. University of Amsterdam, Amsterdam (2007)
33. Wisse, P.E., Oude Luttighuis, P.H.W.M., Ter Doest, H., Abrahamse, M.: Praktijkmodellering van het begrip werkgever. Forum Standaardisatie (2009) (in Dutch)
34. Wisse, P.E.: Op weg naar een stelselmatige aanpak van authenticatie en autorisatie: een gedachtenexperiment. Personal communication (2010) (in Dutch)
35. XBRL International: Extensible Business Reporting Language (XBRL) 2.1. Recommendation 2003-12-31 + Corrected Errata–2008-07-02 (2003),
    `http://www.xbrl.org/Specification/XBRLRECOMMENDATION-`
    `2003-12-31+Corrected-Errata-2008-07-02.rtf`

Anatomy of the
Unified Enterprise Modelling Ontology

Andreas L. Opdahl

Department of Information Science and Media Studies,
University of Bergen, NO-5020 Bergen, Norway
Andreas.Opdahl@uib.no

Abstract. The Unified Enterprise Modelling Language (UEML) aims to become a hub for integrated use of enterprise and information systems (IS) models expressed using different languages. A central part of this hub is an extendible ontology into which modelling languages and their constructs can be mapped, so that precise semantic relations between the languages and constructs can be established by comparing their ontology mappings. The paper presents and discusses ongoing work on reformulating the UEML ontology as an OWL2 DL ontology, the Unified Enterprise Modelling Ontology (UEMO).

Keywords: Ontology, ontological analysis and evaluation, Unified Enterprise Modelling Language (UEML), Unified Enterprise Modelling Ontology (UEMO), OWL2, description logic.

1 Introduction

The Unified Enterprise Modelling Language (UEML) supports *precise semantic definition* of a wide variety of enterprise and IS-modelling languages. It aims to use the definitions to also facilitate *integrated use of models* expressed in those languages [1]. The aim is an important one because information and software technologies are becoming increasingly driven by models, making interoperability between modelling languages and models a helpful step on the way to achieving interoperability between model-driven information and software systems.

To facilitate integrated use of models expressed in a wide variety of languages, the language definitions must be made semantically interoperable. UEML approaches this problem through a structured approach to describing enterprise and IS-modelling constructs in terms of an evolving ontology [2, 3]. So far, 130 constructs from a selection of 10 languages have been mapped into the ontology, although with varying degrees of precision. Whereas the idea of using an ontology to describe and integrate modelling languages is not new in itself, UEML describes and integrates the semantics of modelling constructs in a novel way that combines (1) a systematic, fine-grained approach to describing the semantics of modelling constructs with (2) a systematic approach to structuring and evolving the underlying ontology. UEML thus goes further than other ontology-based approaches to enterprise model interoperability (e.g., [4, 5]) because it is complemented by an extensive framework for systematically describing modelling

M. van Sinderen and P. Johnson (Eds.): IWEI 2011, LNBIP 76, pp. 163–176, 2011.
© IFIP International Federation for Information Processing 2011

constructs and because it has been explicitly designed to evolve and grow over time without becoming overly complex.

It is the common ontology at the heart of UEML that is the focus of this paper. On the meta-ontology (or structure) level it distinguishes itself from comparable approaches by simultaneously (1) promoting states and transformations to first-order concepts alongside things/classes and their properties, (2) providing better support for complex properties, (3) treating relations between things and classes as a type of mutual (or relational, shared) property of things/classes alongside intrinsic properties and (4) considering laws as another type of property of things/classes. On the ontology (or content) level it is distinct (1) by being the first middle-level ontology dedicated to enterprise and IS modelling in general, (2) by being explicitly grounded in Mario Bunge's philosophical ontology [6, 7] and (3) by offering particularly precise and elaborate dynamic and systemic concepts. Because of its grounding in Bunge's ontology and its adaptation to the information systems field (e.g., [8]), the common UEML ontology is ontological in both the philosophical and computer-science senses, although its mathematically formal underpinnings have been less developed so far. A set of OCL-constraints were presented in [9] and later extended and re-written in Prolog [10, 1]. But, beyond that, the UEML ontology has not been formalised so far.

This paper therefore presents a first formalisation of UEML's central ontology concepts by reformulating its classes, properties, states and transformations using OWL2 DL [11]. The purpose of the resulting *Unified Enterprise Modelling Ontology (UEMO)* is threefold. Firstly, we want to contribute towards a more precise UEML, to which the formalisation is a direct contribution. Secondly, we want to make UEML supported by formal reasoning approaches and tools. Although the old UEML ontology was represented in OWL, it did not leverage the full potential of OWL DL as a specification and reasoning language and did not explore the stronger expressiveness of OWL2. Thirdly and finally, we want to be able to show that the core of UEML has nice decision problems, i.e., that it is sound, complete and tractable with respect to many of its anticipated uses.

The rest of the paper is organised as follows. Section 2 presents the Unified Enterprise Modelling Language (UEML). Section 3 presents the backbone of the Unified Enterprise Modelling Ontology (UEMO). Section 4 outlines how UEMO can be used to facilitate interoperability between modelling constructs. Section 5 discusses the results. Finally, Section 6 concludes the paper and suggests paths for further work. Of course, a conference-length paper such as this can only explain a selection of UEMO's most important concepts. Several of our definitions have therefore been simplified because they rely on concepts that are not explained in the paper. Development versions of UEMO are available on http://www.uemlwiki.org/.

2   Theory

Construct description in UEML: UEML describes a modelling language mainly in terms of its modelling constructs. For each construct, both its syntax and semantics are described. The intended semantics of a modelling construct is described in a structured way according to the following six parts (see, e.g., [12]):

1. *Instantiation level:* A modelling construct may be used to represent either individual things (the *instance* level), classes of things (the *type* level) or *both* levels.
2. *Modality:* A modelling construct (or part thereof) may represent either a *fact* about or someone's *belief* about, *knowledge* of, *obligation* within, *intention* for a domain, and so on (in addition the model itself can have yet another modality, e.g., it may represent a possible or wanted future situation).
3. *Classes of things:* Regardless of instantiation level and modality, a modelling construct will represent one or more things (if it is instance level) or classes of things (if it is type level).
4. *Properties of things:* Most modelling constructs will also represent one or more properties that this or these thing(s)/class(es) *possess*. The properties may be *complex*, having other properties as *sub-properties*. In UEML, some complex properties even constrain their sub-properties and their values. Such properties are called *laws* [6, pp. 77-80].
5. *States of things:* Some behavioural modelling constructs represent particular *states* in their things or classes. States are *defined* in terms of a thing's properties by a *state constraint* that *restricts* these properties' values.
6. *Transformations of things:* Behavioural modelling constructs may even represent *transformations* of things/classes from a *pre-* to a *post-state*. Transformations are described by the properties that *define* the pre- and post-states and by a *transformation function* that *prescribes* changes to these properties' values.

Instead of mapping modelling constructs one-to-one with concepts in an ontology, UEML thereby describes each modelling construct as a *scene* of interrelated *roles* that are played by ontology concepts, so that the roles are either *classes/things* (item 3 above), their *properties* (item 4), their *states* (item 5) or their *transformations* (item 6). The roles are interrelated so that classes/things *possess* properties (that characterise the classes); properties *define* states; transformations have *pre-* and *post-states*; state constraints *restrict* states; transformation functions *prescribe* transformations; and by taxonomical/hierarchical relations we will explain later. The scene can be described in further detail by cardinality constraints on the relations between roles; by equivalence and/or disjointness axioms on roles; and by other types of constraints [3].

For example, a scene that describes the Class construct in UML would have a *"class"* role that describes the class of things that UML-Class is intended to represent. Because UML-Class is a very general modelling construct, the "class" role is played by Anything, which we will see is the most general of all classes in UEMO. The scene would also comprise a "name" role that describes the name property that has been assigned to the class and zero or more "attribute" and "operation" properties to describe its attributes and operations, each of them played by a precisely defined ontology property. Further roles would be used to describe associations, including aggregation/composition, and generalization relationships between UML-Classes.

Description logic: Description logic (DL) is a family of knowledge representation languages that are well suited for automated reasoning [13]. The ***SHOIN*** and ***SROIQ*** [11] variants of description logic correspond roughly to the ontology representation languages OWL and OWL2, respectively, so that OWL classes correspond to DL concepts and OWL object properties correspond to DL roles. There are even DL features that correspond to OWL datatype properties, but we will not use them here.

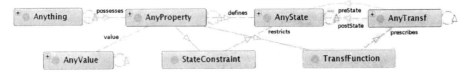

Fig. 1. High-level OWL2 classes that show the structure of UEMO

Description logics can be considered a fragment of 1. order predicate calculus, but with nicer decision problems. [13] and [14] offer introductions to basic DL notation and reasoning.

3   The Unified Enterprise Modelling Ontology (UEMO)

Overall structure: UEMO's concepts are partitioned into *classes of things*, *properties*, *states* and *transformations*, as in the UEML ontology. In addition, UEMO introduces *values* of properties. These five types of ontology concepts are disjoint but interrelated, so that classes of things *possess* properties; properties have *values* and *define* states; and transformations have *pre-* and *post-states*. Furthermore, *state constraints* and *transformation functions* are sub-types of properties that *restrict* states and *prescribe* transformations, respectively The resulting ontology structure is shown in Figure 1. Hence, UEMO has the same structure as the scenes that describe individual modelling constructs, so that each scene can be considered an excerpt from UEMO, possibly with added role names, tighter cardinalities and other constraints.

UEMO defines each concept as an OWL2 *class* (or description logic *concept*) and its interrelations as OWL2 *object properties* (or description logic *roles*) as follows:

Anything ≡ ∃ possesses.AnyProperty ⊓ ∀ possesses.AnyProperty
AnyProperty ≡ ∃ belongsTo.Anything ⊓ ∀ belongsTo.Anything
StateConstraint ≡ AnyProperty ⊓ ∀ restricts.AnyState ⊓ (=1 restricts)
TransformationFunction ≡ AnyProperty ⊓ ∀ prescribes.AnyTransformation ⊓ (=1 prescribes)
AnyState ≡ ∀ restrictedBy.StateConstraint ⊓ (=1 restrictedBy) ⊓
          ∃ definedBy.ConstrainedProperty
AnyTransformation ≡ ∀ prescribedBy.TransformationFunction ⊓ (=1 prescribedBy) ⊓
          ∀ preState.MutableState ⊓ (=1 preState) ⊓ ∀ postState.AnyState ⊓ (=1 postState)
AnyValue ≡ ∀ valueOf.ValuedProperty
Anything ⊓ AnyProperty ⊓ AnyState ⊓ AnyTransformation ⊓ AnyValue ⊑ ⊥

Restrictions like ⋯∀ restricts.AnyState ⊓ (=1 restricts)⋯ are used instead of the conciser ⋯(=1 restricts).AnyState⋯ to limit the ontology to ***SHIN*** expressiveness (e.g., [11], which, however, discuss slightly more powerful DL variants), which is supported by both "OWL1" and OWL2, thus giving access to a broader selection of reasoners and other tools.

Additional *taxonomy relations* organise the ontology concepts into five taxonomies. (1) Classes may *specialise* other classes. The root of the class taxonomy is Anything. (2) Properties may *precede* other properties, so all things that possess a property, such as "being-human", necessarily possess its precedents too, such as "being-alive".

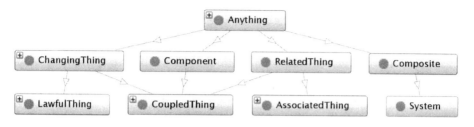

Fig. 2. Top-level classes in UEMO

The root of this taxonomy is AnyProperty. (3) States may *refine* other states (*OR*-decomposition), with AnyState at the root of the taxonomy. (4) Transformations may *elaborate* other transformations (*OR*-decomposition), with AnyTransformation as taxonomical root. (5) Values may *extend* other values. The root of this taxonomy is Any-Value. The five root concepts were shown Figure 1, which also depicted StateConstraint and TransformationFunction as important sub-types of AnyProperty. UEMO comprises several *hierarchical relations* in addition to the taxonomical ones: properties may be *sub-properties* of complex ones; states may be *regions of* composite states (*AND*-decomposition); transformations may be *components of* parallel transformations and *steps in* sequential ones (two ways to *AND*-decompose transformations). We now present each taxonomy in some detail.

Class taxonomy: According to [8], "[A] class is a set of things that possess a common property", where things and their properties are the most basic concepts in Bunge's ontology [6]. Anything is the root of the class taxonomy, so the Anything class in our OWL2 DL reformulation subsumes all the other class concepts in UEMO. Immediately below Anything are ChangingThing and RelatedThing along with Composite and Component (Figure 2). ChangingThing is characterised by possessing at least one *mutable property*, whereas RelatedThing must possess some *relation*, which is a shared (or mutual) property. Composite and Component are both characterised by possessing a *part-whole relation*, in which Composite plays the role of 'whole' and Component the role of 'part'. Composites and Components are not RelatedThings because part-whole relations are ontologically different from regular relations (shared/mutual properties) between other things.

ChangingThing ≡ Anything ⊓ ∃ possesses.SomewhatMutableProperty
RelatedThing ≡ Anything ⊓ ∃ possesses.Relation
Composite ≡ Anything ⊓ ∃ possessesAsWhole.PartWholeRelation
Component ≡ Anything ⊓ ∃ possessesAsPart.PartWholeRelation

The definitions of Composite and Component illustrate how we introduce *sub-roles* (through owl:subPropertyOf axioms on object properties), such as *possessesAsWhole* ⊑ possesses and *possessesAsPart* ⊑ possesses, of the *possesses* role to indicate more specific roles that UEML's properties may play in relation to their things/classes. For example, without sub-roles, it would have been difficult to formally distinguish Composite from Component. It would also have been impossible to limit the current UEMO to **SHIN** expressiveness. We will encounter more sub-roles later.

According to Bunge [6], a CoupledThing is one that interacts with one or more other things so that their histories of states and events depend on one another. Together, these things form a System. Hence, a CoupledThing is both a RelatedThing, a ChangingThing and a Component in a System. In addition, there are LawfulThings (similar to *natural kinds* [6, p. 143]) that possess law properties, which we will say more about later. We have to omit many other UEMO classes, such as the different types of active and executing things and resources, which have been included in the ontology either because they are needed directly to describe modelling constructs as part of the UEML work or indirectly to make other UEMO concepts clearer.

In addition to the named classes, we can use description logic expressions to introduce *anonymous classes* (and *anonymous properties, states* and *transformations*). Such a class can be used to define modelling constructs just like named classes, but does not contribute to making the ontology unwieldy. If it turns out to be useful over time, it can be named and included in the ontology later. For example:

$$UnrelatedThing \equiv Anything \sqcap \forall possesses.(IntrinsicProperty \sqcup PartWholeRelation)$$
$$\equiv AnyThing \sqcap \neg \exists possesses.Relation \equiv \neg RelatedThing$$
$$UnchangingThing \equiv Anything \sqcap \forall possesses.CompletelyImmutableProperty$$
$$\equiv \neg ChangingThing$$

Property taxonomy: In Bunge's ontology [6], properties belong to things and characterise classes. According to [8], "[A] property is modelled via an *attribute* function that maps the thing into some value." Because AnyProperty is the root of the property taxonomy, the AnyProperty class in our OWL2 DL reformulation subsumes all the other property concepts in UEMO, where subsumption between property concepts has been defined to correspond to Bunge's property precedence, i.e., that all things that possess a property necessarily possess its precedents too [6]. Immediately below AnyProperty in the taxonomy is IntrinsicProperty, Relation and PartWholeRelation (Figure 3). IntrinsicProperty belongs to a single thing only. Relation belongs to more than one thing, but is not a part-whole relation. PartWholeRelation belongs to a whole thing (the Composite) and its part thing (the Component).

$$IntrinsicProperty \equiv AnyProperty \sqcap \forall belongsTo.Anything \sqcap (=1 \ belongsTo)$$
$$Relation \equiv AnyProperty \sqcap \forall belongsTo.RelatedThing \sqcap (\geq 2 \ belongsTo) \sqcap$$
$$\neg \exists belongsToWhole.Composite \sqcap \neg \exists belongsToPart.Component$$
$$PartWholeRelation \equiv AnyProperty \sqcap$$
$$\forall belongsToWhole.Composite \sqcap (=1 \ belongsToWhole) \sqcap$$
$$\forall belongsToPart.Component \sqcap (=1 \ belongsToPart) \sqcap$$
$$\forall belongsToPartOrWhole.Component \sqcap (=2 \ belongsToPartOrWhole)$$
$$belongsTo \equiv possesses^{-1}$$

Here, the belongsToPartOrWhole role is introduced so we can assert that the Component and the Composite are different things. Because OWL2 DL prohibits role disjunction, this role has been derived using SWRL [15]:

$$belongsToPart(?c1, ?c2) \rightarrow belongsToPartOrWhole(?c1, ?c2)$$
$$belongsToWhole(?c1, ?c2) \rightarrow belongsToPartOrWhole(?c1, ?c2)$$

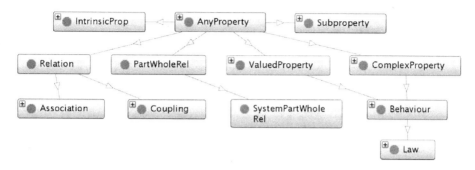

Fig. 3. Top-level properties in UEMO

UEMO thereby circumvents OWL2 DL limitations by using SWRL and its extension SQWRL [16], which allows sets and bags to be used in rules.

These three successors of AnyProperty, i.e., IntrinsicProperty, Relation and Part-WholeRelation, are disjoint, or mutually exclusive, in OWL2 terms, so that no property can be preceded by more than one of them. But they are not incompatible, meaning that the same thing can possess several of them at the same time.

An Association relates (non-coupled) AssociatedThings, whereas a Coupling relates CoupledThings. A SystemPartWholeRelation relates a CoupledThing to its System just like a Component is related to a Composite. A ValuedProperty has a specific *value*, whereas a ComplexProperty has one or more other properties as *sub-properties*. A Behaviour is a Valued- and ComplexProperty that describes either a state (when it is a StateConstraint) or a transformation (when it is a Transformation-Function). A Behaviour that is naturally or socially *enforced* is a Law. Hence, StateLaws are enforced StateConstraints and TransformationLaws are enforced TransformationFunctions, defined along these lines:

Law ≡ Behaviour ⊓ ∀ constrainedSubproperty.LawfullyConstrainedProperty
StateLaw ≡ Law ⊓ StateConstraint ⊓ ∀ constrainedSubproperty.LawfullyConstrainedProperty
TransformationLaw ≡ Law ⊓ TransformationFunction ⊓
        ∃ manipulatedSubproperty.LawfullyManipulatedProperty

Of course, there are many property concepts we cannot discuss here, including more specific types of behaviours and laws. For example, UEMO has socially assigned properties, such as Name, which is an association between a Namegiver and a NamedThing. Information and SocialLaws are other examples of assigned properties. UEMO also has concepts for Mutable- and ImmutableProperties, which come in both strong (e.g., CompletelyImmutableProperty) and weak (e.g., SomewhatMutable-Property) forms, because a property can change in many different ways, i.e., it can be dropped by its thing, it can have its value changed, it can drop a sub-property if it is complex or be dropped by its superior if it is a sub-property.

State taxonomy: According to [8], a state is "[T]he vector of values for all attribute functions of a thing" at a particular time, where an attribute function describes a property by mapping the thing to some value. AnyState is the root of the state taxonomy. Hence, the AnyState class in our OWL2 DL reformulation subsumes all the other state concepts in UEMO, where subsumption between state concepts has been defined to correspond to *OR*-decomposition of states.

A state in UEMO is either mutable or immutable. A MutableState is defined in terms of at least one SomewhatMutableProperty, whereas an ImmutableState is defined only by CompletelyImmutableProperties.

MutableState $\equiv$ AnyState $\sqcap$ $\exists$ definedBy.SomewhatMutableProperty
ImmutableState $\equiv$ AnyState $\sqcap$ $\forall$ definedBy.CompletelyImmutableProperty

UEMO states are also either stable or unstable. A StableState is *restrictedBy* a State-Law, whereas an UnstableState is *restrictedBy* a StateViolation property. Like State-Law, StateViolation is a Behaviour (specifically, a StateConstraint). But, whereas a StateLaw is naturally or socially *enforced*, a StateViolation is only socially *sanctioned*. UnstableState refines MutableState, because the thing must eventually return to a stable state.

StableState $\equiv$ AnyState $\sqcap$ $\forall$ restrictedBy.StateLaw $\sqcap$ (=1 restrictedBy)
UnstableState $\equiv$ MutableState $\sqcap$ $\forall$ restrictedBy.StateViolation $\sqcap$ (=1 restrictedBy)

Transformation taxonomy: According to [8], a transformation of a thing "is a mapping from a domain comprising states to a co-domain comprising states." AnyTransformation is the root of the transformation taxonomy. The AnyTransformation class in our OWL2 DL reformulation therefore subsumes all the other transformation concepts in UEMO, where subsumption between transformation concepts has been defined to correspond to *OR*-decomposition of transformations.

A SelfTransformation in a thing only manipulates the thing's own properties, whereas an ExternalTransformation manipulates at least one Relation property that the thing shares (possesses mutually with) another thing. A Destabilising transformation takes the thing from a Stable- to an UnstableState and a Stabilising takes it back. A Destabilising is always an ExternalTransformation, because nothing destabilises itself, i.e., there are no Destabilising SelfTransformations.

SelfTransformation $\equiv$ AnyTransformation $\sqcap$ $\neg$ $\exists$ manipulatedProperty.Relation
ExternalTransformation $\equiv$ AnyTransformation $\sqcap$ $\exists$ manipulatedProperty.Relation
Destabilising $\equiv$ ExternalTransformation $\sqcap$ $\forall$ prescribedBy.Destabilising $\sqcap$
      (=1 prescribedBy) $\sqcap$ $\forall$ preState.StableState $\sqcap$ (=1 preState) $\sqcap$
      $\forall$ postState.UnstableState $\sqcap$ (=1 postState)
Stabilising $\equiv$ AnyTransformation $\sqcap$ $\forall$ prescribedBy.StabilisingLaw $\sqcap$ (=1 prescribedBy) $\sqcap$
      $\forall$ preState.UnstableState $\sqcap$ (=1 preState) $\sqcap$ $\forall$ postState.StableState $\sqcap$ (=1 postState)

A SequentialTransformation is composed of two or more TransformationSteps, whereas a ParallelTransformation is composed of two or more Transformation-Components. UEMO defines both non-sequential (single-step Firings) and sequential (multi-step Executions) transformations for describing behavioural constructs.

SequentialTransformation $\equiv$ AnyTransformation $\sqcap$
      $\forall$ sequenceOf.TransformationStep $\sqcap$ ($\geq$2 sequenceOf)
TransformationStep $\equiv$ AnyTransformation $\sqcap$ $\exists$ stepIn.SequentialTransformation
ParallelTransformation $\equiv$ AnyTransformation $\sqcap$
      $\forall$ composedOf.TransformationComponent $\sqcap$ (≥ 2 composedOf)
TransformationComponent $\equiv$ AnyTransformation $\sqcap$ $\exists$ componentOf.ParallelTransformation

Value taxonomy: Bunge's ontology [6] does not account for values directly, but treats properties as dichotomous (either possessed by the thing or not). Instead of valued properties such as a "has-age" property that maps to values like "25" and "50", Bunge therefore uses properties such as "has-age-of-25" and "has-age-of-50". UEMO offers valued properties because they are simpler to use. No generality is lost, because valued properties ("property-name" = "value") can trivially be transformed into dichotomous ones ("property-name-of-value").

AnyValue is the root of the value taxonomy, so that the AnyValue class in our OWL2 DL reformulation subsumes all the other value concepts in UEMO, where subsumption between value concepts has been defined to cover both regular subsetting and something we call augmentation (adding new components to tuples). A Set has other values as elements, whereas a Tuple has other values as components. We name inverse roles of values by adding the suffix -Of, e.g., $valueOf \equiv value^{-1}$, $componentOf \equiv component^{-1}$ and $elementOf \equiv element^{-1}$ etc.

AnyValue $\equiv \forall$ valueOf.ValuedProperty
Set $\equiv$ AnyValue $\sqcap \forall$ element.AnyValue $\sqcap \neg \exists$ component.AnyValue
Tuple $\equiv$ AnyValue $\sqcap \forall$ component.AnyValue $\sqcap (\geq 1$ component$) \sqcap \neg \exists$ element.AnyValue

The basic idea is that certain sub-types of values are Constraints that describe States, whereas other sub-types of values are Functions that describe Transformations. However, we have so far only covered transformations that are simple mappings from pre- to post-states, not transformations where inputs arrive and outputs depart at different times, with some outputs possibly being produced before all inputs have been consumed. A fuller definition of transformation functions along the lines discussed, e.g., in [17] has to be left for further work.

4 Using UEMO

The preceding section has formulated UEMO as an OWL2 DL ontology with ***SHIN*** expressiveness (e.g., [11]). While using UEMO to facilitate interoperability between models expressed using different languages remains work in progress, this section suggests how UEMO can facilitate describing and comparing modelling constructs semantically.

Describing modelling ***constructs:*** To describe modelling constructs in terms of UEMO, the ontology must be extended with an additional OWL class (DL concept) for ModellingConstructs and a new OWL object property (DL role) that map ModellingConstructs to the OntologyConcepts they *represent*:

OntologyConcept $\equiv \neg \exists$ represents $\sqcap$
        (Anything $\sqcup$ AnyProperty $\sqcup$ AnyState $\sqcup$ AnyTransformation $\sqcup$ AnyValue)
ModellingConstruct $\equiv \exists$ represents.OntologyConcept $\sqcap \forall$ represents.OntologyConcept

ModellingConstruct formalises the earlier concept of *scene*, so that each role in the scene is an OntologyConcept that the ModellingConstruct *represents*. Sub-roles of the represents role are used to distinguish between the different roles of the scene. For example, the *"class"* role in the scene that describes the Class construct in UML is accounted for by the DL-role *representsClass* ⊑ represents. In consequence, UML-Class can be described as follows (leaving out association, aggregation/composition, generalisation and a few other details for now):

UMLClass ≡ ModellingConstruct ⊓
      ∃ representsClass.Anything ⊓ (=1 representsClass) ⊓
      ∃ representsName.Name ⊓ (=1 representsName) ⊓
      ∀ representsAttribute.(IntrinsicProperty ⊔ AssignedProperty) ⊓
      ∀ representsOperation.FiringLaw ⊓ ∀ representsAssociation.Relation ⊓ ⋯

Further axioms can be introduced for a modelling construct, e.g., to constrain the *relations* between the roles in its scene or their *cardinalities*. The internal consistency of a modelling construct description thereby becomes a *concept satisfiability problem* (e.g., [13]). For UMLClass, this problem has the following form, where T is the set of terminological axioms (the TBox) for ontology concepts and modelling constructs in UEMO:

$T \nvDash$ UMLClass ≡ ⊥

Comparing modelling **constructs:** We approach detailed comparison of modelling constructs as a sub-role matching problem. The above example introduced UMLClass with the sub-roles *representsClass*, *representsName*, *representsAttribute* etc. We now want to compare UMLClass to another ModellingConstruct, GRLGoal, which has sub-roles such as *representsAgent*, *representsTarget* and *representsGoal* [18]. One possible matching of sub-roles is between *representsClass* (of UMLClass) and *representsGoal* (of GRLGoal), which are restricted as follows by their respective modelling constructs:

⋯ ∃ representsClass.Anything ⊓ (=1 representsClass) ⋯   (by UMLClass)
⋯ ∃ representsGoal.Behaviour ⊓ (=1 representsBehaviour) ⋯   (by GRLGoal)

We match the two sub-roles by giving them the same name (ignoring possible name clashes for now), e.g., *representsClassAndGoal*. As a result, the conjunction UMLClass' ⊓ GRLGoal' of the renamed concepts UMLClass' and GRLGoal' contains this combined restriction:

⋯ ∃ representsClassAndBehaviour.(Anything ⊓ Behaviour) ⊓
      (=1 representsClassAndBehaviour) ⋯

We compare the UMLClass and GRLGoal constructs by investigating all possible matchings of UMLClass sub-roles with GRLGoal sub-roles, including combinations where some or all sub-roles of either construct remain *unmatched*. The result will be a large number of candidate matches, each of which combines sub-roles of UMLClass with sub-roles of GRLGoal in a different way. Fortunately, most candidate matches can be immediately discarded, because they contain self-contradictory role restrictions, i.e., restrictions whose conjunction is not satisfiable. In the above example, UMLClass' ⊓ GRLGoal' can be safely discarded because Anything (a UEMO-class concept) and Behaviour (a UEMO-property concept) are disjoint by definition. In other cases, it is the number restrictions or other restrictions on the renamed sub-roles that are self-contradictory. The above test for internal consistency of modelling constructs can be used to eliminate candidate matches too:

$T \nvDash \text{UMLClass}' \sqcap \text{GRLGoal}' \equiv \bot$

We expect that most candidate matches generated by brute-force combination of sub-roles can be immediately discarded because they are not satisfiable. The much smaller set of satisfiable matches must be considered further by other means, most likely involving human inspection and assessment, which can possibly be aided by automatic *ontology classification* that arranges the remaining candidates in a more easily explored subsumption hierarchy. The top match of this hierarchy would be the least restrictive candidate, the one that does not match *any* sub-roles of the two constructs, whereas each leaf would be a candidate that is not restricted further by any other candidate. The search for the best candidate can proceed bottom- up and breadth-first from the leaves of the subsumption hierarchy. The selected best match can be written on the form UMLClass* $\sqcap$ GRLGoal* so that the information represented by UMLClass* and not by GRLGoal* and vice versa can be written

$\text{InformationLostFromUMLClassToGRLGoal} \equiv \text{UMLClass*} \sqcap \neg\text{GRLGoal*}$
$\text{InformationMissingFromUMLClassToGRLGoal} \equiv \neg\text{UMLClass*} \sqcap \text{GRLGoal*}$

These two concepts describe, respectively, the information that will be lost and the information that is missing and must somehow be provided when translating from a UMLClass to a GRLGoal (of course, they also describe the missing/lost information when translating back from GRLGoal to UMLClass).

Comparing modelling *languages:* Not accounted for here is the complementary problem of aligning modelling languages construct-wise, identifying which constructs or groups of constructs in one language that correspond most closely to the constructs or groups in the other, as a necessary preparation for detailed construct comparison.

Facilitating cross-language interoperability: Further work should explore how to facilitate cross-language model-to-model translations based on the detailed construct matchings described here. One approach is to store model elements expressed in one language as OWL individuals and then use complex SPARQL and/or SQWRL queries to retrieve them as model elements expressed in another language. Another strategy is to use construct matches to generate QVT or other transformations, along the lines suggested in [19] which, however, does not build an extensive ontology. To adopt their approach, UEMO must first be extended to account for intended modelling-language and -construct *syntax* in addition to *semantics*.

5   Discussion

UEMO is still evolving and currently comprises 225 OWL classes (or DL concepts), although this number is somewhat inflated because it explicitly defines many *anonymous concepts* that may not be needed in the production version of the ontology. Most of the OWL classes represent UEMO classes and properties, with fewer representing UEML states and transformations so far. Compared to earlier versions of the UEML ontology, many new UEMO properties have been introduced to more precisely describe mutability and immutability, transients and persistence, assignments, complex properties, behaviours and laws. UEMO restricts the OWL classes with 567 subclass and 42 disjointness axioms and connects them with 96 object properties (or DL roles) that are in turn restricted by 97 sub-property (owl:subPropertyOf, aka Bunge-precedence) and 257 other axioms.

The work has shown that a large part of UEMO can be expressed in OWL2 DL and, so far, even in the relatively inexpressive *SHIN* sub-language [11], making a wider range of reasoners and other tools available, because *SHIN* is supported by both "OWL1" and OWL2. In addition, S(Q)WRL [15, 16] has been used to express certain additional constraints. Unfortunately, these "externally expressed" restrictions thereby become out of reach for DL-based reasoners, and further work must consider how they can be best used to reason about modelling languages and constructs. Two other groups of very general constraints seem infeasible to express even in S(Q)WRL, because they may require modal and/or temporal axioms. One group comprises UEMO concepts for transients and persistence and for certain types of mutability. Another includes [6] definitions of couplings and of systems. Further work should attempt to describe as many of these constraints as possible "inside" OWL2 DL, investigating, e.g., whether the modal/temporal axioms may at least have *implications* that can be expressed in DL form.

The present work has contributed both to making UEMO more precise and to supporting it with automatic reasoning tools. It has also indicated that several of the possible uses of UEMO have nice decision problems. UEMO also has the potential to become simpler than the old UEML ontology by exploiting more of OWL's native features. Firstly, it is prepared for using XML-namespaces where the old ontology used elaborate naming schemes. Secondly, where the old ontology introduced "association classes" to account for *role names* and *cardinality constraints*, UEMO uses OWL's built-in sub-role and number restrictions to the same effect. Thirdly, whereas the old ontology represented ontology concepts as OWL *individuals*, UEMO represents its concepts as OWL *classes*. One advantage is that they are thereby better supported by DL reasoning tools, which tend to solve decision problems on the concept (or class) level. Another is that the ontology is thus prepared for representing the semantics not only of modelling constructs, but also of model elements, which can be mapped either to OWL classes in UEMO (e.g., for a particular UML-Class) or to the OWL individuals that instantiate the classes (e.g., for a particular UML-Object).

Space prevents us from discussing several other important features of UEMO, such as the possibility of *parametric definitions* that use place holders (such as <Property> and <Value> below) to define powerful *generic concepts* like these:

$$\text{PossessesProperty<Property>} \equiv \text{AnyState} \sqcap \exists \text{ definedBy.Property}$$
$$\text{PossessesPropertyValue<Property, Value>} \equiv$$
$$\text{AnyState} \sqcap \exists \text{ definedBy.(Property} \sqcap \exists \text{ value.Value)}$$

6 Conclusion and Further Work

The paper has outlined the Unified Enterprise Modelling Ontology (UEMO), which supersedes the *common ontology* of the Unified Enterprise Modelling Language (UEML [1]). UEMO goes further than other ontology-based approaches to enterprise model interoperability (e.g., [4, 5]) because it offers an extensive framework for systematically describing modelling constructs in fine detail and because it has been explicitly designed to evolve and grow over time without becoming overly complex (through the five taxonomies). It is an ontology in both the philosophical and computer-science senses, and the paper has emphasised the latter side. It has formulated UEMO in OWL2 DL with **SHIN** expressiveness, meaning that it so far remains also in "OWL1" DL form. The paper has also outlined potential uses of UEMO as a computer-science ontology and discussed its further development. The paper has thereby contributed both to making UEMO more precise and to supporting it with automatic reasoning tools.

UEMO has already grown large, and a short paper like this can only present a selection of its concepts and features. Further work must present UEMO in fuller detail as an ontology both in the philosophical sense (e.g., grounding its concepts clearly in Bunge's ontology) and the computer-science sense (e.g., defining its concepts in description logic form and detail their use by automated reasoners and other relevant tools). Further work is also needed to extend the ontology with more precise concepts for states and transformations and to properly validate it. The present version of UEMO has already been extensively validated through iterative development, by using several automated reasoners and by cross-checking with earlier ontology versions. But additional validations are needed that use UEMO to describe and support interoperability between existing modelling languages.

Acknowledgements. The author is indebted to all the researchers, assistants and students who contributed to the Domain Enterprise Modelling in Interop-NoE, in particular Giuseppe Berio, Mounira Harzallah and Raimundas Matulevičius.

References

1. Anaya, V., Berio, G., Harzallah, M., Heymans, P., Matulevičius, R., Opdahl, A.L., Panetto, H., Verdecho, M.J.: The Unified Enterprise Modelling Language – Overview and Further Work. Computers in Industry 61(2) (2010)
2. Opdahl, A.L.: A Platform for Interoperable Domain-Specific Enterprise Modelling Based on ISO 15926. In: EDOC 2010 Workshop Proceedings. IEEE CS Press, Los Alamitos (2010)
3. Opdahl, A.L.: Incorporating UML Class and Activity Constructs into UEML. In: Trujillo, J., Dobbie, G., Kangassalo, H., Hartmann, S., Kirchberg, M., Rossi, M., Reinhartz-Berger, I., Zimányi, E., Frasincar, F. (eds.) ER 2010. LNCS, vol. 6413, pp. 244–254. Springer, Heidelberg (2010)
4. Kappel, G., Kapsammer, E., Kargl, H., Kramler, G., Reiter, T., Retschitzegger, W., Schwinger, W., Wimmer, M.: Lifting metamodels to ontologies: A step to the semantic integration of modeling languages. In: Wang, J., Whittle, J., Harel, D., Reggio, G. (eds.) MoDELS 2006. LNCS, vol. 4199, pp. 528–542. Springer, Heidelberg (2006)
5. Ziemann, J., Ohren, O., Jäkel, F.-W., Kahl, T., Knothe, T.: Achieving Enterprise Model Interoperability Applying a Common Enterprise Metamodel. In: Doumeingts, G., Müller, J., Morel, G., Vallespir, B. (eds.) Enterprise Interoperability New Challenges and Approaches. Springer, London (2007)
6. Bunge, M.: Treatise on Basic Philosophy. Ontology I: The Furniture of the World, vol. 3. Reidel, Boston (1977)
7. Bunge, M.: Treatise on Basic Philosophy. Ontology II: A World of Systems, vol. 4. Reidel, Boston (1979)

8. Wand, Y., Weber, R.: On the Ontological Expressiveness of Information Systems Analysis and Design Grammars. Journal of Information Systems 3, 217–237 (1993)
9. Opdahl, A.L., Henderson-Sellers, B.: Template-Based Definition of Information Systems and Enterprise Modelling Constructs. In: Green, P., Rosemann, M. (eds.) Ontologies and Business System Analysis, vol. ch. 6. Idea Group Publishing, USA (2005)
10. Mahiat, J.: A Validation Tool for the UEML Approach. Master thesis, University of Namur (2006)
11. Horrocks, I., Kutz, O., Sattler, U.: The Even More Irresistible SROIQ. In: Proc. of the 10th Int. Conf. on Principles of Knowledge Representation and Reasoning, KR 2006, pp. 57–67 (2006)
12. Opdahl, A.L.: The UEML Approach to Modelling Construct Description. In: Doumeingts, G., Müller, J., Morel, G., Vallespir, B. (eds.) Enterprise Interoperability – New Challenges and Approaches. Springer, Berlin (2007)
13. Donini, F.M., Lenzerini, M., Nardi, D., Schaerf, A.: Reasoning in Description Logic. In: Brewka, G. (ed.) Principles of Knowledge Representation and Planning, pp. 193–238. CSLI Publications, Stanford (1996)
14. Nardi, D., Brachman, R.J.: An Introduction to Description Logics. In: Baader, F., Calvanese, D., McGuinness, D.L., Nardi, D., Patel-Schneider, P.F. (eds.) The Description Logic Handbook: Theory, Implementation, and Applications. Cambridge University Press, Cambridge (2003)
15. Horrocks, I., Patel-Schneider, P.F., Boley, H., Tabet, S., Grosof, B. and Dean, M. SWRL: A Semantic Web Rule Language Combining OWL and RuleML. W3C Member Submission (May 21, 2004)
16. O'Connor, M.J., Das, A.: SQWRL: a query language for OWL. In: OWL – Experiences and Directions Workshop Series (2009)
17. Harel, D., Rumpe, B.: Modelling Languages: Syntax, Semantics and all that Stuff (or, What's the Semantics of "Semantics"?). Technical Report, Technische Universität Braunschweig (2004)
18. Matulevičius, R., Heymans, P., Opdahl, A.L.: Comparing GRL and KAOS using the UEML Approach. In: Gonçalves, R.J., Müller, J.P., Mertins, K., Zelm, M. (eds.) Enterprise Interoperability II – New Challenges and Approaches. Springer, Heidelberg (2007)
19. Roser, S., Bauer, B.: Automatic Generation and Evolution of Model Transformations Using Ontology Engineering Space. J. Data Semantics 11, 32–64 (2008)

Model-Driven Development of Service Compositions for Enterprise Interoperability

Ravi Khadka[1], Brahmananda Sapkota[2], Luís Ferreira Pires[2],
Marten van Sinderen[2], and Slinger Jansen[1]

[1] Utrecht University, P.O. Box 80.089, 3508TB Utrecht, The Netherlands
{ravi,s.jansen}@cs.uu.nl
[2] University of Twente, P.O. Box 217, 7500AE Enschede, The Netherlands
{b.sapkota,l.ferreirapires,m.j.vansinderen}@ewi.utwente.nl

Abstract. Service-Oriented Architecture (SOA) has emerged as an architectural style to foster enterprise interoperability, as it claims to facilitate the flexible composition of loosely coupled enterprise applications and thus alleviates the heterogeneity problem among enterprises. Meanwhile, Model-Driven Architecture (MDA) aims at facilitating the development of distributed application functionality, independent from its implementation using a specific technology platform and thus contributes to deployment in different platforms. In this paper we propose an MDA-based transformation technique for service composition. The contribution of the paper is two-fold. First, our approach shows how enterprise interoperability is supported by service composition at two different technical levels, namely at choreography and orchestration level. Second, the approach contributes to the management of changes that affect enterprise interoperability, by defining a (semi-)automated transformation from choreography to orchestrations in which the interoperability constraints specified at the choreography level are preserved.

Keywords: SOA, MDA, Metamodel Transformation, Enterprise Interoperability, Choreography, Orchestration, Service Composition, Service Interoperability.

1 Introduction

Enterprise interoperability denotes the ability of organizations, hereafter called enterprises, to interoperate in order to achieve certain business goals [13]. To a large extent, the competitiveness and success of modern enterprises is determined by their ability to achieve enterprise interoperability. Advances in Internet technologies have contributed substantially to the propagation and efficiency of cross-organizational collaboration. Nonetheless, important obstacles remain due to business-driven proprietary developments. Therefore, enterprise interoperability problems should be addressed coherently at business and technical levels as a whole [22]. Enterprises are especially challenged by the accelerating pace of changes, such as intra-organizational changes, changes in market demands

M. van Sinderen and P. Johnson (Eds.): IWEI 2011, LNBIP 76, pp. 177–190, 2011.

and opportunities, and, consequently, changes in partners and ways and intent of collaboration, and the changes in supporting technologies. To manage these changes, automatic support is essential.

Service-Oriented Computing (SOC) is one of the promising technologies to realize the necessary automated support for change management. The underlying concept of SOC is service, which is described in [16] as a self-contained, platform-agonistic computational element that supports rapid, low-cost and easy composition of loosely coupled distributed software applications. A service can be described, published, and discovered by an enterprise with a focus on reusing external behavior and hiding implementation details. However, in an enterprise collaboration, no single service alone may be available that fulfills all collaboration goals. A typical approach to this problem is to identify the basic (non-composite) services, based on an analysis of the collaboration goals, and then aggregate them into a larger composite service with the appropriate value-added functionality. We call this process of aggregating services "service composition", which not only realizes a required (composite) service, but also accelerates application development through the application of reuse at service level [11].

Service compositions can be considered at different abstraction levels, notably at choreography and orchestration levels [17,2]. A service choreography is a decentralized perspective, which describes the public message exchanges, and thus defines how participating services should interact with each other. At a lower level, it is necessary to define how to realize the responsibilities specified at the choreography level in terms of the concrete processes. A service orchestration is a centralized coordination of participating services, which defines the message exchanges along with the necessary internal actions, like data transformations and internal function invocations [17]. In an enterprise collaboration, a service choreography specifies requirements in terms of message exchanges to support the collaboration goals, while a service orchestration realizes the required message exchanges in terms of executable processes.

It has been widely recognized that SOC technology and SOA have emerged as evolutionary steps to achieve enterprise interoperability [13]. Enterprises can publish their services to alleviate the heterogeneity problem. The collaboration among these enterprises is realized by composing their individual services through the service composition process. In this phase, we need service interoperability at the technical level to realize enterprise interoperability. In the service composition process we specify the interoperability constraints at service choreography level, which focuses on the message exchanges between the participating services. At a lower level, such as in the service orchestration level, interoperability constraints as specified at the choreography level are preserved. Therefore, an approach is needed to transform a given choreography to one or more orchestration(s). Currently these transformations are mostly performed manually [12], which is a time consuming and error prone. A (semi-)automated transformation from choreography to orchestrations, such that it preserves the interoperability constraints specified at the choreography level and automates the enterprise collaboration process, would represent an improvement. In this paper, we propose an approach to (semi-)automate the transformation from choreography to orchestrations using metamodel transformation techniques from MDA [15]. We refer to this process as model-driven service composition. In this approach, we define the metamodels for choreography and orchestration and mappings between model elements of these metamodels. Our proposed approach of (semi-)automated transformation of choreography into orchestrations improves the productivity of the composition process and correctness of the resulting compositions.

The rest of the paper proceeds as follows: Section 2 introduces our approach to model-driven service composition for enterprise interoperability. Section 3 describes an example scenario that we used for illustrating the proposed approach. Section 4 discusses how this approach was implemented and Section 5 discusses the evaluation of our approach. Section 6 presents related work and finally Section 7 concludes the paper and gives an outlook of future research directions.

2 Approach

Our approach is to perform service composition by (semi-)automatically transforming the given choreography into one or more orchestration(s) using model-driven transformation techniques. In this section, we investigate the relationship between choreography and orchestration, and indicate how model-driven transformation can be useful to relate these concepts.

A choreography describes the public message exchanges, interaction rules and agreements in a service composition at a high level of abstraction [17,2]. A choreography is defined from a decentralized perspective, and specifies how the individual services interact with each other. A service choreography does not describe any internal actions of the participating services, like internal computations or data transformations. A choreography captures message exchanges from a global perspective where all the participating services are treated equally, and as such it provides a convenient starting point to define how the participating services must interact to realize enterprise collaboration. At the choreography level, the interactions among each service participating in the composition are described as a global abstract protocol with which all participating services should comply [2].

After the message exchanges between the participating services are defined in a choreography, we need to define how the added-value of the composite service can be achieved in terms of a concrete implementation. We call the process that realizes the business goal of the enterprise collaboration in terms of executable process an orchestration. There may be one orchestration for each service, or a central authority that coordinates the overall composition process, so called decentralized orchestration and centralized orchestration, respectively [5,4]. In centralized orchestrations, the central authority is called an orchestrator. Orchestrations describe the communication actions and the internal actions, like data transformations or invocations to internal software modules. In an orchestration, execution orders of the interactions and method invocations of the implementations also need to be defined [17,2] in terms of an executable process that contains enough information to enable execution by an orchestration engine.

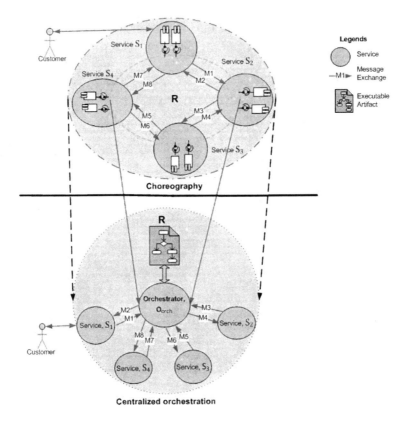

Fig. 1. Transformation from choreography to centralized orchestration

A given choreography can be transformed to either a decentralized or a centralized orchestration. In this paper we only consider the transformation from choreography to centralized orchestration because centralized orchestration is widely used in the service composition process. A diagrammatic representation of the transformation from a choreography to a centralized orchestration is presented in Figure 1. In the choreograph level of Figure 1 the message exchanges and interactions rules are represented by the directed arrows among the services. The overall responsibility of choreography, represented as R, includes message exchange, interactions rules, and the service level constraints. The transformation from choreography to centralized orchestration is achieved by transferring the overall responsibility of choreography R to the orchestrator and establishing the message exchanges, interactions rules, and the interoperability constraints between the orchestrator and the individual services accordingly. The responsibility R is represented as an executable artifact and is depicted as the flow diagram in the orchestration level of Figure 1.

In our approach we specify service choreographies and orchestrations using Web Service Choreography Description Language (WSCDL or CDL in short) [9]

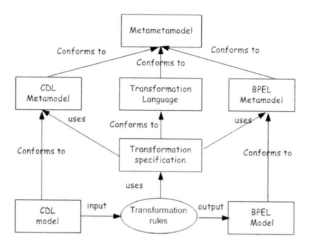

Fig. 2. Model-driven transformation

and Web Service Business Process Execution Language (WSBPEL or BPEL in short) [1], respectively, because of the wide industry acceptance of these languages.

We apply model-driven transformation to (semi-)automate the transformation from a choreography specified in CDL to a centralized orchestration specified in BPEL. The model-driven transformation is diagrammatically presented in Figure 2. In this transformation, we take the CDL metamodel as source metamodel and BPEL metamodel as target metamodel. We used the language syntax of [9] and [1] to develop the metamodels of CDL and BPEL, respectively. We defined the mappings between CDL and BPEL metamodel elements. These mappings are then used to create transformation specifications in Atlas Transformation Language (ATL) [7], and hence executed by ATL transformation engine. The transformation mappings of the metamodel elements of CDL and BPEL are presented in Table 1.

3 Working Example

The Build-To-Order (BTO) application scenario, adopted from [19] is used as an example to illustrate the usability of our approach. We briefly explain this scenario with the sequence diagram shown in Figure 3. The BTO scenario consists of a customer, a manufacturer, and suppliers for CPUs, main boards and hard disks. We consider all the suppliers to be different enterprises. The manufacturer offers assembled IT hardware equipment to its customers. For this purpose, the manufacturer has implemented a BTO business model. It holds a certain part of the individual hardware components in stock and orders missing components if necessary. In the implemented BTO scenario, the customer sends a quote request with details about the required hardware equipment to the manufacturer.

Table 1. Transformation mapping from CDL to BPEL

CDL	BPEL	Remarks
roleType	process per role	*bpel:targerNamespace* attribute is derived from the *cdl:targetNamespace* of cdl:package
participantType	partnerLink	-
relationshipType	partnerLinkType	-
variable	variable	bpel:messageType attribute is derived from the cdl:type of related *cdl:informationType*
channelType	correlationSet	*bpel:properties* is derived from *cdl:name* of *cdl:token* within *cdl:identity*
sequence	sequence	-
Parallel	flow	-
Choice	if-else	*bpel:condition* is manually provided
workunit		
repeat= false , block=false	if-else	*bpel:condition* is manually provided
repeat= true	while	*bpel:condition* is manually provided
block= true	-	no mapping
interaction		
action= request	invoke	current party is mentioned in *cdl:fromRole*
action= request	receive	current party is mentioned in *cdl:toRole*
action= respond	reply	current party is mentioned in *cdl:fromRole*
action= respond	receive	current party is mentioned in *cdl:fromRole* (synchronous reply)
assign	assign	-
finalize	compensationHandler	-
noAction	empty	-
silentAction	sequence with nested empty	BPEL designer have to manually specify the silentActions

The latter sends a quote response back to the customer. As long as the customer and the manufacturer do not agree on the quote, this process is repeated. If a mutual agreement is reached the customer sends a purchase order to the manufacturer. Depending on its hardware stock, the manufacturer has to order the required hardware components from its suppliers. If the manufacturer needs to obtain hardware components to fulfill the purchase order it sends an appropriate hardware order to the respective supplier. In turn, the supplier sends a hardware order response to the manufacturer. Finally, the manufacturer sends a purchase order response back to the customer.

4   Implementation

Based on the BTO application scenario, we specified the choreography in CDL, and (semi-)automatically generated the BPEL based orchestration specification for the Manufacturer as an orchestrator. The orchestration process is specified in BPEL. To implement our proposed approach, we defined the CDL and BPEL

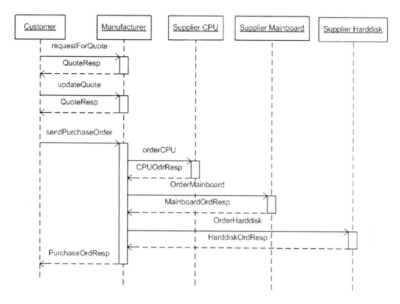

Fig. 3. BTO example

metamodel using Eclipse Modeling Framework (EMF)[1]. EMF is an Eclipse-based modeling framework and has code generation facilities for building tools and other applications based on a structured data model. The transformation specification has been written based on the transformation mapping presented in Table 1 using ATL[2], which contains the ATL transformation engine that runs ATL transformation specifications as transformation rules.

Conceptually, the transformation approach presented in Figure 2 represents the model transformation that takes a CDL model (conforming with the CDL metamodel) and runs the transformation rules in ATL engine to generate a BPEL model (conforming with the BPEL metamodel). However, to execute the ATL transformation rules, an ATL engine expects every model and metamodel (i.e., input/output models and metamodels) to be serialized in XML Metadata Interchange (XMI) format [8], whereas the input/output models (i.e., CDL and BPEL models) in our scenario are in XML format that conforms with the XML schema of CDL and BPEL. Hence, we need a transformation chain that contains the transformations as indicated in Figure 4. This transformation chain is discussed as follows:

4.1 CDL Model (XML) to CDL Model (XMI)

The CDL XML model to CDL XMI model transformation, which is indicated as T1 in Figure 4, is used to transform a CDL model (XML format) to the CDL

---

[1] http://www.eclipse.org/modeling/emf/
[2] http://www.eclipse.org/atl/

model (XMI format) that conforms to CDL metamodel. This XMI model can then be read by the ATL engine to run the transformation specification. We use the eXtensible Stylesheet Language Transformation (XSLT) to implement this transformation, which takes a CDL model in XML and converts it to a CDL model in XMI.

4.2   CDL Model (XMI) to BPEL Model (XMI)

The CDL XMI model to BPEL XMI model transformation, which is indicated as T2 in Figure 4, is the core of our approach and is performed by executing the ATL transformation specification. The ATL engine reads a CDL XMI model as input, executes the transformation rules, and generates a BPEL XMI model as defined in the ATL transformation specification.

4.3   BPEL Model (XMI) to BPEL Process (XML)

After transformation T2 is performed, a BPEL XMI model that conforms to the BPEL metamodel is generated. The BPEL XMI model cannot be executed by orchestration engines, so we perform another transformation, indicated as T3 in Figure 4, which transforms a BPEL XMI model to a BPEL process (in XML). We use AtlanMod MegaModel Management (AM3)[3] for T3 transformation. This transformation performs an XMI-to-XML conversion of a BPEL specification by using the ATL's XML Extraction process [18]. An XML extraction is defined as a transformation from model-driven technical space to another technical space using an XML extractor, which is a tool that implements the extraction process.

Figure 4 shows the transformation chain of our approach which consists of 4 stages.

1. We use the Pi4soa[4] CDL editor to model the choreography specification, which is stored in this tool in the CDL XML format.
2. We use XSLT transformation to transform CDL XML specification to the XMI format that conforms to the CDL metamodel.
3. We execute the transformation specification as transformation rule in ATL engine that generates a BPEL model. The generated BPEL model is in an XMI serialized format that conforms to the BPEL metamodel.
4. We use ATL to transform from the BPEL XMI model to the BPEL XML model. This ATL transformation takes the BPEL metamodel as source metamodel and the XML metamodel as the target metamodel. We use ATL's XML Extraction process to extract the BPEL proces (in XML) from the BPEL XMI model [18]. In this way, a BPEL process in XML format is obtained as output that can be executed by orchestration engines.

---

[3] http://wiki.eclipse.org/AM3
[4] http://sourceforge.net/apps/trac/pi4soa/wiki

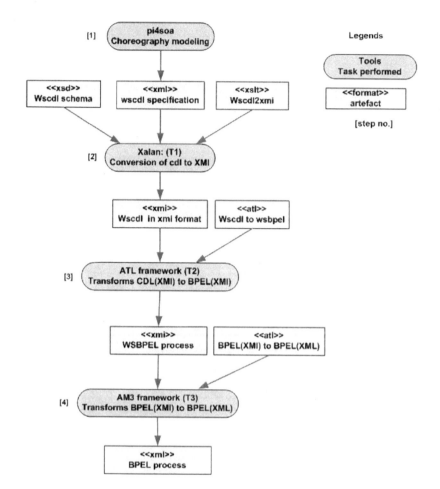

Fig. 4. Transformation Chain

5   Validation and Discussion

We implemented the example described in Section 3 to determine the feasibility of our model-driven transformation approach. We have modeled the choreography of the BTO example by using the Pi4soa choreography editor. The choreography has a higher abstraction level than the orchestration and choreography does not represent the internal details of the participating services in the collaboration, so we could not generate a complete executable BPEL process with necessary internal details. However, our approach successfully generated the BPEL skeleton for the Manufacturer from the given CDL specification. In our approach, the BPEL designer has to manually provide the missing details, like branching conditions, wherever necessary. This is also shown in the transformation mappings given in Table 1, in which we indicated that the BPEL designer has to specify conditions manually. For instance, Listing 1 presents a code snippet of the generated BPEL skeleton in which the BPEL designer has to manually add a condition to replace the empty condition *default=0*.

Listing 1. Conditional branching

```
<flow  name  ="parallel">
 <if  name  ="Choice_CPUnotInStock">
   <condition >"default=0"</condition >
        <sequence>
            <invoke  operation  ="orderCPU"  ../>
        </sequence>
```

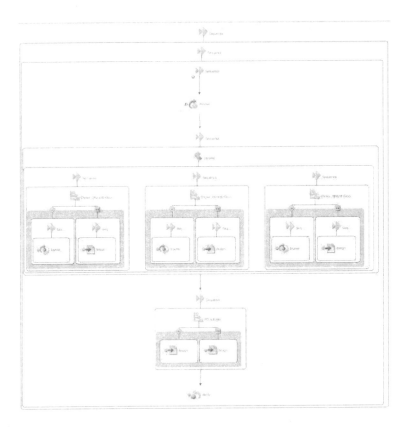

Fig. 5. BPEL process of Manufacturer

After the necessary conditions were added, we validated the BPEL process against the executable schema of BPEL to ensure syntactical correctness. We later imported the BPEL process in the ActiveBPEL designer to check the behavior of the orchestrator, and tested this behavior for correctness, with successful results.

Figure 5 shows the BPEL process of Manufacturer of BTO example in the ActiveBPEL designer.

The proposed approach is also validated for Purchase Order scenario [10] and tested with successful results.

6   Related Work

In this section we discuss existing Model-Driven SOA based approaches for enterprise interoperability as well as choreography to orchestration transformation approaches.

6.1   Model-Driven SOA Based Approaches for Enterprise Interoperability

Recently, model-based initiatives for enterprise interoperability have achieved significant attention in academic research and various interoperability frameworks have been proposed. The IDEAS Interoperability Framework [6] focuses on structuring the interoperability into business, knowledge, semantics, and architecture and platform issues. The ATHENA Interoperability Framework (AIF) [3] is a Model-Driven Interoperability (MDI) framework that has evolved from IDF. The AIF framework focus on the solution approaches for enterprise interoperability and defines different level of interoperations: enterprise/business, process, service, and information/data. The service level interoperability of the AIF framework is concerned with identifying, composing, and executing various services. The Platform-Independent Model for Service-Oriented Architecture (PIM4SOA) metamodel supports the execution and composition of services. PIM4SOA tool facilitates the transformation of PIM4SOA model (e.g., generated from higher level tooling) to a BPEL model. The AIF framework prescribes model-driven interoperability [3] and explicitly provides solution approach (PIM4SOA) for services. The PIM4SOA Eclipse plugin can be used for identifying, composing, and executing the services. However, compared to our approach PIM4SOA lacks the (semi-)automated transformation from choreography to orchestration. Though both the approaches are model-driven, our approach aims to achieve automation in enterprise collaboration and enterprise interoperablity.

6.2   Choreography to Orchestration Transformation

The work of [14] presents the mapping rules for the derivation of a BPEL process from a CDL specification. These mapping rules inspired the mappings shown in Table 1. In [14], the mappings are implemented in a recursive XSLT script, as a proof-of-concept, to realize the transformation. The transformation is bi-directional, i.e., the XSLT script can generate a BPEL process from a CDL specification, and vice-versa.

In [19], Rosenberg et al. proposed a top-down modeling approach to generate a BPEL process from a given CDL specification. This transformation also considers Service Level Agreements (SLAs), which are defined as annotations to the CDL specification, and are transformed into policies that can be enforced by a BPEL engine during execution. This transformation approach is implemented in Java 1.5 using a simple Swing-based graphical user interface.

Weber et al. [23] present a CDL to BPEL transformation in the context of a virtual organization, which is possibly also applicable to other domains. This transformation introduces the concept of information gap, which is the term used to mention the different levels of detail between a choreography and an orchestration, and indicates that the sum of orchestrations contains more knowledge than the choreography they implement. Given a choreography, their approach generates executable processes and respective WSDL specifications for each role. This transformation is implemented in Java.

In our approach, we use metamodel-based transformations, in which we define the abstract syntax (metamodel) of both the source and target models, and use ATL as transformation language. We follow MDA principles to perform the core transformation (T2) in the transformation chain, which allows us to express the mappings from source model to target model at a higher abstraction level than in case a programming language is used. Our approach falls under the "Transformation Language Support" category as described in [20]. In transformation language support, the transformation uses a language that provides a set of constructs for explicitly expressing, composing, and applying transformation. Our approach uses metamodels to express the mapping from source model to target model at a higher level of abstraction when compared with the other approaches. XSLT-based transformations require experience and considerable effort to define and maintain the transformation, whereas transformations written using general-purpose programming language tend to be hard to write, comprehend, and maintain the transformation. Hence, our metamodel-based transformation approach is favorable and is more efficient than other available techniques (i.e., Direct Model Manipulation, Intermediate Representation) [20,21], used in aforementioned related works.

7   Conclusion

In this paper, we presented a model-driven approach to service composition, based on combining concepts from Service-Oriented Architecture (SOA) and Model-Driven Architecture (MDA). The approach aims at facilitating enterprise collaboration by addressing enterprise interoperability problems caused by system heterogeneity and business-technology misalignment in the context of continuous change. The heart of the proposed model-driven service composition is the definition of a (semi-)automatic transformation from service choreography to service orchestrations. The approach has been illustrated with an implementation prototype and validated with a working example. We use service choreography to define service interoperability constraints in terms of message exchanges among collaborating enterprises. In our approach such constraints are preserved in the transformation to service orchestration level. We successfully validated the approach using a Build-To-Order (BTO) application scenario as example, where we represented the generated service orchestration as a BPEL process and tested the behavior of the BPEL process for correctness. We achieved the two objectives of our research, namely supporting enterprise interoperability by service composition at choreography and orchestration level and guaranteeing consistency between these levels by defining an (semi-)automated transformation from choreography to orchestrations. Our transformation represents an improvement over the currently existing manual transformations. In particular, our transformation automatically preserves the interoperability constraints when going from choreography to orchestration level.

As future work we can still improve our approach in several ways. For instance, automatic generation of WSDL specification for each participant from the choreography description can ease the deployment and testing of the behavior of the generated BPEL process. We can further contribute to enterprise interoperability by including SLAs in the choreography description and transforming them to BPEL policies [19]. Additionally, transformation T1 of our approach, which is currently an XSLT-based transformation (see Figure 4), can also be performed using ATL by XML injection [18] so our approach is solely based on metamodel transformations.

References

1. Alves, A., Arkin, A., Askary, S., Barreto, C., Bloch, B., Curbera, F., Ford, M., Goland, Y., Guizar, A., Kartha, N., Liu, K.C., Khalaf, R., Konig, D., Marin, M., Mehta, V., Thatte, S., Van der Rijn, D., Yendluri, P., Yiu, A.: Web Services Business Process Execution Language Version 2.0. OASIS, pp. 1–126 (2007), http://docs.oasis-open.org/wsbpel/2.0/OS/wsbpel-v2.0-OS.html
2. Barros, A., Dumas, M., Oaks, P.: Standards for web service choreography and orchestration: Status and perspectives. In: Bussler, C.J., Haller, A. (eds.) BPM 2005. LNCS, vol. 3812, pp. 61–74. Springer, Heidelberg (2006)
3. Berre, A., Elvesæter, B., Figay, N., Guglielmina, C., Johnsen, S., Karlsen, D., Knothe, T., Lippe, S.: The ATHENA Interoperability Framework. In: 3rd International Conference on Interoperability for Enterprise Software and Applications (I-ESA 2007), pp. 771–782. Springer, Madeira (2007) ISBN 9781846288579
4. Binder, W., Constantinescu, I., Faltings, B.: Decentralized orchestration of composite web services. In: Proccedings of the International Conference on Web Services, ICWS 2006, pp. 869–876. IEEE Computer Society, Los Alamitos (2006)
5. Chafle, G., Chandra, S., Mann, V., Nanda, M.: Decentralized orchestration of composite web services. In: Proceedings of the 13th International World Wide Web Conference on Alternate Track Papers & Posters, pp. 134–143. ACM, New York (2004)
6. IDEAS: A Gap Analysis Required Activities in Research, Technology and Standardisation to close the RTS Gap - Roadmaps and Recommendations on RTS activities, IDEAS, Deliverable D.3.4, D 3.5, D 3.6 (2001)
7. Jouault, F., Allilaire, F., Bézivin, J., Kurtev, I.: ATL: A model transformation tool. Science of Computer Programming 72(1-2), 31–39 (2008)

8. Jouault, F., Allilaire, F., Bézivin, J., Kurtev, I., Valduriez, P.: ATL: a QVT-like transformation language. In: Companion to the 21st ACM SIGPLAN Symposium on Object-Oriented Programming Systems, Languages, and Applications, pp. 719–720. ACM, New York (2006)

9. Kavantzas, N., Burdett, D., Ritzinger, G., Lafon, Y.: Web Services Choreography Description Language Version 1.0, W3C Candidate Recommendation, World Wide Web Consortium (November 2005)

10. Khadka, R.: Model-Driven Development of Service Compositions: Transformation from Service Choreography to Service Orchestrations. Master's thesis, University of Twente (August 2010), http://essay.utwente.nl/59677/

11. Khadka, R., Sapkota, B.: An Evaluation of Dynamic Web Service Composition Approaches. In: Proceeding of the 4th International Workshop on Architectures, Concepts and Technologies for Service Oriented Computing, ACT4SOC 2010, pp. 67–79. INSTICC Press, Athens (2010)

12. Kopp, O., Leymann, F.: Choreography Design Using WS-BPEL. Data Engineering 31(2), 31–34 (2008)

13. Li, M., Cabral, R., Doumeingts, G., Popplewell, K.: Enterprise interoperability research roadmap. An Enterprise Interoperability community document (2006)

14. Mendling, J., Hafner, M.: From inter-organizational workflows to process execution: Generating BPEL from WS-CDL. In: Chung, S., Herrero, P. (eds.) OTM-WS 2005. LNCS, vol. 3762, pp. 506–515. Springer, Heidelberg (2005)

15. Miller, J., Mukerji, J., et al.: MDA Guide Version 1.0. 1. Object Management Group (2003), http://www.omg.org/cgi-bin/doc?omg/03-06-01

16. Papazoglou, M.: Web services: principles and technology. Addison-Wesley, Reading (2008)

17. Peltz, C.: Web services orchestration and choreography. Computer 36(10), 46–52 (2003)

18. Ribarić, M., Gašević, D., Milanović, M., Giurca, A., Lukichev, S., Wagner, G.: Model-Driven engineering of rules for web services. Generative and Transformational Techniques in Software Engineering II, pp. 377–395 (2008)

19. Rosenberg, F., Enzi, C., Michlmayr, A., Platzer, C., Dustdar, S.: Integrating quality of service aspects in top-down business process development using WS-CDL and WS-BPEL. In: Proceedings of the 11th IEEE International Enterprise Distributed Object Computing Conference, EDOC 2007, p. 15. IEEE Computer Society, Los Alamitos (2007)

20. Sendall, S., Kozaczynski, W.: Model transformation: The heart and soul of model-driven software development. IEEE Software 20(5), 42–45 (2003)

21. Sendall, S., Kozaczynski, W.: Model Transformation the Heart and Soul of Model-Driven Software Development. Tech. rep. (2003)

22. van Sinderen, M.: Challenges and solutions in enterprise computing. Enterprise Information Systems 2(4), 341–346 (2008)

23. Weber, I., Haller, J., Mulle, J.: Automated derivation of executable business processes from choreographies in virtual organisations. International Journal of Business Process Integration and Management 3(2), 85–95 (2008)

A Data-Centric Approach for Privacy-Aware Business Process Enablement

Stuart Short and Samuel Paul Kaluvuri

Sap Labs France, 805, Avenue du Docteur Maurice Donat,
BP 1216 - 06254 Mougins Cedex, France
{Stuart.Short,Samuel.Paul.Kaluvuri}@sap.com

Abstract. In a SOA context, enterprises can use workflow technologies to orchestrate available business processes and their corresponding services and apply business rules or policies to control how they can be used and who can use them. This approach becomes a bit more complex when a set of business processes includes services that derive outside the company's domain and therefore can be difficult to align with existing rules/policies. In the privacy and security domain, access control and policy languages are used to define what actions can be performed on resources, by whom, for what purpose and in what context. In this paper we propose an approach for dealing with the inclusion of internal and/or external services in a business process that contains data handling policies.

Keywords: privacy; policy; BPM; SOA; web services.

1 Introduction

Privacy on the internet or in information systems usually refers to data that is of a personal or sensitive nature [2]. This information can be used to identify somebody (personal identifiable information) and may be used in a manner that was not intended. With the onslaught of tougher laws (e.g. Sarbanes-Oxley SOX [18]) and regulations, businesses and more to the point, system administrators, are being asked to put in place mechanisms (e.g. Control Objectives for Information and related Technology CobiT [19] that can enable a compliant environment and ensure that information is being handled correctly.

It can be a difficult task to translate the idea of privacy into technology, let alone develop privacy preserving mechanisms [5]. Furthermore, there may be issues over the use of personal information for genuine business interests on the one hand and the right of the individual to maintain control over how their personal data is used [6] [7] on the other hand. This trade-off [8] has lead to an increase in both corporate self-regulation and government intervention [9] in the form of data protection and privacy laws [10]. One way for an organization to deal with privacy concerns is to control its processes and the flow of information. Business Process Management is a systematic way to achieve this goal although its use is mainly to create business value and operational efficiency for competitive advantage [11] [12].

M. van Sinderen and P. Johnson (Eds.): IWEI 2011, LNBIP 76, pp. 191–203, 2011.

Service Oriented Architectures (SOA) are commonly used as a way to design business processes and loosely coupled services (a set of related business functions) can be dynamically composed or orchestrated to meet the needs of the designer and end-users. Although traditional workflows rarely leave the boundaries of the enterprise for security, privacy, sharing ability, firewalls reasons [13] there has been a definite move towards collaborative workflows. With the existing SOA and BPM approach combined with greater collaboration and tougher regulations on how data is consumed, process designers need to be able to track how data flows and ensure that the business processes are compliant.

In this paper we propose a two-fold solution for dealing with the inclusion of internal and/or external services in a business process. Firstly, in a workflow, policy or system administrators are able to describe policies on activities in a business process and data objects. Furthermore they are able to identify inconsistencies with activities or web services that are mapped or linked together in a process. For instance, if an activity states that it can be used by certain participants in a certain context and the following activity disagrees with one of these elements then the binding with a data object will trigger an alert or warning on the designer's interface.

The second part of the proposed solution permits the workflow to import policies that are attached to an external or internal service. In the former case, when the service is consumed with the data handling policies, it would be seen as accepting a Service Level Agreement (SLA) with an external party and confirming that the consumer of the service will adhere to whatever rules are in place. Once the SLA is imported with the service the policy administrator is prompted to align the naming of potential recipients to the system's identity management engine. This ensures consistency of integration and lessens the chance of ambiguity.

The paper is outlined as follows: Section 2 first lists the requirements for a privacy-enabled BPM. The idea of data-centricity in BPM is detailed in Section 3. The underlying approach to a prototype implementation is then discussed in Section 4. We finally compare the approach presented in this paper with related work and outline future directions for investigation.

2 Requirements for a Privacy-Enabled BPM

When designing a process an administrator can apply access control by assigning roles to activities ensuring that only those who are authorized to perform a given task can do so. Our approach extends this principle by allowing the process designer to include not only role assignment but also to express how the web service and the data contained within should be consumed and how long it can be used for. Furthermore the nature of web services permits their use in different contexts and environments, therefore the data handling or service consumption policies should always stay with the web service so that the initial requirements are respected. In order to do this a policy structure is needed that is capable of describing the aforementioned conditions and permit a means to evaluate whether a web service is consumable thereby making the business process compliant.

The following are functional requirements for a BPM engine that will assist a process designer in being compliant both with internal and external web services used in a process:

2.1 Policy Language

In order to express policies on a web service in a business process, the workflow engine should use a language that has a well-defined structure. An example of this can be seen in XACML [4]. This language uses the structure of Subject, Action and Resource (plus optional conditions or rules that may have to be satisfied) and provides a processing model that renders a decision on whether a resource should be accessed or not.

2.2 Policy Viewer

To facilitate the writing of policies, the BPM application should allow the designer the ability to define policies and to assign them to activities in the business process. Therefore a policy viewer should be integrated into the BPM suite that links with an identity management engine and allows for the mapping of roles or recipients from web services to the roles specified in the identity management engine, if not done so already.

2.3 Sticky Policies

Furthermore, there should be a means to import policies that belong to internal and external web services, into the viewer. In our solution we propose a way to include the policies in the web service description language file and then to populate the properties of the viewer. In this way we are ensuring that downstream usage of web services respects the original intention of use specified in the services' policies. Sticky policies [20] [24] are strictly associated to a piece of data and should be composed whenever data aggregation happens. Expressing a condition for each piece of data is a means for a data provider to declare how personal data is to be used. Even if privacy policy languages like P3P [1], EPAL [22] or Prime [23] exist they lack the notion of sticky policies or the complex composition of services or policies for resolving possible conflicts [21].

2.4 Policy Checker

Once the binding of a web service to a task or activity is completed and the policies have been attached, there should be a means to check if there are policy conflicts between services. For example, when it is stated that a web service should not be consumed for marketing purposes and the subsequent activity/web service in the process permits this, then there is a conflict of purpose or, in other terms, a violation of the web services policy.

2.5 Policy Language

By including a validity period for a web service's policy, the process designer can be reminded that the service's policy is out-of-date and he needs to reload/re-import the WSDL [3] file. This feature ensures that the service consumer has the most current policy and therefore remains compliant.

3 Privacy in BPM/Web Services

Web services are consumed in a business process purely on the basis of their business and technical functionality however this approach is limited when it comes to dealing with privacy concerns. Services can be aligned to business rules and assigned to be used by specific users however this approach is time-consuming and is limited in its expressivity. A web service policy is a way to stipulate how the service has to be consumed, for example, it can be stated that the service can be only consumed by certain entities such as a person and they have the right to do a certain action in a specific context. Sticking a policy to a service means that when the service is invoked, the data that is sent and received will adhere to the stated policy that travels with it. This facilitates process composition by identifying the appropriate web services. The process designer should be allowed to narrow the scope of certain policies as long as it is not compromised. For instance, if the web service stated that the data within a service can only be consumed within a certain time period, e.g. 50 days, perhaps internal practices deem this retention period too long, then this should be narrowed to comply. This would be also the case for the purpose of using the service and for the proposed recipient.

3.1 Policy Model Overview

Privacy of data in a business process can be achieved by attaching data privacy policies (privacy policies) onto data objects.. Hence directly attaching a privacy policy to a data object would make a business process more rigid and not offer the process designer the opportunity to change the services as and when required for process optimization.

In the proposed model (Fig. 1) the privacy policies are attached to an input and output of an activity. This in effect implies that an activity states its intentions of using the data that is required by it (consumption), this is the input privacy policy, while the output privacy policy states how the data that is generated by an activity should be used.

The output of an activity if it has to be used again by any other activity in a business process has to be mapped to data fields contained in a single data object or many data objects. The output privacy policy attached to an activity is then attached to the data fields that are mapped to the output of an activity. Through this method, privacy policies can be attached to data fields in a data object.

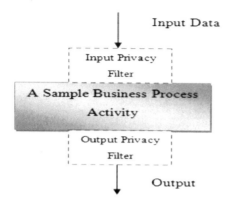

Fig. 1. Input and Output of an Activity

3.2 Privacy-Aware BPM Use Case

This section introduces a scenario that illustrates the need for data handling policies in a business process. When a bank customer/borrower submits an application for a loan, the loan origination process is initiated. This process entails the formalization, evaluation and eventual decision on the borrower's request. In order to do this, three main actors may be involved within the bank, namely, pre-processing clerk, post-processing clerk and a manager.

The pre-processing clerk receives a loan request from a customer and starts the application. Once the loan applicant's identity has been verified the post-processing clerk evaluates the customer's credit rating both through internal and external rating mechanisms. The latter is a trusted third-party credit bureau that can derive information about the applicant from various sources including publicly available records. In the event that the rating meets the requirements of the bank, the clerk selects the appropriate bundled product and forwards the application to the manager for final evaluation and eventual signature. On approval a loan account is then opened for the loan applicant.

Supposing that the information in the loan origination scenario contained restrictions on how it should be processed then it should be possible to include these in a BPM while designing a process. Furthermore, a system administrator should be able to test whether there are inconsistencies between policies. For example, the loan applicant may inform the pre-processing clerk that she wishes to express restrictions on who can perform a task, for what purpose and how long the data can remain in the system. The applicant states that the information supplied may only be used for administrative needs and may not be used for marketing; that marketing research analysts may not read this information and that the information is only to be used for the lifespan of the application unless successfully processed. The clerk includes these requirements while inputting the customer's information and an alert is triggered, at design time, if the subsequent consuming service or activity conflicts with this.

The credit bureau could specify that only a manager could request information from its service, with the intention of administrative purposes and may only store the information for a certain period of time. Given that the bureau is an external service there should be a means for it to express itself in these terms and also for the consuming service to receive this information and align it with its own system requirements.

4 Privacy-Enabled BPM/Web Services

When we talk about privacy we are referring to enabling a system with the means to deal with expressions on how data is processed. In the context of BPM and SOA we would see this as providing a means for process designers to control how data is handled in a web service composition, respecting the privacy concerns of parties to the orchestration. Whether these web services are internal or external, the down-stream usage of data maintains the original conditions of use. This data-centric approach can involve the use of data handling policies (DHP) 2 that can be attached to data. In the loan origination process example, the bank may have a policy that the sensitive information or personal identifiable information (PII) of the customers who apply for a loan, will not be sent to an entity that will use this information for other reasons than is intended by the current process. The PII could be attributes such as age, address or ethnic background. It can specify that the data provided by the customer in a loan application will only be consumed for a certain reason (purpose), for a certain length of time (retention period) and by a certain person (potential recipient). The process designer has to ensure that any external services that are used in the process have to comply with these data handling policies.

When the process under-design has a large amount of activities, a privacy manager tool is required to handle these policies and inform the process designer of the conflicts. In the loan origination scenario, the credit bureau should not receive information about the loan applicant that is not needed in the rating check.

4.1 Policy Language Structure

A privacy model is required that encapsulates the key privacy attributes in a business process. The model also has to facilitate the policies to be saved in existing standard languages like XACML:

```
<Subject>
    <Attribute AttributeId="urn:oasis:names:tc:xacml:1.0:subject:subject-id"
            DataType="urn:oasis:names:tc:xacml:1.0:data-type:rfc822Name">
        <AttributeValue>PostProcessorClerk</AttributeValue>
    </Attribute>
</Subject>
<Resource>
    <Attribute AttributeId="urn:oasis:names:tc:xacml:1.0:resource:resource-id"
            DataType="http://www.w3.org/2001/XMLSchema#string">
        <AttributeValue>Ethnic_Background</AttributeValue>
    </Attribute>
</Resource>
```

```
<Action>
    <Attribute AttributeId="urn:oasis:names:tc:xacml:1.0:action:action-id"
            DataType="http://www.w3.org/2001/XMLSchema#string">
        <AttributeValue>Deny</AttributeValue>
    </Attribute>
</Action>
```

The privacy attributes considered in the proposed model are Purpose Specification, Recipient Specification and Retention Obligation.

4.1.1 Purpose Specification

The purpose attached to data is useful in regulating the unintended usage of the data. The data that is collected by a service to do a certain task (for example: providing an insurance quote) must be used only for that purposes that the data provider intends. The purpose is the intention of using the data provided or the intention for which the data should be used. Purposes can vary within different domains. However, having a purpose attached to a data gives the data owner (or data generator) some control over the downstream usage of the data.

This ability to specify the purpose, for which data can be used, helps the process designers (PD) to understand clearly how the data from external enterprise services should be used. It also provides some level of guarantee to them (PD) about how their data is consumed by the external enterprise services. This has a positive effect on collaboration as organizations can know the intent of data consumption by all participating parties.

4.1.2 Recipient Specification

The Recipient specification allows the data provider and the data consumer to be aware of the users/roles that have access to the data. A data provider can stipulate that the data provided by it should only be accessed by only Managers or any role higher than that.

A recipient is the user/role that has the access to the data that is being consumed or a user/role that can access the data being provided. The recipient specification is of vital importance when enterprises are sharing sensitive information. Recipient specification is closely related with access control policies. In a business process access control, information is usually associated with activities (tasks) and not on the data itself. This is where the recipient specification proves useful by providing the process designer the means to explicitly state the recipients for the data that is generated or provided to an activity.

Recipient specification has more significance in automated activities, because the data that is provided to these services could be stored in databases. If the automated activity is invoking a external web service, process designers would be wary to provide sensitive information without knowing who has access to the data stored by these external services.

4.1.3 Retention Obligation

The retention period of data is of vital importance in information security. In business processes, there are two major compulsions to have a data retention policy in place for organizations, namely, compliance to government regulations and improving the trust of consumers in an organization. When data is a business process consumed by automated activities which have external services, running on servers located in different geographical locations and governed by different data protection regulations, it becomes challenging for a process designer to design a business process that adheres to the data protection regulations that are in place. For example, a business process designed for travel booking by the HR portal of an enterprise located in France uses an external service that books the hotels in China and is governed by Chinese data protection laws, a process designer would be wary to share his personal information (governed by data protection laws in France) to a service that runs under Chinese data protection laws which are very strict and always under the ambit of the state.

Thus by adding a data retention clause in the privacy policy in the business process, an external service that is consuming data is "obliged" to accept the data retention period set by the process designer.

4.2 Human and Automated Activities

Business Process Management software permits an orchestration of services to fit a business need, for instance, a process designer may wish to establish a new loan approval process that involves different services within the organization. Authorizations can be assigned to the process as a whole and to the individual parts or activities. This is done in line with the roles or groups that have been defined in the identity management engine, which is accessible by the BPM. This ensures that there is an accepted system-wide authorization schema in place that should be adhered to when designing processes.

Human activities in BPM are an illustration of this as the designer can assign limited users to an activity and thereby enable them to contribute (view, edit, append or generate) to both the input and output of that activity. The authorized person may be allowed to perform the allocated task however there is no means to prevent the input data being used in a manner that was not intended. In a banking scenario, a bank clerk may be authorized to collect customer information for the purpose of a loan application but perhaps the customer does not wish that this data be used by the bank's marketing department and be a potential target for an insurance policy.

Automated activities do not allow for the same access control as they are web services that are consumed in the business process. The designer selects the appropriate methods and attaches them to the automated activity. Exposing business processes as web services facilitates system integration as any technology can be used, such as Java and .NET, and the designer just needs to locate, identify and communicate through a WSDL file. Also this approach provides for greater efficiency as services can be easily reused in other business processes.

Given the automated nature of these type of activities and the lack of access control and user information, privacy preservation becomes more critical. As this may be an external service there may be a possibility that it resides on a server in a country that has different data protection laws. Therefore information exchanged with this service should be regulated in some manner.

4.3 Policy Consistency Check

To facilitate the process designer to specify privacy policies on the aforementioned activity types in a BP and to check for the consistency of these properties, a privacy validator tool has been developed as a plugin for SAP Netweaver BPM (Fig. 2). The tool has a User Interface for the process designer to attach policies on activities, perform the consistency check and inform the process designer of any policy mismatches. In this instance the Clerk PostProcessor has filled in a data retention period that will conflict with the period specified in the previous activity, input customer data. When the policy check is run there is a warning on the UI and the error details detailed in the Problems tab.

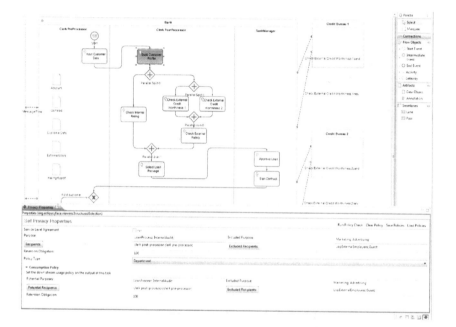

Fig. 2. Policy Checker

A web service provider can specify the location of an associated data handling policy file to the WSDL file through the usage of the documentation tag available in WSDL. The documentation tag can contain the URL of the policy file. When the process designer imports a WSDL file for automated activities in the process under-design, the privacy validator tool will extract the URL from the WSDL file, retrieve the file contained in the specified location, parse it and display it in the privacy view for the process designer to view the policy. A wizard permits the mapping of roles to the internal user management system in the case of external services in order to comply to its internal structures. A sample WSDL containing the URL of the policy file is shown below:

```
<wsdl:definitions
targetNamespace="http://example.com/sample/ws/"
  xmlns:wsdl="http://schemas.xmlsoap.org/wsdl/"
  xmlns:xs="http://www.w3.org/2001/XMLSchema"
  xmlns:tns="http://example.com/sample/ws/">
  <wsdl:documentation>
  @PolicyLink=Yes
  @PolicyURL=http://example.com/samplePrivacyPolicy.xml
  </wsdl:documentation>
  <wsdl:types>
  <!-- --- -->
</wsdl:types>
```

In a business process, the context data, that is the data generated by an activity or the data provided to an activity is stored in Data Objects (DO). A DO contains the actual data that acts as an input to an activity or collected as an output from an acitivity. In a privacy aware workflow, the data should have an associated data handling policy when it is consumed by activities in the BPM. The privacy tool developed will enable the process designer to attach policies to activities. The policy of an activity consists of two parts: Consumption Policy and Provider Policy. Consumption Policy states how an activity will be consuming the data provided to it. While the Provider policy specifies how the data that is provided by an activity should be used.

When the output of an activity is mapped into the data fields of a data object, the provider policy of that activity is attached to those data fields. When the outputs of two or more activities are mapped into the same data field, the provider policies of those activities are merged into a single policy for the data field. However, if the policies of those activities are conflicting with each other, the process designer is informed through a warning message. This data object has a data handling policy that is mapped as an input to another activity and the consumption policy of the activity is

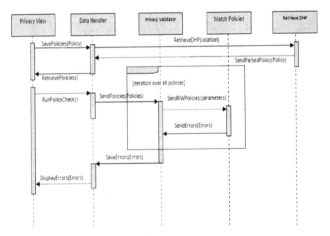

Fig. 3. Sequence Diagram of Policy Checking

matched against the policy of the data object and if there are any conflicts the process designer is informed through an error message. The process designer can thus, choose to change the policies on an activity to resolve the conflict or if it is an external service, he/she can negotiate with the service provider for an acceptable policy. The sequence diagram [Fig. 3.] gives an overview of the steps involved in the policy check.

5 Related Art

In [6] the model chooses the approach of assigning a purpose to the workflow considering it as a unit of work that cannot be interrupted. The user roles have purposes associated to them. When an activity in a workflow that has a user role includes a purpose that is conflicting with the purpose of the workflow, then the user role is denied access to perform the task. However, a workflow is an orchestration of activities, both human and automated and each activity can have a purpose associated with it and especially automated activities that consume external services should have downstream usage associated with them. And though denying access to a user role that is conflicting with the purpose of the workflow enforces privacy at run time, it does not aid in the design of privacy aware business processes. Also there is no data retention period specified. For compliance purposes data retention periods would be necessary and also external services used in workflows might want the organization to assure that the data it is providing would be deleted after a certain amount of time.

In the CoopFlow approach [15], the privacy on a workflow results abstracting the workflow of an organization and providing only the minimal amount of activities that are needed for cooperation between workflows of different organizations. The privacy in this context is on the internal activities of an organization and not on the data. Though data privacy could be a result of the abstraction of some activities and some internal data, it is not the main aim of this methodology.

The proposed XML-based notation called BPeX[16], describes a Business Process Model as a hierarchical tree-based structure. The model preserves all the relationships between the different activities and entities of a business process model. The BPeX, is then extended to support P3P policies. The policies are attached to a pool. It then attaches a purpose to each BPM element. The recipient information is attached to message flows that go outside the pool. The policy enforcement is done by using an XPath Matching on the BPeX file. A Boolean value "isP3pCompliant" is used as a flag to state the compliance of each activity with the P3P policy.

The policies are nevertheless attached to the pool and not at the activity level which can hamper the consumption of external services that have their own privacy policies. Activities can have different purposes, or recipients, for example, an external web service which is used as automated activity, can have its own privacy policy. The recipient list is attached to message flows from an internal pool to an external pool, which is based on an assumption that internally every office and every department within the organization have no privacy restrictions on them, which is not the case in most of the organizations.

In [17] a subject notion is introduced that is added to the workflow design; the subject is the user. The workflow management system can then access the subject attribute, and from that retrieve the user's privacy policy and thus can enforce the privacy policies of the user in the workflow. It also introduces auxiliary data properties that are attached to data elements and these can be used in real time for various functions in the workflow. The privacy properties of the user are then retrieved for each activity that is performed by the user and then the policies based on the policy of the user's data is hidden or generalized. They do not consider the bindings of activities in a business process.

6 Conclusion

This paper discussed privacy issues in the context of service oriented architectures in business process management. A solution based on data handling policies was used to add conditions to the use activities or web services in a BPM application. Furthermore the solution allowed for the import of policies attached to web services. A consistency check is able to be carried out by deploying bound activities in design time. Following alerts, the process designer is aware of any conflicting issues and is able to either remove the activity/web service or amend the consuming service's policy in order to adhere to the previous activity/web service. The proposal needs to integrate fully with a BPM application and also with a standard policy language and engine. Furthermore the approach will be evaluated in terms of scalability and compared to other matching mechanisms. These issues will be investigated in the context of the European project Primelife. Recent interest in moving towards data-oriented architectures [25] and other work in data centric security management [26] may influence future work.

Acknowledgements. The research leading to these results has received funding from the European Community's Seventh Framework Programme (FP7/2007-2013) under grant agreement n° 216483. The information in this document is provided "as is", and no guarantee or warranty is given that the information is fit for any particular purpose. The above referenced consortium members shall have no liability for damages of any kind including without limitation direct, special, indirect, or consequential damages that may result from the use of these materials subject to any liability which is mandatory due to applicable law.

References

1. Platform for Privacy Preferences (P3P) Project, http://www.w3.org/P3P/
2. Primelife, European project, http://www.primelife.eu/
3. WSDL specifications, http://www.w3.org/TR/wsdl
4. XACML specifications,
   http://www.oasis-open.org/committees/
   tc_home.php?wg_abbrev=xacml#XACML20
5. Miller, S., Weckert, J.: Privacy, the Workplace and the Internet. Journal of Business Ethics, 255–265 (2000)
6. Eddy, E.R., Stone, D.L., Stone-Romero, E.F.: The effects of information management policies on reactions to human resource information systems: An integration of privacy and procedural justice perspectives. Personnel Psychology 52(2), 335–358 (1999)

7. Culnan, M., Smith, H., Bies, R.: Law Privacy and Organizations: The Corporate Obsession to know v. the individual right not to be known. In: Sitkin, S., Bies, R. (eds.) The Legalistic Organization, Thousand Oaks, CA, pp. 199–211 (1994)
8. Milne, G.R., Gordon, M.E.: Direct mail privacy-efficiency trade-offs within an implied social contract framework. Journal of Public Policy & Marketing 12(2), 206–215 (1993)
9. Milberg, S.J., Smith, H., Burke, S.J.: Information Privacy: Corporate Management and National Regulation. Organization Science, 35–57 (2000)
10. Dresner, S.: Data protection roundup. Privacy Laws Bus (U.K.), January, vol. (33), pp. 2–8 (1996)
11. Noel, J.: BPM and SOA: Better Together. White paper, IBM (2005)
12. Malinverno, P., Hill, J.B.: SOA and BPM are Better Together. Gartner, 3–11 (2007)
13. Chen, Q., Hsu, M.: Inter-Enterprise Collaborative Business Process Management. In: International Conference on Data Engineering, pp. 253–260 (2001)
14. Jafari, M., Safavi-Naini, R., Sheppard, N.P.: Enforcing Purpose of User via workflows. WPES (November 2009)
15. Chebbi, I., Tata, S.: Workflow abstraction for privacy preservation. In: Weske, M., Hacid, M., Godart, C. (eds.) WISE Workshops 2007. LNCS, vol. 4832, pp. 166–177. Springer, Heidelberg (2007)
16. Chinosi, M., Trombetta, A.: Integrating Privacy Policies into Business Processes. Journal of Research and Practice in Information Technology 41(2), 155–170 (2009)
17. Alhaqbani, B., Adams, M., Fidge, C., ter Hofstede, A.H.M.: Privacy-Aware Workflow Management. BPM Center Report BPM-09-06, BPMcenter.org (2009)
18. Sarbanes Oxley Act of 2002 (2002),
    http://uscode.house.gov/download/pls/15C98.txt
19. Information Systems Audit and Control Association (ISACA), CobiT4.1:
    http://www.isaca.org/Knowledge-Center/
    cobit/Documents/COBIT4.pdf
20. Ashley, P., Powers, C., Schunter, M.: From privacy promises to privacy management: a new approach for enforcing privacy throughout an enterprise. In: NSPW 2002: Proceedings of the 2002 Workshop on New Security Paradigms, pp. 43–50. ACM, New York (2002)
21. Bandhakavi, S., Zhang, C.C., Winslett, M.: Super-sticky and declassifiable release policies for flexible information dissemination control. In: WPES 2006: Proceedings of the 5th ACM Workshop on Privacy in Electronic Society, pp. 51–58. ACM, New York (2006)
22. EPAL: Enterprise privacy authorisation language,
    http://www.zurich.ibm.com/pri/projects/epal.html
23. Prime: Privacy and identity management for europe (prime),
    https://www.prime-project.eu/primeproducts/
24. Mont, M.C., Pearson, S., Bramhall, P.: Towards accountable management of identity and privacy: Sticky policies and enforceable tracing services. Technical report (2003),
    http://www.hpl.hp.com/techreports/2003/HPL-2003-49.pdf
25. Data4BPM(BEDL),
    http://public.dhe.ibm.com/software/dw/wes/
    1004_nandi/1004_nandi.pdf
26. Grandison, T., Bilger, M., Graf, M., Swimmer, M., Schunter, M., Wespi, A., Zunic, N., O'Connor, L.: Elevating the Discussion on Security Management - The Data Centric Paradigm. In: Proceedings of the 2nd IEEE/IFIP International Workshop on Business-driven IT Management, pp. 89–93. IEEE Press, Piscataway (2007)

Agent-Supported Collaboration and Interoperability for Networked Enterprises

Ingo Zinnikus, Xiaoqi Cao, and Klaus Fischer*

German Research Center for Artificial Intelligence, Saarbrücken, Germany
{Ingo.Zinnikus,Xiaoqi.Cao,Klaus.Fischer}@dfki.de
http://www.dfki.de/~kuf

Abstract. The paper presents an agent-supported framework for improving solutions for enterprise interoperability and enterprise collaboration. We present the context of COIN in the European research area and explain the basic approach and system architecture COIN is aiming at. Special emphasis is put on how agents can support enterprise interoperability as well as enterprise collaboration services. The framework adopts a modeling approach for the description and execution of business processes. With this a system engineer can describe the interaction protocols that should be used at an intuitive level and transform the model down to executable code. Private partner processes can be integrated using a mapping approach to bridge technical interoperability gaps.

1 Motivation

According to the COIN vision, by 2020 enterprise collaboration and interoperability services will become an invisible, pervasive and self-adaptive knowledge and business utility at disposal of networked enterprises from any industrial sector and domain in order to rapidly set-up, efficiently manage and effectively operate different forms of business collaborations, from the most traditionally supply chains to the most advanced and dynamic business ecosystems [1].

In the area of business process modeling and enactment, progress has been made to bridge the notorious gap between business and IT. Still, the business perspective itself is split into a *value perspective* with regards to strategical considerations and a *process perspective* which concentrates on conceptual modeling of business activities. The latter perspective has received exceptional attention in research and commercial tool development. Recent empirical studies among researchers and practitioners confirmed critical areas of concern: *standardization of modeling approaches* and *model-driven process execution* are considered important [2]. Model-driven process design and execution could improve 'plug-and-play' functionality and rapid prototyping for testing in order to decrease

---

* The paper is mainly based on work performed in the project COIN (EU FP7 Project 216256; www.coin-ip.eu) funded by the European Community within the IST-Programme of the 7th Framework Research Programme. The authors also thank the contribution from other partners in the COIN consortium.

M. van Sinderen and P. Johnson (Eds.): IWEI 2011, LNBIP 76, pp. 204–215, 2011.

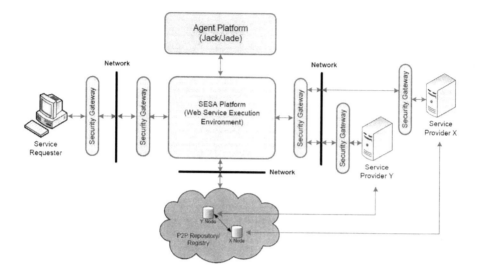

Fig. 1. The COIN Service Provisioning Platform

time to market. These tendencies are valid not only for intra-business process execution but also for modeling inter-organizational processes.

The gap between business and IT perpective was already a focus in the ATHENA project funded by the European Commission (IP, FP6). A core idea in the ATHENA project was to bring together different approaches and to combine them into a new framework: a modelling approach for designing collaborative processes, a model-driven development framework for SOAs and, among others, an agent-based approach for flexible execution.

The COIN Project continues this line of research. The main objectives of COIN are to design and develop a pervasive, adaptive service platform to host baseline and innovative COIN services for enterprise interoperability (EI) and enterprise collaboration (EC) and make them available under innovative on-demand, utility-oriented business models to enterprises (and SMEs in particular) for running their business in a secure, reliable and efficient way.

One of the main ideas of COIN is to unify EC and EI services in a unifying architecture. COIN adds a service provisioning platform for registering and executing (semantically annotated) services as baseline to the collaboration platform. The core of this service provisioning platform is a generic service platform (GSP) which is built on top of the basic infrastructure of the Internet and the Web. Innovative services to support EC and EI are designed as an extension to the GSP. These innovative services can access Web services registered in the GSP or can be built directly with traditional Internet technology. Proof-of-concept tools to support end users in the execution of collaborative processes in networked enterprises are developed on top of the COIN platform.

The COIN service provisioning platform (see Figure 1) is based on the WSMO [3] framework and the corresponding set of languages and specifications for describing ontologies, services, goals and mediators. Agent technologies are used in the GSP for intelligent service coordination and negotiation.

This paper describes an agent-based modeling framework with embedded support for solving interoperability issues. The rest of the paper is organized as follows: we describe the approach for modeling collaborative processes in Section 2 and describe the agent-based modeling environment in Section 3. Related work is discussed in Section 4. Finally, Section 5 concludes.

2   Collaborative Processes

Following the main objectives of COIN as described in the last section, the design and execution of collaborative business processes is in the main focus of COIN. Figure 2 presents COIN's approach to collaborative business process design. The situation in the figure is simplified to the collaboration of two partners but of course COIN aims at the collaboration of any number of partners. In such a setting each partner has its private process from which so-called *view* (or *public*) processes are derived. On the other hand, a collaborative process is defined where the collaborative process can take advantage of the processes and services specified in the view processes. The approach seems to be centralized, however, this is only a conceptual description. It is actually not prescribed how the collaborative process is developed nor is it prescribed how the resulting collaborative process is eventually executed (cf. [4]). However, to assume that the collaborative process is executed by any of the participating parties or by a third party is a straightforward solution once the collaborative process has been defined.

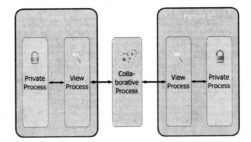

Fig. 2. COIN's Approach to Collaborative Process Design and Execution

The view processes mediate between the private processes that are already available in the local environment of the individual partners and the collaborative process. In the design of collaborative processes already existing view processes might be used or new view processes might be derived by the requirements that are specified in the collaborative process.

Complex interactions between the partners in collaborative environments imply a number of interoperability problems occurring in cross-organizational scenarios which have to be solved:

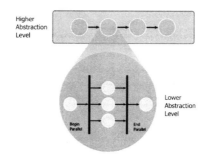

Fig. 3. Reducing Complexity in Collaborative Processes

- changing the protocol and integration of a new partner should be possible in a rapid manner (scalability)
- the execution of the message exchange should be flexible, i.e. in case a partner is unavailable or busy, the protocol should nevertheless proceed
- the different partners (may) expect different atomic protocol steps (service granularity)
- the partners expect and/or provide differing data structures

The collaborative processes are specified on a technology-independent level (using the Business Process Modeling Notation, BPMN) and transformed to a platform-independent level so that refinements and modifications in the interaction of the partners can be made on the respective levels and code generated automatically. Flexibility is achieved by applying a BDI (belief-desire-intention) agent-based approach for the actual execution layer. BDI agents provide flexible behavior for exception-handling in a natural way (compared to e.g. BPEL where specifying code for faults often leads to complicated code). The problem of different service granularities is envisaged by specifying a collaborative protocol which allows adaptation to different service granularities. Finally, the mediation of the data is tackled with using transformations which are specified at design-time and executed at run-time by transforming the exchanged messages based on the design-time transformations.

In the top-down approach a business process engineer starts of with the definition of a high-level process in BPMN. When she is more or less satisfied with the high-level definition she starts to work on the grounding of the collaborative process. The process model is transformed into an agent model which captures the structure of the high-level process. On the agent model, *refinement* of processes and interactions is done, i.e. adding concrete data structures for storing instance data and fleshing out the messaging within the public process. For the integration of the private processes, agents invoke Web services described by WSDL interfaces.

3   Agent-Based Modeling of Collaborative Processes

The graphical agent modeling framework developed at DFKI [5] directly supports service interaction and complex workflow patterns (for a more complete discussion of supported workflow and service interaction patterns see [6]). Enriched with concepts for supporting Web service invocation, it allows modeling and executing collaborative processes. The framework is expressive enough to capture the most important workflow and service interaction patterns identified in research on workflow modeling [7,8].

The overall procedure for specifying collaborations can be summarized as follows (see Figure 4):

- In a first step, the domain roles and participants are specified, using BPMN models for collaborative processes.
- Next, the interaction protocol(s) between the roles are derived by transformation and refinement on PIM level.

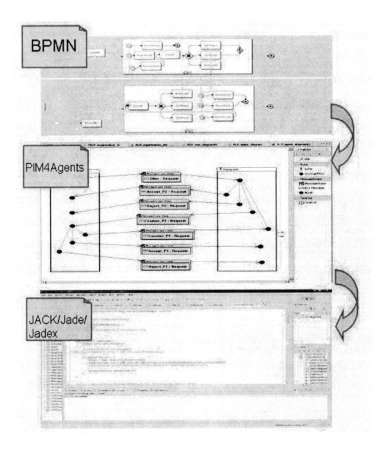

Fig. 4. Transformations for executable collaborative processes

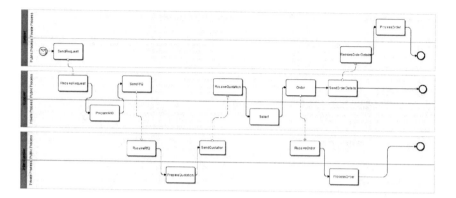

Fig. 5. Abstract collaborative process with lanes representing public and private processes

- The local behavior of the participants complementing the protocol description is defined in plans. The interoperability gap between the global data and the private processes (services) is bridged with a mapping on the PIM level.
- Executable code is generated from the model and deployed in a Web-based COIN environment to allow humans to use the modeled process.

With this approach, it is possible to model complex processes and generate executable code for agent-based platforms.

As an application example for collaborative processes, we consider negotiations between business partners as scenario to illustrate the approach. Following the approach presented in the previous section, we conceive negotiations in COIN as examples and instances of interactions between organizations which try to reach an agreement on some issues. A concrete example is the selection of a part provider in a 3-tier manufacturing supply-chain where the acceptance of a bid is the result of a possibly multi-lateral interaction between e.g. retailer, manufacturers/suppliers and e.g. raw material vendors. Note that supply chains are only used as illustration (concerning agents in supply chains, see e.g [9]). The approach is not restricted to supply chains; a different scenario could even involve n-to-n interaction between collaborating partners. In the following, we demonstrate the application of the model-driven methodology with an example which is based on a supply-chain scenario.

3.1 Deriving the Roles and Participants

As a first step, the collaborative process is specified with a graphical editor for BPMN (see Figure 5). Parties involved in the collaboration are specified (derived from pools). A domain role is designed for each lane in the collaboration. These roles are performed by agents which are abstract types that can be instantiated by concrete agent instances. Each agent in the scenario uses plans which describe the procedural knowledge the agent has about the domain.

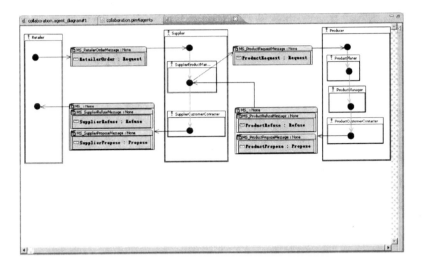

Fig. 6. Specifying the collaboration

3.2 Modeling the Interaction

The next step in the methodology is to derive the interaction between the roles in the domain by transforming the abstract process into an agent interaction model. The interaction view provides the constructs necessary to specify complex protocols which abstract from the concrete behavior of the participants.

In Figure 6, the interaction protocol for the collaboration is depicted. Pool-like boxes for Retailer and n-tier suppliers indicate the activities which are related to participants. In-between the pools, the messages exchanged are defined. MessageFlows (indicated by filled circles/nodes in a pool) allow defining the control flow of the protocol at each participant site. E.g., after receiving the starting request, the retailer contacts the suppliers which reply by sending a quotation or refusing the request. Note that the criteria for the decision are not defined in the interaction view but locally in the behavior model of the participants. Furthermore, the number of suppliers is left open at design-time. This reduces the complexity of the interaction model.

3.3 Modeling the Local Behavior of the Participants

The next step in the methodology consists in refining the local behavior of the participants corresponding to the interaction protocol. The behavior extends and complements the protocols by specifying additional information for generating executable code. In order to be consistent, the behavior has to comply with the interaction protocol.

In fact, an ongoing line of research is the automatic projection of the interaction protocol into local behavior models for the participating agents [10]. The results of the projection are plan skeletons which can then be further refined to specify e.g. decision conditions in more detail.

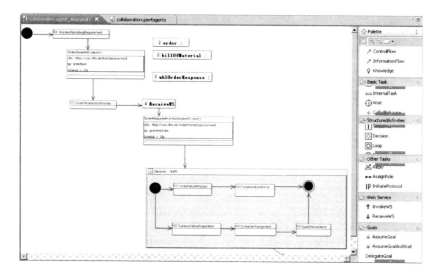

Fig. 7. Local behavior for participant

The plan for the supplier (see Figure 7) contains the detailed specification of the steps necessary for executing the supplier parts of the interaction protocol.

After receiving a request for quotation, the private process for generating a quotation is invoked. The service is exposed as a web service described in WSDL. Both synchronous and asynchronous invocation are supported. After receiving the response of the private process, the participant prepares the reply to the 2-tier supplier.

The plan for integrating the private process (service) also allows abstracting from peculiarities of the service interface (service granularity). The private process might require a complex interaction with a specific order of invocations. These local protocol issues can be encapsulated in the local behaviour of a participant. From a global perspective, the interaction appears as an atomic step.

The plan model is obviously more complicated than the interaction protocol description since the model contains the control flow as well as the information flow (data such as *order* or *billOfMaterial*). The control flow describes the sequence of tasks to be executed, whereas the information flow concerns the way data is transferred from one task to the other.

3.4 Mediating Data Heterogeneity

Concerning the integration of private processes, two cases can be distinguished:

(i) Integrating consortial partners: Partners define the shared process together. The common information/data model may also be defined together. Roughly speaking, two alternatives are possible, analogous to the local-as-view (LAV) vs. global-as-view (GAV) distinction in the fields of data integration (cf. [11]) and Enterprise Information Integration (cf. [12]).

In a LAV approach, the common data structure is defined independently from the local data model of each partner. Each partner then defines a (local) mapping from the common information model to the local model. The mapping in turn can be executed (at run-time) either by the consumer of the service or the partner service itself. The first solution is the one preferred by Semantic Web service descriptions, where the service provider describes the grounding to e.g. WSDL. The grounding is used by a service consumer who invokes the service. The second solution means that the service consumer always sends the same message (e.g. a SOAP message) to a partner service and does not care about the local data model. This is reasonable if specifying as well as testing the mapping is tedious and the mapping underlies many changes.

In the GAV approach, each element in the global model is defined in terms of local sources. Adding a new source (i.e. partner) affects the global model. The LAV approach is preferable for cases where the global model is stable and new partners are frequently joining (or leaving) the collaboration space.

(ii) **Integrating partners external to the collaboration:** For the integration of external partners service discovery as well as process and data mediation have to be realized. Service discovery using the COIN GSP can be based on the service requirements which are specified implicitly or explicitly for a service invocation task. Integrating the discovered services requires data transformations which are either provided by the service descriptions or based on a mapping to the common information model.

The data structure for the global (public) process is agreed among the partners. This means that, as long as the interfaces of the private processes are not aligned, mismatches between public and private data structure are to be expected. In order to bridge this gap, we developed a mapping tool (Figure 8) which allows to import the data structure of the private service and align it with the data of the public process. In more detail, the data structure of the service is described in XML schema which is imported and 'lifted' to Ecore format supported by the Eclipse developing environment. The mapping tool allows specifying the mediation between the Ecore format of the private process and the Ecore format of the public process. Currently, apart from one-to-one mappings, also one-to-many mappings are supported, as well as operations such as concatenation etc. For executing this mapping, an XSLT transformation is derived and used at runtime. The approach is open in the sense that other executable transformations are supported.

3.5   Generating Executable Agent-Code

The modeling framework provides code generation for several agent-platforms. Currently, the agent platforms Jade and JACK are supported. Code generation for Jadex is under development. The specified models can be transformed e.g. into Java-based Jade code. The transformation leads to code which can be

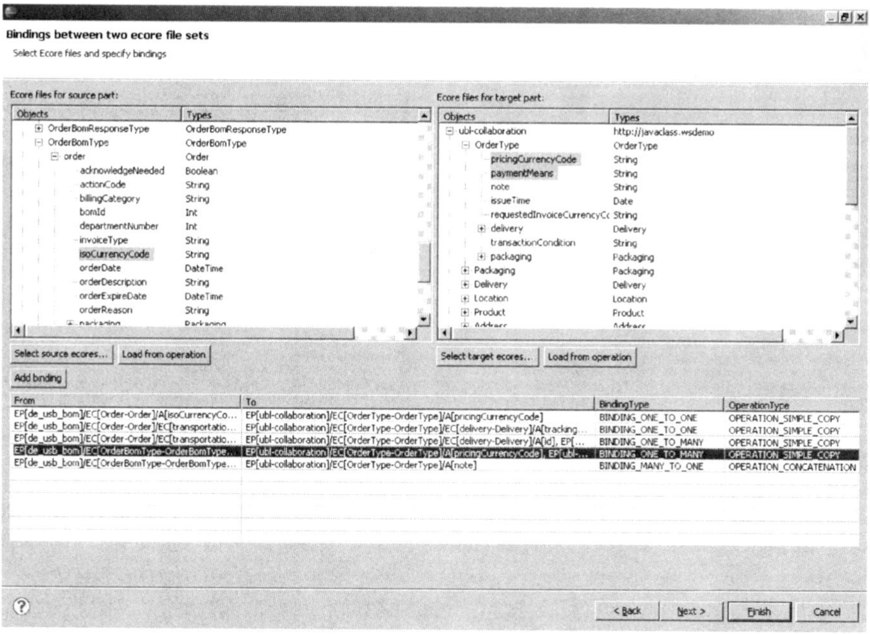

Fig. 8. Integrated tool support for defining maping on PIM level

further refined if necessary, e.g. to invoke an evaluation service or to deploy the collaboration protocol in a Web-based environment to involve human users.

4 Related Work

Extensions for modeling choreographies in BPMN have been proposed by [13]. The new version BPMN 2.0[1] includes notation diagrams for choreographies involving complex interactions patterns. Tool support for version 2.0 is slowly improving. However, recent empirical studies suggest that the 'core' subset of the notation used in realistic scenarios will remain rather stable and small [14]. It remains to be seen whether the 'new' elements will be used in a large scale in higher-level process models.

Besides the huge amount of literature on business process modeling, enterprise application integration and SOAs, the relation between agents and SOAs has already been investigated. [15] cover several important aspects, [16] propose the application of agents for workflows in general. [17] provide an overview of agent-based modeling approaches for enterprises. [18] describe the TROPOS methodology for a model-driven design of agent-based software systems. However, the problems related to integration of agent platforms and service-oriented architectures are out of scope for their approach. [19] map BPMN models to

---

[1] http://www.bpmn.org/

BDI agents but do not consider an integration of agents and Web services. [20] and [21] present a technical and conceptual integration of an agent platform and Web services. [22] integrate Web services into agent-based workflows, [23] integrate BDI agents and Web services. However, the model-driven approach and the strong consideration of problems related to cross-organizational settings have not been investigated in this context. Furthermore, our focus on a tight and lightweight integration of BDI-style agents fits much better to a model-driven, process-centric setting than the Web service gateway to a JADE agent platform considered by e.g. [20]. A good starting point for details on the semantic web is [24].

5   Conclusion

In this article we presented an agent-supported modeling framework for collaborative processes that is integrated with a service-oriented environment. We presented the context of COIN in the European research area and explained the basic approach and system architecture COIN is aiming at. Special emphasis was put on how a model-driven, agent-based framework can support enterprise interoperability as well as enterprise collaboration services.

References

1. COIN Consortium: COIN Integrated Project: Collaboration and Interoperability for Networked Enterprises, http://www.coin-ip.eu/
2. Indulska, M., Recker, J., Rosemann, M., Green, P.: Business Process Modeling: Current Issues and Future Challenges. In: van Eck, P., Gordijn, J., Wieringa, R. (eds.) CAiSE 2009. LNCS, vol. 5565, pp. 501–514. Springer, Heidelberg (2009)
3. Roman, D., Keller, U., Lausen, H., de Bruijn, J., Lara, R., Stollberg, M., Polleres, A., Feier, C., Bussler, C., Fensel, D.: Web service modeling ontology. Applied Ontology 1(1), 77–106 (2005)
4. Müller, J.P., Roser, S., Bauer, B.: Architectures for cross-enterprise business integration. In: Sherif, H.M. (ed.) Handbook of Enterprise Integration, pp. 337–354. Auerbach Publications, Taylor & Francis (2009)
5. Warwas, S., Hahn, C.: The DSML4MAS development environment. In: Sierra, C., Castelfranchi, C., Decker, K.S., Sichman, J.S. (eds.) AAMAS (2). IFAAMAS, pp. 1379–1380 (2009)
6. Hahn, C., Zinnikus, I.: Modeling and executing service interactions using an agent-oriented modeling language. In: Bellahsène, Z., Léonard, M. (eds.) CAiSE 2008. LNCS, vol. 5074, pp. 37–40. Springer, Heidelberg (2008)
7. Barros, A., Dumas, M., ter Hofstede, A.: Service interaction patterns. In: van der Aalst, W.M.P., Benatallah, B., Casati, F., Curbera, F. (eds.) BPM 2005. LNCS, vol. 3649, pp. 302–318. Springer, Heidelberg (2005)
8. van der Aalst, W.M.P., ter Hofstede, A., Kiepuszewski, B., Barros, A.: Workflow patterns. Distributed and Parallel Databases 14(3), 5–51 (2003)
9. Chaib-draa, B., Müller, J.: Multiagent based Supply Chain Management. SCI. Springer-Verlag New York, Inc., Secaucus (2006)

10. Hahn, C., Zinnikus, I., Warwas, S., Fischer, K.: From agent interaction protocols to executable code: a model-driven approach. In: Proceedings of the 8th International Conference on Autonomous Agents and Multiagent Systems, Budapest, Hungary, Richland, SC, May 10-15, vol. 2, pp. 1199–1200 (2009)

11. Lenzerini, M.: Data integration: a theoretical perspective. In: PODS 2002: Proceedings of the Twenty-First ACM SIGMOD-SIGACT-SIGART Symposium on Principles of Database Systems, pp. 233–246. ACM, New York (2002)

12. Halevy, A.Y., Ashish, N., Bitton, D., Carey, M., Draper, D., Pollock, J., Rosenthal, A., Sikka, V.: Enterprise information integration: successes, challenges and controversies. In: SIGMOD 2005: Proceedings of the 2005 ACM SIGMOD International Conference on Management of Data, pp. 778–787. ACM, New York (2005)

13. Decker, G., Puhlmann, F.: Extending BPMN for Modeling Complex Choreographies. In: Chung, S. (ed.) OTM 2007, Part I. LNCS, vol. 4803, pp. 24–40. Springer, Heidelberg (2007)

14. Muehlen, M.Z., Recker, J.: How much language is enough? Theoretical and Practical Use of the Business Process Modeling Notation. In: Bellahsène, Z., Léonard, M. (eds.) CAiSE 2008. LNCS, vol. 5074, pp. 465–479. Springer, Heidelberg (2008)

15. Singh, M.P., Huhns, M.N.: Service-oriented Computing — Semantic, Processes, Agents. John Wiley & Sons, Ltd., Chichester (2005)

16. Vidal, J.M., Buhler, P., Stahl, C.: Multiagent systems with workflows. IEEE Internet Computing 8(1), 76–82 (2004)

17. Cabri, G., Leonardi, L., Puviani, M.: Service-oriented agent methodologies. In: 5th IEEE International Workshop on Agent-Based Computing for Enterprise Collaboration, ACEC 2007 (2007)

18. Penserini, L., Perini, A., Susi, A., Mylopoulos, J.: From stakeholder intentions to software agent implementations. In: Martinez, F.H., Pohl, K. (eds.) CAiSE 2006. LNCS, vol. 4001, pp. 465–479. Springer, Heidelberg (2006)

19. Endert, H., Küster, T., Hirsch, B., Albayrak, S.: Mapping BPMN to agents: An analysis. In: First International Workshop on Agents, Web-Services and Ontologies Integrated Methodologies, AWESOME 2007, p. 164 (2007)

20. Greenwood, D., Calisti, M.: Engineering web service — agent integration. In: IEEE International Conference on Systems, Man and Cybernetics, vol. 2, pp. 1918–1925 (2004)

21. Dickinson, I., Wooldridge, M.: Agents are not (just) web services: Considering BDI agents and web services. In: AAMAS 2005 Workshop on Service-Oriented Computing and Agent-Based Engineering, SOCABE (2005)

22. Savarimuthu, B.T.R., Purvis, M., Purvis, M., Cranefield, S.: Agent-based integration of web services with workflow management systems. In: Fourth International Joint Conference on Autonomous Agents and Multiagent Systems, AAMAS 2005, pp. 1345–1346 (2005)

23. Bozzo, L., Mascardi, V., Ancona, D., Busetta, P.: Coows: Adaptive BDI agents meet service-oriented computing extended abstract. In: Proceedings of the Third European Workshop on Multi-Agent Systems, EUMAS 2005 (2005)

24. Lausen, H., Ding, Y., Stollberg, M., Fensel, D., Hernandez, R.L., Han, S.K.: Semantic web portals: state-of-the-art survey. Journal of Knowledge Management 9(5), 40–49 (2005)

Author Index